The Chaldean

GW01403398

Genesi

Containing the description of the creation, the fall of man, the deluge, the tower of Babel, the times of the patriarchs

George Smith

(Editor: A. H. Sayce)

Alpha Editions

This edition published in 2024

ISBN : 9789366381657

Design and Setting By
Alpha Editions
www.alphaedis.com
Email - info@alphaedis.com

Contents

PREFACE BY THE EDITOR.

IT is now five years since the present volume was first laid before the public by Mr. George Smith, just before setting out on his last ill-fated expedition to the East. It naturally awakened extreme interest and curiosity. The earlier chapters of Genesis no longer stood alone. Parallel accounts had been discovered by the author among the clay records of ancient Babylonia, which far exceeded in antiquity the venerable histories of the Bible. All those who had a theory to support, or a tradition to overthrow, turned eagerly to the newly-discovered documents, which possessed an equal interest for the students of history, of religion, and of language.

The five years that have elapsed since the publication of "The Chaldean Account of Genesis" have been five years of active work and progress among Assyrian scholars. The impulse given to Assyrian research by Mr. Smith has survived his death; numberless new tablets and fragments of tablets have been brought to Europe from Assyria and Babylonia; fresh students of the inscriptions have risen up in this country and on the continent, more especially in Germany; and the scientific spirit which has been introduced into the study of the Assyrian language has immeasurably increased our knowledge of it. Thanks to the labours of men like Oppert, Lenormant and Guyard in France, or of Schrader, Delitzsch, Haupt and Hommel in Germany, texts which were obscure and doubtful at the time of Mr. Smith's death have now become almost as clear as a page of the more difficult portions of the Old Testament. The Assyrian student, moreover, has an advantage which the Hebrew student has not; he possesses dictionaries and vocabularies compiled by the Assyro-Babylonians themselves, and these frequently throw light on a word which otherwise would be a "hapax legomenon."

The more backward condition of our knowledge of Assyrian, however, was not the only difficulty against which Mr. Smith had to contend. He was pressed for time when writing the present volume, which had to be finished before his departure for the East. The class of texts, also, which he had brought to light was a new class hitherto unknown, or almost unknown, to the Assyrian decipherer. He had to break fresh ground in dealing with them. Their style differed considerably from that of the texts previously studied; they had a vocabulary of their own, allusions of their own, and even, it may be added, a grammar of their own. If the texts had been complete the difficulty perhaps would not have been so great; but it was enormously increased by their mutilated condition. The skill and success with which Mr. Smith struggled against all these difficulties show more plainly than ever what a loss Assyrian research has sustained in him.

Nevertheless, even the genius of Mr. Smith could not do more than give a general idea of the contents of the fragments, and not always even this. A comparison of the translations contained in the present edition with those contained in the preceding ones will show to what an extent the details of translation have had to be modified and changed, sometimes with important consequences. Thus the corrected translation of the fragments relating to the Tower of Babel will remove the doubts raised by Mr. Smith's translation as to his correctness in associating them with that event; thus, too, the corrected rendering of a passage in the Izdubar Epic will show that the practice of erecting a Bethel or sacred stone was familiar to the early Babylonians. In some instances Mr. Smith has misconceived the true character of a whole text. What he believed to be a record of the Fall, for instance, is really, as M. Oppert first pointed out, a hymn to the Creator.

On the other hand, the fresh materials that have been acquired by the British Museum during the last five years, or a closer examination of the treasures it already possessed, have enabled us to add to the number of cuneiform texts which illustrate the earlier portions of Genesis. Mr. Rassam, for example, has brought home a fragment of the Deluge tablet, which not only helps us to fill up some of the *lacunæ* in the text, but is also important in another way. It is written, not in Assyrian, but in Babylonian cuneiform characters, and comes, not from an Assyrian, but from a Babylonian library. But it agrees exactly with the corresponding parts of the Assyrian editions of the story, and thus furnishes us with a proof of the trustworthiness of the Assyrian copies of the old Babylonian texts. The text, again, which relates to the destruction of a country by a rain of fire, though long contained in the British Museum Collection, was first noticed by myself as being apparently the Babylonian version of the biblical account of the destruction of Sodom and Gomorrah.

Numerous alterations and insertions have had to be made in the text which accompanies the translations. The latter necessarily occupied the main part of Mr. Smith's attention; he had neither time nor inclination to enter very elaborately into the questions raised by them, or the illustrations they might receive from elsewhere. In fact, any adequate treatment of the great Izdubar Epic, for instance, demanded a special acquaintance with the method and results of Comparative Philology, as well as a more intimate knowledge of its history and character than was possible at the time when Mr. Smith wrote.

A large proportion of the cuneiform texts from which the translations contained in the present volume are made has not yet been published. I have, however, gone carefully over them all with the exception of a small portion of the Izdubar Epic, and endeavoured to bring the translations up to the level of our present knowledge of the Assyrian language. I am indebted to the ready kindness and accurate eye of Mr. Pinches for copies of almost all the unpublished portions of the Izdubar legends. In these he has corrected several faulty readings, more especially that of the name of the pilot of Xisuthrus, which ought to be Nes-Hea, "the lion of Hea." Mr. Pinches assures me that the name of the deity composing the second part of the name is invariably written with the numeral 40, the symbol of the god Hea, except once when the scribe has miswritten 50, the symbol of Bel, and he has pointed out to me a passage in a bilingual tablet where the name is explained in Assyrian by Nes-Hea. Unfortunately, the texts given in pp. 103-124 cannot be found, and here therefore I have been obliged to leave Mr. Smith's translations unaltered.

The reader, however, must remember that no translations of these mutilated tablets can be more than approximately correct. Even if the meaning of all the words were well known, and they were divided from one another (which is not the case), the broken condition of so many of the inscriptions would make a good deal of the translation more or less conjectural. This must be doubly the case where the signification of the words is either unknown or only half known. I have always endeavoured to indicate a doubtful word or passage by a query; but there must be instances in which the meaning that I believe ought to be assigned to particular words will be corrected by the further progress of discovery. This is even more true of what may be termed the commentary accompanying the translations. Surprises are constantly in store for the Assyrian decipherer, and a tiny fragment may suddenly throw a new light on a question he had supposed to be settled. In fact, in Assyriology, as in all other branches of science, there is no finality; we cannot be more than approximately exact at any given time, and every month enables us to introduce fresh corrections and improvements into our work.

A fresh illustration of the fact has been afforded even while the present volume has been passing through the press. Mr. Pinches has come across two fragments (one marked S 669, the other unnumbered) which belong to two separate copies or editions of a very interesting work. This is nothing less than a list of the ancient epics and legends of Chaldea, along with the names of their reputed authors, many of whom, however, are probably as mythical as the famous Rishis of India. The list shows how numerous these early poems were, and how few of them, comparatively, we possess at present. Both fragments belong to the same part of the list, and we are therefore ignorant of many of the ancient compositions it must originally have contained. Some of the works mentioned receive their names from the heroes celebrated in them, others are named from their opening lines. A distinction is drawn between those that belonged to the Accadian period, and were written by Accadian poets in the Accadian language, and those that were of Semitic Babylonian origin. The interest of the list is enhanced by the great antiquity of the poems it records, none of them being later than about 2000

B.C. Here is a translation of the text as restored from a comparison of the two fragments according to the copies I have made of them:—

OBVERSE.

- 1. *Ca* ....

- 2. This is the work (*literally* from the mouth) of .

- 3. "*a khus ba a ri* ....

- 4. the god .... *tsu bu nu*" .... [Accadian.]

- 5. This is the work of Nupatuv ....

- 6. "The mighty lady, the winged one, Nigirra," or "Bel" ....

- 7. "He restored Til-enni," or "Life."

- 8. "May Merodach the great lord firmly defend." [Semitic.]

- 9. This is the work of Basa-Gula, the scribe ...

- 10. "The king of the sphere in their front," or "the lord" .... [Acc.]

- 11. This is the work of En-me-duga ....

- 12. .... "head, thy lustre" .... [Acc.]

- 13. This is the work of Elum ....

- 14. .... *ci bat* ....

REVERSE.

- 1. ....

- 2. (This is the work of ....) ragas, the scribe, the man (of a non-existent tablet).

- 3. ..... "the gods" [Acc.]. This is the work of ....

- 4. .... "the bull of Bit-Esir (the firmament)," or "The great fortress of the royal crown" ....[Acc.]

- 4 -

- 5. This is the work of Cus-dib the son of....

- 6. .... *nun-na* [Acc.]. This is the work of Elum-ban-cudur, the son of Khumetis, the scribe, the man of (a non-existent) tablet.

- 7. .... "the *paggalti* which over heaven are placed" [Sem.].
- 8. (This) is the work of Gimil-Gula, the son of Il-khigal the scribe, the man of a non-existent tablet.

- 9. "The day of calling, the long day at the dawning of light" (?) [Acc.]. This is the work of Ekur (Esiru), the son of Nunna-tur.

- 10. The hero Izdubar. This is the work of Sin-lici-unnini the scribe ....

- 11. The hero Etana. This is the work of Nis-Sin the scribe ....

- 12. The hero the Fox. This is the work of Kak-Merodach the son of Eri-Turnunna, the man of a non-existent tablet.

- 13. (The hero) 'Sidu. This is the work of 'Sidu-labiri the prince, the man of a non-existent tablet.

- 14. .... *a tu gab* [Acc.]. This is the work of Lig-Dimir the scribe, the man (of a non-existent tablet).

What is meant by the phrase "the man of a non-existent tablet," I do not know. Possibly it signifies that the autograph of the author no longer existed at the time the list was drawn up. "The Bull of the firmament" was a legend which was probably connected with the second month of the year, originally, it would seem, the first, which like the zodiacal sign after which it was named, was called the month of "the directing bull."

Future excavations will doubtless bring to light some of the poems mentioned in the list and not previously known. I have myself lately come across two fragments (S 802 and S 316) which belong to legends hitherto unknown, but they are too short to be worth translating. What curious revelations, however, we may yet expect from the cuneiform records may be judged from a small and well preserved tablet recently brought to England, which contains a catalogue of the gardens belonging to Merodach-Baladan, the contemporary of Hezekiah, and grouped according to the districts in which they were situated. Merodach-Baladan must have been fond of horticulture, since the catalogue contains the names of no less than sixty-seven seed-gardens, besides six other pleasure-grounds. Many of them were named from the localities in whose neighbourhood they were, but others bore such significant titles as "the forest of reeds," "the small enclosure," or "the garden of the waters of the city." As the tablet was copied by a scribe named Merodach-sum-iddin, probably in the time of Nebuchadnezzar or his successors, it is evident that some of the contents of the library of Babylon escaped the destruction brought upon that city by Sennacherib in B.C. 692.

I may add that since the greater part of this edition has been in type, I have found myself able to explain the name of the hero which in default of the true transcription has been provisionally read Izdubar. The name is composed of three ideographs, the first of which is the determinative prefix of wood, while the two latter are rendered *saptu saplitu*, "the lower lip," in Semitic Assyrian. Now M. Lenormant has shown that Izdubar was originally the Accadian Fire-god, and Mr. Boscawen has pointed out that the fire-stick was once used in Babylonia; it is therefore evident that the three ideographs composing the name represent the lower piece of wood, with a lip or groove in it, which formed the most important part of the primitive fire-machine. I believe the Accadian pronunciation of the name will turn out to be Kibirra.

A. H. SAYCE.

May 21st, 1880.

Chapter I.
THE DISCOVERY OF THE GENESIS LEGENDS.

Cosmogony of Berosus.—Discovery of Cuneiform Inscriptions.—
Historical texts.—Babylonian origin of Assyrian literature.—Mythological
tablets.—Discovery of Deluge texts.—Mutilated condition of tablets.—
Lecture on Deluge tablets.—"Daily Telegraph" offer.—Expedition to
Assyria.—Fragments of Creation tablets.—Solar Myth.—Second journey to
Assyria.—Tower of Babel.—Clay records.—List of texts.—Legend of
Oannes.—List of early legends and their authors.

IT has long been known from the fragments of the Chaldean historian,
Berosus, preserved in the works of various later writers, that the Babylonians
were acquainted with traditions referring to the Creation, the period before
the Flood, the Deluge, and other matters of which we read in the book of
Genesis.

Berosus, however, who recorded these events, is stated by Eusebius and
Tatian to have been a contemporary of Alexander the Great, and to have
lived into the reign of Antiochus Soter. His date lies, therefore, between B.C.
330 and 260. As this was three hundred years after the captivity of the Jews
in Babylon, the great antiquity of these traditions could not be proved with
certainty, much less their independence of the accounts which we have in
Genesis.

On the discovery and decipherment of the cuneiform inscriptions, Oriental
scholars hoped that copies of the Babylonian histories and traditions would
one day be found, and that earlier and more satisfactory evidence as to these
primitive histories than had previously been accessible, would thus be gained.

In the mound of Kouyunjik, opposite the town of Mosul, Mr. Layard
discovered part of the Royal Assyrian library, and further collections, also
forming part of this library, have been subsequently found by Mr. H. Rassam,
Mr. Loftus, and Mr. George Smith. Sir Henry Rawlinson, who made the
preliminary examination of Mr. Layard's treasures, and was the first to
recognize their value, estimated the number of fragments brought from this
Library at over twenty thousand.

The attention of decipherers was in the first instance drawn to the later
historical inscriptions, particularly to those of the Assyrian kings
contemporary with the Hebrew monarchy; and in this department of
research a very large number of texts of great importance rewarded the toil
of Assyrian scholars. Inscriptions of Tiglath Pileser, Shalmaneser, Sargon,
Sennacherib, Esarhaddon, Nebuchadnezzar, Nabonidus, and numerous

other ancient sovereigns, bearing directly on the Bible, and throwing new light upon parts of ancient history previously obscure, for a long time occupied almost exclusively the attention of students, and overshadowed any work in other divisions of Assyrian literature.

Although it was known that Assyria borrowed its civilization and written characters from Babylonia, yet, as the Assyrian nation was throughout the greater part of its independent existence hostile to the southern and older kingdom, it could not be guessed beforehand that the peculiar national traditions of Babylonia would have been transported to Assyria.

Under these circumstances, for some years after the cuneiform inscriptions were first deciphered, nothing was looked for or discovered bearing upon the events described in Genesis; but, as new texts were brought into notice, it became evident that the Assyrians borrowed their literature largely from Babylonian sources, and it appeared likely that search among the fragments of Assyrian inscriptions would yield traces at least of some of these ancient Babylonian legends.

Attention was early drawn to this fact by Sir Henry Rawlinson, who pointed out several coincidences between the geography of Babylonia and the account of Eden in Genesis, and suggested the great probability that the accounts in Genesis had a Babylonian origin.

While preparing the fourth volume of Cuneiform Inscriptions for the trustees of the British Museum, Mr. George Smith noticed references to the Creation in a tablet numbered K 63 in the Museum collection, as well as allusions in other tablets to similar legends; he therefore searched through a series of tablets he had previously classed as "Mythological," in order to find, if possible, some of these legends. This series of mythological tablets was one of six into which he had divided the Museum collection of cuneiform inscriptions for convenience of working. By placing all the tablets and fragments of the same class together, he had been able to complete several texts, to find easily any subject required, and to get, whenever it was needed, a general idea of the contents of the collection.

The mythological division contained all the tablets which related to Assyrian mythology, and all the legends in which the gods took a leading part, together with prayers and similar subjects.

A steady search among these fragments soon brought to light half of a curious tablet which had evidently contained originally six columns of text; two of these (the third and fourth) were still nearly perfect; two others (the second and fifth) were imperfect, about half being lost, while the remaining columns (the first and sixth) were entirely gone. A statement in the third column that "the ship" had rested on the mountain of Nizir, followed by an account of the sending forth of a dove, and its finding no resting-place and returning, convinced Mr. Smith that he had discovered a portion at least of the Chaldean account of the Deluge. He then proceeded to read through the document, and found it was in the form of a speech from the hero of the Deluge to a person whose name might be transcribed as Izdubar. The same name had already been read on the fragment of another tablet numbered K 231, which turned out to belong to the same series of tablets as the newly-found account of the Deluge. Mr. Smith was thus encouraged to make a search for other portions of the series.

The search was a long and heavy work, for there were thousands of fragments to be examined, and these were so small, and contained so little of the text, that it was extremely difficult to ascertain their meaning. The search, however, proved successful. A fragment of another copy of the Deluge was found containing a second account of the sending forth of the birds. Several other portions of the same tablet were gradually collected and fitted one after another into their places until the greater part of the second column was filled up. Portions of a third copy were next discovered, which, when joined together, completed a considerable part of the first and sixth columns. Mr. Smith now translated the text he had so laboriously pieced together, and published his discovery to the world at a meeting of the Society of Biblical Archæology, December 3rd, 1872. By this time he had made out that the series of Izdubar legends, as we may term them, contained twelve tablets or books. Of this series the tablet describing the Deluge was the eleventh and K 231 the sixth.

The interest excited by Mr. Smith's discovery was naturally very great. Immediately after the meeting of the Society of Biblical Archæology, Mr. E. Arnold, in the name of the proprietors of the "Daily Telegraph," asked the fortunate discoverer to reopen, at their cost, the excavations in Assyria in the hope of finding the missing portions of the story of the Deluge. The trustees of the British Museum granted Mr. Smith leave of absence for the purpose, and he accordingly started for the ruins of Nineveh, and there engaged in researches, the history of which is related in his work entitled "Assyrian Discoveries." Hardly had he begun his excavations on the site of the palace of Assur-bani-pal at Kouyunjik, when he came across a new fragment of the Chaldean account of the Deluge belonging to the first column of the tablet, containing the command to build and fill the ark, and nearly filling up the most considerable blank in the story. Some other fragments, found afterwards, still further completed this tablet, which was already the most perfect one in the Izdubar series. The trench in which the fragment in question was discovered must have passed very near the part of the Library in which the Assyrians kept a series of inscriptions relating to the early history of the world. The same trench soon afterwards yielded a fragment of the sixth tablet, describing the destruction of the bull of Istar by Izdubar and Hea-bani, an incident often depicted on early Babylonian gems. The next discovery was a fragment which referred to the creation of the world; it formed the upper corner of a tablet, and gave a fragmentary account of the creation of animals. Two other portions of this legend were found further on in the trench, one of which contained a mutilated account of the war between the gods and evil spirits.

In the following year Mr. Smith was again in Assyria, in charge of an expedition sent out by the trustees of the British Museum, and succeeded in bringing home fresh fragments relating to the early traditions and legends of Babylonia. Among these is the fragment which seems to describe the building of the Tower of Babel. Then followed the disastrous expedition of 1875-6, in the course of which Mr. Smith fell a victim to over-fatigue and his zeal for Assyrian research. The subsequent explorations of Mr. Hormuzd Rassam, though rich in other results, have added very little to our knowledge of the old Babylonian legends; and it seems probable that the missing portions of the tablets which contained them have irretrievably perished. We must wait for further light upon the subject until the cities and libraries of Babylonia have been excavated. After all, the early Babylonian legends, of which copies were made for the Assyrian Library at Kouyunjik, were but a selected few; the Assyrians took little interest in that part of Babylonian literature which had no connection with their own history or beliefs, and we have reason to congratulate ourselves that among the traditions they borrowed from their older and more civilized neighbours were so many which bear upon the earlier chapters of Genesis.

The fragmentary condition of the legends we possess, however, is much to be lamented. The chief difficulties with which the Assyrian scholar has to contend, when dealing with them, are due to the mutilated state of the tablets. If the inscriptions were perfect, their translation would be a comparatively easy matter. As it is, so skilled a decipherer as Mr. Smith himself was deceived by the defective character of the text into imagining that a hymn addressed to the Creator was the Babylonian version of the Fall of Man.

The fragmentary and scattered character of these legends is explained by the nature of the material of which the tablets are composed, and the changes undergone by them since they were written. They consist of fine clay and were inscribed with cuneiform characters while in a soft state; they were then baked in a furnace until hard, and afterwards transferred to the library. The library seems to have been in an upper storey of the palace, and after the destruction of Nineveh, the fall of the building in which it was placed naturally caused the tablets contained in it to be broken to pieces. Many of them were cracked and scorched by the heat of the burning ruins. Subsequently the ruins were turned over in search of treasure, and the tablets still further broken; while, to complete their destruction, the rain, soaking through the ground every spring, saturates them with water containing chemicals, and these chemicals form crystals in every available crack. The growth of the crystals further splits the tablets, some of them being literally shivered to pieces.

REVERSE OF INSCRIBED TERRA COTTA TABLET CONTAINING THE ACCOUNT OF THE DELUGE, SHOWING THE VARIOUS FRAGMENTS OF WHICH IT WAS COMPOSED AT THE TIME OF MR. SMITH'S TRANSLATION.

Some idea of the mutilated condition of the Assyrian tablets, and of the work required by the restoration of a single text, will be gained from the engraving above, which exhibits the appearance of one of the Deluge tablets at the time Mr. Smith published his translation of it. In this tablet there are no less than sixteen fragments.

The clay records of the Assyrians are by these means so broken up, that a single text is in some cases divided into over one hundred fragments; and it is only by collecting and joining these together that the old texts can be restored. Many of the fragmentary tablets which have been more than twenty years in the British Museum have been added to considerably by the fragments recently brought to England by Mr. Smith and Mr. Rassam; and yet there probably remain from ten to twenty thousand fragments still buried in the ruins, without the recovery of which it is impossible to complete these valuable Assyrian inscriptions.

It is, nevertheless, out of these imperfect materials that we have at present to piece together our knowledge of the early legends of Babylonia and Assyria. Most, if not all, of them, are, it must be remembered, of Chaldean or Babylonian origin, the Assyrians having either slavishly copied Babylonian originals or simply put into a new form the story they had borrowed from their southern neighbours. Such as they are, however, they are presented to the reader as faithfully translated as our existing knowledge of the Assyrian language allows; it is for him to draw his inferences and make his comparisons. The greater number of them, as we shall see, mount back to a date earlier than the second millennium before the Christian era, and even where the actual text belongs to a later period, the legend which it embodies claims a similar antiquity. We may classify them in the following order:—

1. An account of the Creation of the world in six days, parallel to that in the first chapter of Genesis, and probably in its present form not older than the 7th century B.C.

2. A second account of the Creation, derived from the Library of Cuthah, and belonging to the oldest period of Babylonian literature.

3. A history of the conflict between Merodach, the champion of the gods, and Tiamat, "the Deep," the representative of chaos and evil. To this we may add the bilingual legend of the seven evil spirits and their fight against the moon.

4. The story of the descent of the goddess Istar or Venus into Hades, and her return.

5. The legend of the sin of the god Zu, punished by Bel, the father of the gods.

6. A collection of five tablets giving the exploits of Dibbara the god of the pestilence.

7. The story of the wise man who put forth a riddle to the gods.

8. The legend of the good man Atarpi, and the wickedness of the world.

9. The legend of the tower of Babel, and dispersion.

10. The story of the Eagle and Etana.

11. The story of the ox and the horse.

12. The story of the fox.

13. The legend of Sinuri.

14. The Izdubar legends: twelve tablets, with the history of Izdubar, and an account of the flood.

15. The story of the destruction of Sodom and Gomorrah. Besides these there are fragments of other legends, which show that there was a considerable collection of such primitive stories still quite unknown to us. In fact we have little chance of becoming acquainted with them until the libraries of Babylonia are excavated. Thus for example we learn from Berosus that the Babylonians ascribed their civilization to certain wonderful creatures who ascended out of the Persian Gulf, and more especially to a being called Oannes. But of all this the library of Nineveh tells us nothing, although an Accadian Reading-book compiled for Assyrian students contains an excerpt which seems to be taken from the legend of Oannes. It is as follows:—

- 1. To the waters their god

- 2. had returned.

- 3. To the glistening house

- 4. he descended (as) an icicle.

- 5. (On) a seat of snow

- 6. he grew not old in wisdom.

- 7. The wise people

- 8. with his wisdom he filled.

Two fragments, belonging to two editions of the same text, have just been found, containing a list of the numerous legends and epics current among the ancient Babylonians, along with the names of their authors. Among them are found several of which translations are given further on in this volume; but there are also several of which we hear for the first time. The great Izdubar Epic, it may be noted, is ascribed to a certain Sin-lici-unnini ("O Moon-god, receive my cry!"). A fuller account of the fragments and their contents will be found in the Introduction.

Chapter II.
BABYLONIAN AND ASSYRIAN LITERATURE.

Babylonian literature.—Kouyunjik library.—Fragmentary
condition.—Arrangement of tablets.—Subjects.—
Dates.—Babylonian source of literature.—Literary
period.—Babylonian Chronology.—Accad.—Sumir.—
Extinction of the Accadian language.—Izdubar legends.—
Creation.—Syllabaries and bilingual tablets.—Assyrian
copies.—Difficulties as to date.—Library of Senkereh.—
Assyrian empire.—City of Assur.—Library at Calah.—
Sargon of Assyria.—Sennacherib.—Removal of Library to
Nineveh.—Assur-bani-pal or Sardanapalus.—His
additions to library.—Description of contents.—Later
Babylonian libraries.

IN order to understand the position to which we must assign the legends of
early Chaldea, it is necessary to give some account of the literature of the
Ancient Babylonians and their copyists, the Assyrians. As has been already
stated, the fragments of burnt brick on which these legends are inscribed
were found in the débris which covers the palaces called the South West
Palace and the North Palace at Kouyunjik; the former building being of the
age of Sennacherib, the latter belonging to the time of Assur-bani-pal. The
tablets, which are of all sizes, from one inch long to over a foot square, are
generally in fragments, and in consequence of the changes which have taken
place in the ruins the fragments of the same tablet are sometimes scattered
widely apart. They were originally deposited, it would seem, in one of the
upper chambers of the palace, from which they fell on the destruction of the
building. In some of the lower chambers the whole floor has been found
covered with them, in other cases they lay in groups or patches on the
pavement, and there are occasional clusters of fragments at various heights
in the earth which covers the ruins. Other fragments are scattered singly
through all the upper earth which covers the floors and walls of the palace.
Different fragments of the same tablet or cylinder are found in separate
chambers which have no immediate connection with each other, showing
that their present distribution has nothing to do with the original position of
the tablets of which they formed part.

The inscriptions show that the tablets were arranged according to their
subjects. Stories or subjects were continued on other tablets of the same size
and form as those on which they were commenced, in some cases the
number of tablets in a series and on a single subject amounting to over one
hundred.

Each subject or series of tablets had a title, the title consisting of the first phrase or part of a phrase in it. Thus, the series of Astrological tablets, numbering over seventy tablets, bore the title "When the gods Anu (and) Bel," this being the commencement of the first tablet. At the end of every tablet in each series was written its number in the work, thus: "the first tablet of When the gods Anu, Bel," "the second tablet of When the gods Anu, Bel," &c. &c.; and, further to preserve the proper position of each tablet, every one except the last in a series had at the end a catch phrase, consisting of the first line of the following tablet. There were besides, catalogues of these documents written like them on clay tablets, and other small oval tablets with titles upon them, apparently labels for the various series of works. All these arrangements show the care taken with respect to literary matters. There were regular libraries or chambers, probably on the upper floors of the palaces, appointed for the reception of the tablets, and custodians or librarians to take charge of them. These regulations were all of great antiquity, and like the tablets had a Babylonian origin.

Judging from the fragments discovered, it appears probable that there were in the Royal Library at Nineveh over 10,000 inscribed tablets, treating of almost every branch of knowledge existing at the time.

In considering a subject like the present one it is a point of the utmost importance to define as closely as possible the date of our present copies of the legends, and the most probable period at which the original copies may have been inscribed. By far the greatest number of the tablets brought from Nineveh belong to the age of Assur-bani-pal, who reigned over Assyria from B.C. 670, and every copy of what we will term the Genesis legends yet found was inscribed with one exception during his reign. The statements made on the tablets themselves are conclusive on this point, and have not been called in question, but it is equally stated and acknowledged on all hands that most of these tablets are not the originals, but are only copies from earlier texts. It is unfortunate that the date of the original copies is never preserved, and thus a wide door is thrown open for difference of opinion on the point. The Assyrians acknowledged that this class of literature was borrowed from Babylonian sources, and of course it is to Babylonia that we have to look to ascertain the approximate dates of the original documents. But here we are met by the following difficulty. It appears that at an early period in Babylonian history a great literary development took place, and numerous works were produced which embodied the prevailing myths, religion, and science of the day. Written many of them in a noble style of poetry, and appealing to the strongest feelings of the people on one side, or registering the highest efforts of their science on the other, these texts became the standards of Babylonian literature, and later generations were content to copy them instead of composing new works for themselves. Clay, the material on which they were written, was everywhere abundant, copies were multiplied, and the veneration in which the texts were held fixed and stereotyped their style. Even the language in which they were written remained the language of literature up to the period of the Persian conquest. Thus it happens that texts of Rim-agu, Sargon, and Khammuragas, who lived at least a thousand years before Nebuchadnezzar and Nabonidus, are composed in the same language as the texts of these later kings, there being no sensible difference in style to match the long interval between them.

We have, however, clear proof that, although the language of devotion and literature remained fixed, the speech of the bulk of the people was gradually modified; and in the time of Assur-bani-pal, when the texts of the Genesis legends which we possess were copied by Assyrian scribes, the common speech of the day was widely different from that of literature. The private letters and despatches of this age which have been discovered differ considerably in language from the contemporary public documents and religious writings, showing the change the language had undergone since the style of the latter had been fixed. So, too, in our own country the language of devotion and the style of the Bible differ in several respects from those of the English of to-day.

These considerations show the difficulty of fixing the age of a cuneiform document from its style, and the difficulty is further increased by the uncertainty which hangs over all Babylonian chronology—an uncertainty that can be cleared away only when the ruined cities of Babylonia are excavated.

Chronology is always a thorny subject, and dry and unsatisfactory to most persons besides; some notice must, however, be taken of it here, in order to fix something like an approximate date or epoch for the original composition of the Genesis legends.

The so-called Assyrian Canon affords us an exact chronology up to the year B.C. 909, and a series of contemporaneous monuments, together with one or two chronological allusions in later inscriptions, enables us to work back from this date to a period falling between B.C. 1450 and 1400 when Assyria was brought into close relation with the southern kingdom of Babylonia. Babylonia was at the time under the sway of a foreign dynasty of Kossæan princes from the mountains of Elam, which was overthrown, as we learn from the Assyrian records, about B.C. 1270. It had been in possession of the country for a considerable time, since a fragmentary list which gives the names of the first nine sovereigns composing it does not come down to the time when the first of the princes who came into close contact with Assyria was reigning. Indeed, a considerable interval must be allowed between the latter period and the last of the nine kings mentioned in the list, in which to insert the isolated names of more than one monarch of the dynasty incidentally mentioned on later monuments. Supposing that not more than fifteen kings preceded Cara-indas in B.C. 1450, and that the average length of their reigns was twenty years, we should have B.C. 1750 as the approximate date of the leader of the dynasty. He could not have been later than this, and there are many reasons which would lead us to suppose that he was earlier.

Khammuragas was the leader of the dynasty in question. He had conquered the rulers of the two kingdoms into which Babylonia was at this time divided. One of these was a queen, with whom ended a dynasty, famous in the annals of early Babylonia, whose seat was at Agané or Agadé, near Sepharvaim. She had been the successor of Naram-Sin, the son of Sargon, who, like his father, had extended his power far and wide, and had even penetrated as far as the shores of the Mediterranean. Sargon had been a great patron of learning as well as a conqueror; he had established a famous library at Agané, and had caused a work on astronomy and astrology to be compiled, which remained the standard authority on the subject up to the end of the Assyrian Empire. It was entitled, "The Illumination of Bel," and was in seventy-two books. Berosus, the historian, seems to have translated it into Greek.

Like the Babylonians and Assyrians of a later day, Sargon and his subjects belonged to the Semitic stock, and were therefore related to the Hebrews and the Arabians. But they were really intruders in Chaldea. The primitive inhabitants of the country, the builders of its cities, the inventors of the cuneiform system of writing, and the founders of the culture and civilization which was afterwards borrowed by the Semites, were of a wholly different race. They spoke an agglutinative language of the same character as that of the modern Turks or Finns, and were originally divided into two sections— the inhabitants of Sumir or Shinar, the plain country, and the Accadians or "Highlanders," who had descended from the mountains of Elam subsequently to the first settlement of their kinsfolk in Shinar. At some date between B.C. 3000 and 2000, the Semitic population which bordered upon Babylonia on the west, and had long been settled in some of its western cities, such as Ur (now Mugheir), conquered Shinar or Sumir. The Accadians, however, maintained their independence for a considerable time after this conquest, until, finally, Accad also was reduced under the sway of the Semitic kings. The old population of the country was gradually absorbed, and its language became extinct. The extinction of the Accadian or Sumerian language had already taken place—at all events among the educated classes— at the time that Sargon founded his library at Agané, and one of the chief reasons which led to the compilation of the great work on astronomy, was the necessity of preserving the astronomical and astrological observations recorded in a language which was beginning to be forgotten. At the same time Semitic translations of other portions of the old Accadian literature were made. The library at Agané, however, was not the only place where the work of translation went on; many other libraries existed, and their scribes and readers had alike become Semites, who required works written in their own tongue. The Semitic translations of Accadian works which were made for the library of Erech, one of the earliest seats of Semitic power, must have been considerably older than those made for the library of Sargon.

The extinction of the Accadian language and the translation of Accadian works into Semitic Babylonian are important facts for settling the chronology of a document or inscription. Wherever we can show that a Babylonian or Assyrian text is translated from an Accadian original, or wherever we have a copy of that original itself, we may feel pretty sure that we are dealing with something older than the eighteenth century before the Christian era.

Mr. Smith believed that the "Exploits of the God Dibbara" was one of the oldest of the mythological texts which have come down to us, though he admitted that the mention of Assyria in it was in favour of a somewhat later date.

It notices a large number of peoples or states, the principal being the people of the coast, Subartu or Syria, Assyria, Elam, the Kassi, the Sutu, Goim, Lullubu, and Accad.

The Izdubar legends, containing the story of the Flood, and possibly also the history of Nimrod, were probably written in the south of the country, and at least as early as B.C. 2000. These legends were, however, traditions before they were committed to writing, and were common in some form to the whole of Chaldea.

The account of the Creation in days, though probably of late Assyrian origin in its present form, may nevertheless rest on older traditions. At present, however, it is not possible to assign to it any great antiquity.

It should, of course, be remembered, that the texts we possess at present are written in Semitic Babylonian or Assyrian—Babylonian and Assyrian being but slightly varying dialects of the same language. They are, however, mostly translations of earlier Accadian documents, and belong to the same period as that which witnessed the foundation of the library of Agané. We shall not be far wrong, therefore, in dating them in their present form about B.C. 2000. The translations then made were copied by successive generations of librarians and scribes, the latest copies of which we know being those that have been brought from the library of Kouyunjik.

To the same early period belonged various other literary compositions, among which we may particularize a long work on terrestrial omens, compiled for Sargon of Agané, as well as the syllabaries, grammars, phrasebooks and vocabularies, and other bilingual tablets by means of which a knowledge of the old language of Accad was conveyed to the Babylonian or Assyrian scholar.

On the other hand, a series of tablets on evil spirits, which contained a totally different tradition of the Creation from that in days, goes back to the Accadian epoch; and there is a third account from the City of Cutha, closely agreeing in some respects with the account handed down by Berosus, which must be placed about the same date.

In spite of the indications as to peculiarities of worship, names of states and capitals, historical allusions and other evidence, it may seem hazardous to many persons to fix the dates of original documents so high, when our only copies in many cases are Assyrian transcripts made in the reign of Assurbani-pal, in the seventh century B.C.; but one or two considerations may show that this is a perfectly reasonable view, and no other likely period can be found for the original composition of the documents unless we ascend to a greater antiquity. In the first place, it must be noticed that the Assyrians themselves state that the documents were copied from ancient Babylonian copies, and in some cases state that the old copies were partly illegible even in their day. Again, in more than one case there is actual proof of the antiquity of a text. We may refer, for example, to a text an Assyrian copy of part of which is published in "Cuneiform Inscriptions," vol. ii. plate 54, Nos. 3 & 4. In a collection of tablets discovered by Mr. Loftus at Senkereh, belonging, according to the kings mentioned in it, to about B.C. 1600, is part of an ancient Babylonian copy of this very text, the Babylonian copy being about one thousand years older than the Assyrian one.

Similarly a fragment of a Babylonian transcript of the Deluge tablet has recently been brought from Babylonia, and serves not only to fill up some of the breaks in our Assyrian copies, but also to verify the text of the latter.

It is unfortunate that so many of the documents embodying the Genesis traditions are in such a sadly mutilated condition, but there can be no doubt that future explorations will reveal more perfect copies, and numerous companion and explanatory texts, which will one day clear up the difficulties which now meet us at every step of our examination of them.

So far as known contemporary inscriptions are concerned, we cannot consider our present researches and discoveries as anything like sufficient to give a fair view of the literature of Assyria and Babylonia; and however numerous and important the Genesis legends may be, they form but a small portion of the whole literature of the country.

It is generally considered that the earliest inscriptions of any importance which we now possess belong to the time of Lig-Bagas, king of Ur, who first united under his sway the petty kingdoms into which Chaldea was previously split up, and whose age is generally assigned to about three thousand years before the Christian era.

The principal inscriptions of this period consist of texts on bricks and on signet cylinders, and some of the latter may be of much greater antiquity. Passing down to a time when the country was again divided into the kingdoms of Karrak, Larsa, and Agané, we find a great accession of literary material, almost every class of writing being represented by contemporary specimens. Each of the principal cities had its library, and education seems to have been widely diffused. From Senkereh, the ancient Larsa, and its neighbourhood have come our oldest specimens of these literary tablets, the following being some of the contents of this earliest known library:—

1. Mythological tablets, including lists of the gods, and their manifestations and titles.

2. Grammatical works, lists of words, and explanations.

3. Mathematical works, calculations, tables of cube and square roots, and tables of measures.

4. Works on astronomy, astrology, and omens.

5. Legends and short historical inscriptions.

6. Historical cylinders, one of Kudur-mabuk, B.C. 1800 (?) (the earliest known cylinder), being in the British Museum.

7. Geographical tablets, and lists of towns and countries.

8. Tablets containing laws and law cases, records of sale and barter, wills and loans.

Such are the inscriptions a single library of Babylonia has produced, and beside these there are numerous texts, only known to us through later copies, but which certainly had their origin as early as this period.

Passing down from this period, for some centuries we find only detached inscriptions, accompanied by evidence of the gradual shifting of both political power and literary activity from Babylonia to Assyria.

In Assyria the first centre of literature and seat of a library was the city of Assur (Kileh Shergat), and the earliest known tablets date about B.C. 1500.

Beyond the scanty records of a few monarchs nothing of value remains of this library, and the literary works contained in it are only known from later copies.

A revival of the Assyrian empire began under Assur-natsir-pal, king of Assyria, who ascended the throne B.C. 885. He rebuilt the city of Calah (Nimroud), and this city became the seat of an Assyrian library. Tablets were procured from Babylonia by Shalmaneser, son of Assur-natsir-pal, B.C. 860, during the reign of Nabu-bal-idina, king of Babylon, and these were copied by the Assyrian scribes, and placed in the royal library. Rimmon-nirari, grandson of Shalmaneser, B.C. 812, added to the Calah library, and had tablets written at Nineveh. Assur-nirari, B.C. 755, continued the literary work, some mythological tablets being dated in his reign.

Tiglath Pileser, B.C. 745, enlarged the library, and placed in it various copies of historical inscriptions. It was, however, reserved for Sargon, who founded the last Assyrian dynasty, B.C. 721, to make the Assyrian royal library worthy of the empire. Early in his reign he appointed Nabu-zuqub-cinu principal librarian, and this officer set to work to make new copies of all the standard works of the day. During the whole of his term of office copies of the great literary works were produced, the majority of the texts preserved belonging to the early period previous to Khammuragas.

With the accession of Sargon came a revival of literature in Assyria; education became more general, ancient texts were brought from Babylonia to be copied, and the antiquarian study of early literature became fashionable.

Sennacherib, son of Sargon, B.C. 704, continued to add to his father's library at Calah, but late in his reign he removed the collection from that city to Nineveh (Kouyunjik), where from this time forth the national library remained until the fall of the empire.

Esarhaddon, son of Sennacherib, B.C. 681, further increased the national collection, most of the works he added being of a religious character.

Assur-bani-pal, son of Esarhaddon, the Sardanapalus of the Greeks, B.C. 670, was the greatest of the Assyrian sovereigns, and he is far more memorable on account of his magnificent patronage of learning than on account of the greatness of his empire or the extent of his wars.

Assur-bani-pal added more to the Assyrian royal library than all the kings who had gone before him, and it is to tablets written in his reign that we owe almost all our knowledge of the Babylonian myths and early history, beside many other important matters.

The agents of Assur-bani-pal sought everywhere for inscribed tablets, brought them to Nineveh, and copied them there; thus the literary treasures of Babylon, Borsippa, Cutha, Agané, Ur, Erech, Larsa, Nipur, and various other cities were transferred to the Assyrian capital to enrich the great collection there.

The fragments brought over to Europe give us a good idea of this library and show the range of the subjects embraced by its collection of works. Among the different classes of texts, the Genesis stories and similar legends occupied a prominent place; these, as they will be further described in the present volume, need only be mentioned here. Accompanying them we have a series of mythological tablets of various sorts, varying from legends of the gods, psalms, songs, prayers, and hymns, down to mere allusions and lists of names. Many of these texts take the form of charms to be used in sickness and for the expulsion of evil spirits; some of them are of great antiquity, being older than the Izdubar legends. One fine series deals with remedies against witchcraft and the assaults of evil spirits. Izdubar is mentioned in one of these tablets as lord of the oaths or pledges of the world.

Some of the prayers were for use on special occasions, such as on starting on a campaign, on the occurrence of an eclipse, &c. Astronomy and astrology were represented by various detached inscriptions and reports, but principally by the great work of which mention has already been made, and many copies of which were in the Library of Assur-bani-pal.

Among the Astrological tablets is a fragment which professes to be copied from an original of the time of Izdubar.

Historical texts formed another section of the library, and these included numerous copies of inscriptions of early Babylonian kings; there were besides, chronological tablets with lists of kings and annual officers, inscriptions of various Assyrian monarchs, histories of the relations between Assyria and Babylonia, Elam, and Arabia, treaties, despatches, proclamations, and reports on the state of the empire and military affairs.

Natural history was represented by bilingual lists of mammals, birds, reptiles, fishes, insects, and plants, trees, grasses, reeds, and grains, earths, stones, &c. These lists are classified according to the supposed nature and affinities of the various species, and show considerable advance in the sciences. Mathematics had a place in the library, there being tables of problems, figures, and calculations; but this branch of learning was not studied so fully as in Babylonia.

Grammar and Lexicography were better represented, since there were many works on these subjects, including lists of the characters, the declension of the noun, the conjugation of the verb, examples of syntactical construction, reading-books, interlinear translations of Accadian texts, and the like. All these tablets were copied from Babylonian originals. In legal and civil literature the library was also rich, and the tablets serve to show that the same laws and customs prevailed in Assyria as in Babylonia. There are codes of laws, law cases, records of sale, barter, and loans, lists of property, lists of titles and trades, of tribute and taxes, &c.

In Geography the Assyrians were not very advanced; but there are lists of countries and their productions, of cities, rivers, mountains, and peoples.

Such are some of the principal contents of the great library from which we have obtained our copies of the Creation and Flood legends. Most of the tablets were copied from early Babylonian ones which have in most cases disappeared; but the copies are sufficient to show the wonderful progress in culture and civilization already made by the people of Chaldea long before the age of Moses or even Abraham. Babylonian literature, which had been the parent of Assyrian writing, revived after the fall of Nineveh, and Nebuchadnezzar and his successors made Babylon the seat of a library rivalling that of Assur-bani-pal at Nineveh. Of this later development of Babylonian literature we know very little, explorations being still required to bring to light its texts. A few fragments only, discovered by wandering Arabs or recovered by chance travellers, have as yet turned up, but there is in them evidence enough to promise a rich reward to future excavators.

Chapter III.
CHALDEAN LEGENDS TRANSMITTED THROUGH BEROSUS AND OTHER ANCIENT AUTHORS.

Berosus and his copyists.—Cory's translation.—Alexander
Polyhistor.—Babylonia.—Oannes, his teaching.—
Creation.—Belus.—Chaldean kings.—Xisuthrus.—
Deluge.—The Ark.—Return to Babylon.—
Apollodorus.—Pantibiblon.—Larancha.—Abydenus.—
Alorus, first king.—Ten kings.—Sisithrus.—Deluge.—
Armenia.—Tower of Babel.—Kronos and Titan.—
Dispersion from Hestiæus.—Babylonian colonies.—
Tower of Babel.—The Sibyl.—Titan and Prometheus.—
Damascius.—Tauthe.—Moymis.—Kissare and
Assorus.—Triad.—Bel.

BY way of introduction to the native versions of the early legends left us by the Babylonians, it is advisable to glance at the principal fragments bearing on them which are found in the classical writers of Greece and Rome. Several others might have been quoted, but their origin is doubtful, and they are of less importance for the subject in hand. Those who wish to consult them may turn to Cory's "Ancient Fragments" (2nd edition, 1876), whose translations, as being fairly scholarlike and correct, are here given without alteration.

Berosus, from whom the principal extracts are copied, lived, as has already been stated, about B.C. 330 to 260, and, from his position as a Babylonian priest, had the best means of knowing the Babylonian traditions.

The others are later writers, who copied in the main from Berosus, most of whose notices may be taken as mere abridgments of his statements.

EXTRACT I. FROM ALEXANDER POLYHISTOR (CORY, p. 56).

Berosus, in the first book of his history of Babylonia, informs us that he lived in the age of Alexander, the son of Philip. And he mentions that there were written accounts, preserved at Babylon with the greatest care, comprehending a period of above fifteen myriads of years; and that these writings contained histories of the heaven and of the sea; of the birth of mankind; and of the kings, and of the memorable actions which they had achieved.

And in the first place he describes Babylonia as a country situated between the Tigris and the Euphrates; that it abounded with wheat, and barley, and ocrus, and sesame; and that in the lakes were found the roots called gongæ, which are fit for food, and in respect to nutriment similar to barley. There were also palm-trees and apples, and a variety of fruits; fish also and birds, both those which are merely of flight, and those which frequent the water. Those parts of the country which bordered upon Arabia were without water, and barren; but that which lay on the other side was both hilly and fertile.

At Babylon there was (in these times) a great resort of people of various races, who inhabited Chaldea, and lived in a lawless manner like the beasts of the field.

OANNES AND OTHER BABYLONIAN MYTHOLOGICAL FIGURES FROM CYLINDER.

In the first year there appeared, from that part of the Erythræan sea which borders upon Babylonia, an animal endowed with reason, by name Oannes, whose whole body (according to the account of Apollodorus) was that of a fish; under the fish's head he had another head, with feet also below similar to those of a man, subjoined to the fish's tail. His voice, too, and language were articulate and human; and a representation of him is preserved even to this day.

This being was accustomed to pass the day among men, but took no food at that season; and he gave them an insight into letters and sciences, and arts of every kind. He taught them to construct houses, to found temples, to compile laws, and explained to them the principles of geometrical knowledge. He made them distinguish the seeds of the earth, and showed them how to collect the fruits; in short, he instructed them in every thing which could tend to soften manners and humanize their lives. From that time, nothing material has been added by way of improvement to his instructions. And when the sun had set this being Oannes used to retire again into the sea, and pass the night in the deep, for he was amphibious. After this there appeared other animals like Oannes, of which Berosus proposes to give an account when he comes to the history of the kings. Moreover, Oannes wrote concerning the generation of mankind, of their different ways of life, and of their civil polity; and the following is the purport of what he said:—

"There was a time in which there existed nothing but darkness and an abyss of waters, wherein resided most hideous beings, which were produced of a two-fold principle. There appeared men, some of whom were furnished with two wings, others with four, and with two faces. They had one body, but two heads; the one that of a man, the other of a woman; they were likewise in their several organs both male and female. Other human figures were to be seen with the legs and horns of a goat; some had horses' feet, while others united the hind quarters of a horse with the body of a man, resembling in shape the hippocentaurs. Bulls likewise were bred there with the heads of men; and dogs with fourfold bodies, terminated in their extremities with the tails of fishes; horses also with the heads of dogs; men, too, and other animals, with the heads and bodies of horses, and the tails of fishes. In short, there were creatures in which were combined the limbs of every species of animals. In addition to these, fishes, reptiles, serpents, with other monstrous animals, which assumed each other's shape and countenance. Of all which were preserved delineations in the temple of Belus at Babylon.

COMPOSITE ANIMALS FROM CYLINDER.

"The person who was supposed to have presided over them was a woman named Omoroka, which in the Chaldean language is Thalatth; which in Greek is interpreted Thalassa, the sea; but according to the most true interpretation it is equivalent to Selene the moon. All things being in this situation, Belus came, and cut the woman asunder, and of one half of her he formed the earth, and of the other half the heavens, and at the same time destroyed the animals within her (or in the abyss).

"All this" (he says) "was an allegorical description of nature. For, the whole universe consisting of moisture, and animals being continually generated therein, the deity above-mentioned (Belus) cut off his own head; upon which the other gods mixed the blood, as it gushed out, with the earth, and from thence men were formed. On this account it is that they are rational, and partake of divine knowledge. This Belus, by whom they signify Hades (Pluto), divided the darkness, and separated the heavens from the earth, and reduced the universe to order. But the recently-created animals, not being able to bear the prevalence of light, died. Belus upon this, seeing a vast space unoccupied, though by nature fruitful, commanded one of the gods to take off his head, and to mix the blood with the earth, and from thence to form other men and animals, which should be capable of bearing the light. Belus formed also the stars, and the sun, and the moon, and the five planets." (Such, according to Alexander Polyhistor, is the account which Berosus gives in his first book.)

(In the second book was contained the history of the ten kings of the Chaldeans, and the periods of the continuance of each reign, which consisted collectively of an hundred and twenty sari, or four hundred and thirty-two thousand years; reaching to the time of the Deluge. For Alexander, enumerating the kings from the writings of the Chaldeans, after the ninth, Ardates, proceeds to the tenth, who is called by them Xisuthrus, in this manner):—

"After the death of Ardates, his son Xisuthrus reigned eighteen sari. In his time happened the great deluge; the history of which is thus described. The deity Kronos appeared to him in a vision, and warned him that upon the fifteenth day of the month Dæsius there would be a flood, by which mankind would be destroyed. He therefore enjoined him to write a history of the beginning, progress, and conclusion of all things, down to the present term, and to bury it in Sippara, the city of the Sun; and to build a vessel, and take with him into it his friends and relations; and to convey on board every thing necessary to sustain life, together with all the different animals, both birds and quadrupeds, and trust himself fearlessly to the deep. Having asked the Deity whither he was to sail, he was answered, 'To the Gods;' upon which he offered up a prayer for the good of mankind. He then obeyed the divine admonition, and built a vessel five stadia in length, and two in breadth. Into this he put everything which he had prepared, and last of all conveyed into it his wife, his children, and his friends.

After the flood had been upon the earth, and was in time abated, Xisuthrus sent out birds from the vessel; which not finding any food, nor any place whereupon they might rest their feet, returned to him again. After an interval of some days, he sent them forth a second time; and they now returned with their feet tinged with mud. He made a trial a third time with these birds; but they returned to him no more: from whence he judged that the surface of the earth had appeared above the waters. He therefore made an opening in the vessel, and upon looking out found that it was stranded upon the side of some mountain; upon which he immediately quitted it with his wife, his daughter, and the pilot. Xisuthrus then paid his adoration to the earth: and, having constructed an altar, offered sacrifices to the gods, and, with those who had come out of the vessel with him, disappeared.

They who remained within, finding that their companions did not return, quitted the vessel with many lamentations, and called continually on the name of Xisuthrus. Him they saw no more; but they could distinguish his voice in the air, and could hear him admonish them to pay due regard to the gods; and he likewise informed them that it was upon account of his piety that he was translated to live with the gods, and that his wife and daughter and the pilot had obtained the same honour. To this he added that they should return to Babylonia, and, as it was ordained, search for the writings at Sippara, which they were to make known to all mankind; moreover, that the place wherein they then were was the land of Armenia. The rest having heard these words offered sacrifices to the gods, and, taking a circuit, journeyed towards Babylonia.

The vessel being thus stranded in Armenia, some part of it yet remains in the Gordyæan (or Kurdish) mountains in Armenia, and the people scrape off the bitumen with which it had been outwardly coated, and make use of it by way of an antidote and amulet. In this manner they returned to Babylon and when they had found the writings at Sippara they built cities and erected temples, and Babylon was thus inhabited again."—*Syncel. Chron.* xxviii.; *Euseb. Chron.* v. 8.

BEROSUS, FROM APOLLODORUS (CORY, p. 51).

This is the history which Berosus has transmitted to us. He tells us that the first king was Alorus of Babylon, a Chaldean; he reigned ten sari (36,000 years); and afterwards Alaparus and Amelon, who came from Pantibiblon; then Ammenon the Chaldean, in whose time appeared the Musarus Oannes, the Annedotus from the Erythræan sea. (But Alexander Polyhistor, anticipating the event, has said that he appeared in the first year, but Apollodorus says that it was after forty sari; Abydenus, however, makes the second Annedotus appear after twenty-six sari.) Then succeeded Megalarus from the city of Pantibiblon, and he reigned eighteen sari; and after him

Daonus, the shepherd from Pantibiblon, reigned ten sari; in his time (he says) appeared again from the Erythræan sea a fourth Annedotus, having the same form with those above, the shape of a fish blended with that of a man. Then reigned Euedorachus (or Euedoreschus) from Pantibiblon for the term of eighteen sari; in his days there appeared another personage from the Erythræan sea like the former, having the same complicated form between a fish and a man, whose name was Odakon. (All these, says Apollodorus, related particularly and circumstantially whatever Oannes had informed them of; concerning these Abydenus has made no mention.) Then reigned Amempsinus, a Chaldean from Larancha; and he being the eighth in order reigned ten sari. Then reigned Otiartes,[1] a Chaldean, from Larancha; and he ruled eight sari. And, upon the death of Otiartes, his son Xisuthrus reigned eighteen sari; in his time happened the great Deluge. So that the sum of all the kings is ten; and the term which they collectively reigned an hundred and twenty sari.—*Syncel. Chron.* xxxix.; *Euseb. Chron.* v.

BEROSUS, FROM ABYDENUS (CORY, p. 53).

So much concerning the wisdom of the Chaldeans.

It is said that the first king of the country was Alorus, and that he gave out a report that God had appointed him to be the shepherd[2] of the people; he reigned ten sari; now a sarus is esteemed to be three thousand six hundred years, a neros six hundred, and a sossus sixty.

After him Alaparus reigned three sari; to him succeeded Amillarus from the city of Pantibiblon, who reigned thirteen sari; in his time there came up from the sea a second Annedotus, a demigod very similar in form to Oannes; after Amillarus reigned Ammenon twelve sari; who was of the city of Pantibiblon; then Megalarus of the same place reigned eighteen sari; then Daos the shepherd governed for the space of ten sari, he was of Pantibiblon; in his time four double-shaped personages came up out of the sea to land, whose names were Euedokus, Eneugamus, Eneubulus, and Anementus; afterwards in the time of Euedoreschus appeared another, Anodaphus. After these reigned other kings, and last of all Sisithrus, so that in all the number amounted to ten kings, and the term of their reigns to an hundred and twenty sari. (And among other things not irrelative to the subject he continues thus concerning the Deluge): After Euedoreschus some others reigned, and then Sisithrus. To him the deity Kronos foretold that on the fifteenth day of the month Dæsius there would be a deluge of rain: and he commanded him to deposit all the writings whatever which were in his possession in Sippara the city of the sun. Sisithrus, when he had complied with these commands, sailed immediately to Armenia, and was presently inspired by God. Upon the third day after the cessation of the rain Sisithrus sent out birds by way of experiment, that he might judge whether the flood had subsided. But the birds, passing over an unbounded sea without finding any place of rest, returned again to Sisithrus. This he repeated with other birds. And when upon the third trial he succeeded, for the birds then returned with their feet stained with mud, the gods translated him from among men. With respect to the vessel, which yet remains in Armenia, it is a custom of the inhabitants to form bracelets and amulets of its wood.—*Syncel. Chron.* xxxviii.; *Euseb. Præp. Evan.* lib. ix.; *Euseb. Chron.* v. 8.

OF THE TOWER OF BABEL (CORY, p. 55).

They say that the first inhabitants of the earth, glorying in their own strength and size and despising the gods, undertook to build a tower whose top should reach the sky, in the place where Babylon now stands; but when it approached the heaven the winds assisted the gods, and overturned the work upon its contrivers, and its ruins are said to be still at Babylon; and the gods introduced a diversity of tongues among men, who till that time had all spoken the same language; and a war arose between Kronos and Titan. The place in which they built the tower is now called Babylon on account of the confusion of tongues, for confusion is by the Hebrews called Babel.—*Euseb. Præp. Evan.* lib. ix.; *Syncel. Chron.* xliv.; *Euseb. Chron.* xiii.

OF THE DISPERSION, FROM HESTIÆUS (*Cory*, p. 74).

The priests who escaped took with them the implements of the worship of the Enyalian Zeus, and came to Senaar in Babylonia. But they were again driven from thence by the introduction of a diversity of tongues; upon which they founded colonies in various parts, each settling in such situations as chance or the direction of God led them to occupy.—*Jos. Ant. Jud.* i. c. 4; *Euseb. Præp. Evan.* ix.

OF THE TOWER OF BABEL, FROM ALEXANDER POLYHISTOR (CORY, p. 75).

The Sibyl says: That when all men formerly spoke the same language some among them undertook to erect a large and lofty tower, that they might climb up into heaven. But God sending forth a whirlwind confounded their design, and gave to each tribe a particular language of its own, which is the reason that the name of that city is Babylon. After the deluge lived Titan and Prometheus, when Titan undertook a war against Kronos.—SYNC. xliv.; JOS. ANT. JUD. i. c. 4.; EUSEB. PRÆP. EVAN. ix.

THE THEOGONIES, FROM DAMASCIUS (CORY, p. 92).

But the Babylonians, like the rest of the barbarians, pass over in silence the One principle of the universe, and they constitute two: Tauthe[3] and Apason,[4] making Apason the husband of Tauthe, and denominating her the mother of the gods. And from these proceeds an only-begotten son, Moymis,[5] which I conceive is no other than the intelligible world proceeding from the two principles. From them also another progeny is derived, Dache and Dachus;[6] and again a third, Kissare and Assorus, from which last three others proceed, Anus (Anu), and Illinus (Elum), and Aus (Hea). And of Aus and Dauke (Davcina, "lady of the earth,") is born a son called Belus, who, they say, is the fabricator of the world, the Demiurgus.

Chapter IV.
BABYLONIAN MYTHOLOGY.

IN their accounts of the Creation and of the early history of the human race the Babylonian divinities figure very prominently, but it is often difficult to identify the deities mentioned by the Greek authors, because the phonetic reading of many of the names of the Babylonian gods is still very obscure, and the classical writers frequently replace them by the deities of their own mythology, whom they imagined to correspond with the Babylonian names.

In this chapter it is proposed to give a general account only of certain parts of the Babylonian mythology, in order to show the relationship between the deities and their titles and work.

Babylonian mythology was local in origin; each of the gods had a particular city which was the special seat of his worship, and it is probable that the idea of weaving the gods into a system, in which each should have his part to play, did not arise until after the Semitic occupation of the country. The antiquity of this systematized mythology may, however, be seen from the fact, that two thousand years before the Christian era it was already completed, and its deities definitely connected into a system which remained with little change down to the close of the kingdom.

In early times the gods were worshipped only at their original cities or seats, the various cities or settlements being independent of each other; but it was natural as wars arose, and some cities gained conquests over others, and kings gradually united the country into monarchies, that the conquerors should impose their gods upon the conquered. Thus arose the system of different ranks or grades among the gods. Colonies, again, were sent out at times, and the colonies, as they considered themselves sons of the cities they started from, also considered their gods to be sons of the gods of the mother cities. Political changes in early times led to the rise and fall of various towns and consequently of their deities, and gave rise to numerous myths relating to the different personages in the mythology. In some remote age there appear to have been three great cities in the country, Erech, Eridu, and Nipur, and their divinities Anu, Hea, and Bel were considered the "great gods" of the country. Subsequent changes led to the decline of these states, but their deities still retained their position to the end of the Babylonian system.

These three leading deities formed members of a circle of twelve gods, also called "great." These gods and their titles are given as:

1. Anu, meaning "the sky" in Accadian, king of angels and spirits, lord of the city of Erech.

2. Bel, Elum or Mul in Accadian, lord of the lower world, father of the gods, creator, lord of the city of Nipur.

3. Hea, "god of the house of water," maker of fate, lord of the deep, god of wisdom and knowledge, lord of the city of Eridu.

4. Sin, the Moon-god, Acu or Agu in Accadian, lord of crowns, maker of brightness, lord of the city of Ur.

5. Merodach, "the glory of the Sun," just prince of the gods, lord of birth, lord of the city of Babylon.

6. Rimmon, the Air-god, Mirmir in Accadian, the strong god, lord of canals and atmosphere, lord of the city of Muru.

7. Samas, the Sun-god, Utuci in Accadian, judge of heaven and earth, director of all, lord of the cities of Larsa and Sippara.

8. Ninip, warrior of the gods, destroyer of the wicked, lord of the city of Nipur.

9. Nergal, "illuminator of the great city" (Hades), giant king of war, lord of the city of Cutha.

10. Nusku, holder of the golden sceptre, the lofty god.

11. Belat, wife of Bel, mother of the great gods, lady of the city of Nipur.

12. Istar, Gingir in Accadian, eldest of heaven and earth, raising the face of warriors.

Below these deities there was a large body of gods forming the bulk of the pantheon, and below these were arranged the Igigi, or 300 angels of heaven, and the Anunnaki, or 600 angels of earth. Below these again came various classes of spirits or genii called Sedu, Vadukku, Ekimu, Gallu, and others; some of these were evil, some good.

The relationship of the various principal gods and their names, titles and offices will appear from the following remarks.

At the head of the Babylonian mythology stands a deity who was sometimes identified with the heavens, sometimes considered as the ruler and god of heaven. This deity is named Anu, his sign is the simple star, the symbol of divinity, and at other times the Maltese cross. In the philosophic theology of a later age, Anu represents abstract divinity, and he appears as an original principle, perhaps as the original principle of nature. He represents the universe as the upper and lower regions, and when these were divided the upper region or heaven was called Anu, while the lower region or earth was called Anatu; Anatu being the female principle or wife of Anu. Anu is termed the old god, and the god of the whole of heaven and earth; one of the manifestations of Anu was under the two forms Lakhmu and Lakhamu, which probably correspond to the Greek forms Dache and Dachus, see p. 44.[7] These forms are said to have sprung out of the original chaos, and they are followed by the two forms Sar and Kisar (the Kissare and Assorus of the Greeks). Sar means the upper hosts or expanse, Kisar the lower hosts or expanse; these are also forms or manifestations of Anu and his wife. Anu is further called lord of the old city, and bears the name of Alalu. His titles generally indicate height, antiquity, purity, divinity, and he may be taken as the general type of divinity. Anu was originally worshipped at the city of Erech, which was called the city of Anu and Anatu, and the great temple there was called the "house of Anu," or the "house of heaven."

Anatu, the wife or consort of Anu, is generally only a female form of Anu, but is sometimes contrasted with him; thus, when Anu represents height and heaven, Anatu represents depth and earth; she is also the lady of darkness, the mother of the god Hea, the mother of heaven and earth, the female fish-god, and is often identified with Istar or Venus. Anatu, however, had no existence in Accadian mythology. She is the product of the imagination of the Semites, whose grammar drew a distinction between the masculine and feminine genders.

Anu and Anatu had a numerous family; among their sons are numbered Lugal-edin, "the king of the desert," Latarak, Ab-gula, Kusu, and the air-god, whose name was Ramman or Rimmon, in Accadian Mirmir. Rimmon is god of the region of the atmosphere, or space between the heaven and earth, he is the god of rain, of storms and whirlwind, of thunder and lightning, of floods and watercourses. He was in high esteem in Syria and Arabia, where he bore the name of Dadda; in Armenia he was called Teiseba. Rimmon is always considered an active deity, and was extensively worshipped.

Another important god, a son of Anu, was the god of fire, whose name was Gibil in Accadian. The fire-god takes an active part in the numerous mythological tablets and legends, and is considered to be the most potent deity in relation to witchcraft and spells generally.

The most important of the daughters of Anu was named Istar; she was in some respects the equivalent of the classical Venus. Her worship was at first subordinate to that of Anu, and as she was goddess of love, while Anu was god of heaven, it is probable that the first intention in the mythology was only to represent love as heaven-born; but in time a more sensual view prevailed, and the worship of Istar became one of the darkest features in Babylonian mythology. As the worship of this goddess increased in favour, it gradually superseded that of Anu, until in time his temple, the house of heaven, came to be regarded as the temple of Venus.

The planet Venus, as the evening star, was identified with Istar of Erech, while the morning star was Anunit, goddess of Agané.

Istar, however, was worshipped under a great variety of forms. Each city, each state, had its own special Istar and its own special worship of her. In the syncretic age of Babylonian theology, these various forms and modes of worship were amalgamated together, and epithets of the goddess which were originally peculiar to particular localities, were applied to the single goddess of the state religion. Thus, according to the legends of one part of Babylonia, Istar was the daughter of the Moon-god, according to those of another part of the country she was the daughter of Anu. Hence in the mythology of a later period she appears sometimes as the daughter of the one deity, sometimes as the daughter of the other.

A companion deity with Anu is Hea, who is god, of the sea and of Hades, in fact of all the lower regions. In some of his attributes he answers to the Kronos of the Greeks, in others to their Poseidon. Hea is called god of the lower region, he is lord of the sea or abyss; he is also lord of generation and of all human beings and bears the titles: lord of wisdom, of mines and treasures; of gifts, of music, of fishermen and sailors, and of Hades or hell. It has been supposed that the serpent was one of his emblems, and that he was the Oannes of Berosus; but these conjectures have not yet been proved. The wife of Hea was Davkina, the Davke of Damascius, who is the goddess of the lower regions, the consort of the deep; and their principal son was Maruduk or Merodach, the Bel of later times.

Merodach, god of Babylon, appears in all the earlier inscriptions as the agent of his father Hea; he goes about the world collecting information, and receives commissions from his father to set right all that appears wrong. He is called the redeemer of mankind, the restorer to life, and the raiser from the dead. He is an active agent in creation, but is always subordinate to his father

Hea. In later times, after Babylon had been made the capital, Merodach, who was god of that city, was raised to the head of the Pantheon. Merodach afterwards came to be identified with the classical Jupiter, but the name Bel, "the lord," was only given to him in times subsequent to the rise of Babylon, when the worship of the older Bel, the Accadian Elum, was falling into decay. The wife of Merodach was Zirat-panit, perhaps the Succoth Benoth of the Bible. Besides Merodach, Hea had a numerous progeny, his sons being principally river-gods.

Nebo, the god of knowledge and literature, who was worshipped at the neighbouring city of Borsippa, was a favourite deity in later times, as was also his consort Tasmit "the Hearer." Nebo, whose name signifies "the prophet," was called Timkhir in Accadian, and had his temple in the island of Dilvun, called "the island of the gods" by the Accadians, now Bahrein. Here he was worshipped under the name of Enzak.

A third great god was united with Anu and Hea, named Enu, Mul, and Elum in Accadian, and Bel in Semitic Babylonian; he was the original Bel of the Babylonian mythology, and was lord of the surface of the earth and the affairs of men. Elum was lord of the city of Nipur, and in the Semitic period had a consort named Belat or Beltis. He was held to be the most active of the gods in the general affairs of mankind, and was so generally worshipped in early times that he came to be regarded as the national divinity, and his temple at the city of Nipur was regarded as the type of all others. The extensive worship of Bel, and the high honour in which he was held, seem to point to a time when his city, Nipur, was the metropolis of the country.

Belat, or Beltis, the wife of Bel, is a famous deity celebrated in all ages, but as the title Belat only signified "lady," or "goddess," it was a common one for many goddesses, and the notices of Beltis probably refer to several different personages.

Bel had, like the other gods, a numerous family; his eldest son was the moon-god, called Agu or Acu in Accadian, in later times generally termed Sin. Sin was presiding deity of the city of Ur, and early assumed an important place in the mythology. The moon-god figures prominently in some early legends, and during the time when the city of Ur was capital of the country his worship became very widely-spread and popular throughout the country.

Ninip, god of hunting and war, was another celebrated son of Bel; he was worshipped with his father at Nipur. Ninip was also much worshipped in Assyria as well as Babylonia, his character as presiding genius of war and the chase making him a favourite deity with the warlike kings of Assyria. Originally he was a form of the sun-god.

Sin the moon-god had a son Samas, the sun-god. Samas is an active deity in some of the Izdubar legends and fables, but he is generally subordinate to Sin. In the Babylonian system the moon takes precedence of the sun, as befitted a nation of astronomers, and the Samas of Larsa was probably considered a different deity from Samas of Sippara.

Among the other deities of the Babylonians may be counted Nergal, god of Cutha, who like Ninip, presided over hunting and war, and Anunit, the goddess of one of the quarters of Sippara, and of the city of Agané.

The following table will exhibit the relationship of the principal deities as it had been drawn up by the native writers on the cosmogony; but it must be noted that it belongs to a late age of syncretic philosophy, when the scholars of Assur-bani-pal's court were endeavouring to resolve the old deities of Accad into mere abstractions, and so explain the myths which described the creation of the world.

Tamtu or Tiamtu (the sea).	Absu (Apason?) (the deep).
Mummu (chaos).	
Lakhmu	Lakhamu
Kisar (Kissare) (lower expanse).	Sar (Assorus) (upper expanse).

Anu (heaven).	Anatu	Elum, or Bel. (earth).	Beltis.

Rimmon (atmosphere).	Gibil (fire-god).	Hea (Saturn) (the deep).	Istar (Venus).

Hea (Saturn).   Davkina (Davke).

Merodach.   Zirat-panit.

Nebo.   Tasmit.

Elum. Beltis.

Sin.   Ningal.   Ninip.

Samas. Istar.

Chapter V.
BABYLONIAN LEGEND OF THE CREATION.

Mutilated condition of tablets.—List of subjects.—
Description of chaos.—Tiamat.—Generation of Gods.—
Damascius.—Comparison with Genesis.—Three great
gods.—Doubtful fragments.—Fifth tablet.—Stars.—
Moon.—Sun.—Abyss or chaos.—Creation of moon.—
Creation of animals.—Monotheism.—Hymn to
Merodach.—The black-headed race or Adamites.—
Garden of Eden.—The flaming sword.—The fall.—The
Sabbath.—Sacred tree.—Hymn to the Creator.

IT is extremely unfortunate that the legend of the Creation in days has reached us in so fragmentary a condition. It is evident, however, that in its present form it is of Assyrian, not of Babylonian, origin, and was probably composed in the time of Assur-bani-pal. It breathes throughout the spirit of a later age, its language and style show no traces of an Accadian original, and the colophon at the end implies by its silence that it was not a copy of an older document. No doubt the story itself was an ancient one; the number seven was a sacred number among the Accadians, who invented the week of seven days, and kept a seventhday Sabbath, and excavations in Babylonia may yet bring to light the early Chaldean form of the legend. But this we do not at present possess.

So far as the fragments can be arranged, they seem to observe the following order:—

•   1. Part of the first tablet, giving an account of the Chaos and the generation of the gods.

•   2. Fragment of subsequent tablet, perhaps the second on the foundation of the deep.

•   3. Fragment of tablet placed here with great doubt, possibly referring to the creation of land.

•   4. Part of the fifth tablet, recording the creation of the heavenly bodies.

•   5. Fragment of the seventh? tablet, recording the creation of land animals.

These fragments indicate that the series included at least seven tablets, the writing on each tablet being in one column on the front and back, and probably including over one hundred lines of text.

The first fragment in the story is the upper part of the first tablet, giving the description of the void or chaos, and part of the generation of the gods. The translation is as follows:

- 1. At that time above, the heaven was unnamed:

- 2. below the earth by name was unrecorded;

- 3. the boundless deep also (was) their generator.

- 4. The chaos of the sea was she who bore the whole of them.

- 5. Their waters were collected together in one place, and

- 6. the flowering reed was not gathered, the marsh-plant was not grown.

- 7. At that time the gods had not been produced, any one of them;

- 8. By name they had not been called, destiny was not fixed.

- 9. Were made also the (great) gods,

- 10. the gods Lakhmu and Lakhamu were produced (the first), and

- 11. to growth they ....

- 12. the gods Sar and Kisar were made next.

- 13. The days were long; a long (time passed), (and)

- 14. the gods Anu (Bel and Hea were born of)

- 15. the gods Sar and (Kisar).......

On the reverse of this tablet there are only fragments of the eight lines of colophon, but the restoration of the passage is easy; it reads:—

- 1. First tablet of "At that time above" (name of Creation series).

- 2. Palace of Assur-bani-pal king of nations, king of Assyria,

- 3. to whom Nebo and Tasmit gave broad ears

- 4. (his) seeing eyes regarded the engraved characters of the tablets;

- 5. this writing which among the kings who went before me

- 6. none of them regarded,

- 7. the secrets of Nebo, the literature of the library as much as is suitable,

- 8. on tablets I wrote, I engraved, I explained, and

- 9. for the inspection of my people within my palace I placed.

This colophon will serve to show the value attached to the documents, and the date of the present copies.

The fragment of the obverse, broken as it is, is precious as giving the description of the chaos or desolate void before the Creation of the world, and the first movement of creation. This corresponds with the first two verses of the first chapter of Genesis.

1. "In the beginning God created the heaven and the earth.

2. And the earth was without form and void; and darkness was upon the face of the deep. And the spirit of God moved upon the face of the waters."

On comparing the fragment of the first tablet of the Creation with the extract from Damascius, we do not find any statement as to there being two principles at first called Tauthe and Apason, and these producing Moymis, but in the Creation tablet the first existence is called Mummu Tiamatu, a name meaning "the chaos of the deep." The compound Mummu Tiamatu, in fact, combines the two names Moymis and Tauthe of Damascius. Tiamatu must also be the same as the Thalatth of Berosus, which we are expressly told was the sea. It should, therefore, be corrected to Thavatth, as M. Lenormant proposed some years ago. It is evident that, according to the notion of the Babylonians, the sea was the origin of all things, and this also agrees with the statement of Genesis i. 2. where the chaotic waters are called tĕhôm, "the deep," the same word as the Tiamat of the Creation text and the Tauthe of Damascius.

The Assyrian word *Mummu* is probably connected with the Hebrew *mĕhûmâh*, confusion, its Accadian equivalent being *Umun*. Besides the name of the chaotic deep called *tĕhôm* in Genesis, which is, as has been said, evidently the Tiamat of the Creation text, we have in Genesis the word *tohû*, waste, desolate, or formless, applied to this chaos. The correspondence between the inscription and Genesis is complete, since both state that a watery chaos preceded the creation, and formed, in fact, the origin and groundwork of the universe. We have here not only an agreement in sense, but, what is rarer, the same word used in both narratives as the name of this chaos, and given also in the account of Damascius.

Next we have in the inscription the creation of the gods Lakhmu and Lakhamu; these are male and female personifications of motion and production, and correspond to the Dache and Dachus of Damascius, and the moving *rûakh*, the wind, or spirit of Genesis. The next stage in the creation was the production of Sar and Kisar, representing the upper expanse and the lower expanse, and corresponding with the Assorus and Kissare of Damascius. The resemblance in these names is probably even closer than is here represented, since Sar is generally read Assur as a deity in later times, being an ordinary symbol for the supreme god of the Assyrians.

So far as can be made out from the mutilated text, the next step in the creation of the universe was (as in Damascius) the generation of the three great gods, Anu, Elum, and Hea, the Anus, Illinus, and Aus of that writer. Anu here symbolizes the heaven, Elum the earth, and Hea the sea.

It is probable that the inscription went on to relate the generation of the other gods, and then passed to the successive acts of creation by which the world was fashioned.

The successive forms Lakhmu and Lakhamu, Sar and Kisar, are represented in some of the lists of the gods as names or manifestations of Anu and Anatu. These lists were compiled at a time when a school of monotheists had risen in Chaldea, and an attempt was made on the part of its adherents to resolve the various deities of the popular creed into forms of "the one god" Anu. In each case there appears to be a male and female principle, which principles combine in the formation of the universe.

As has been already remarked, the conception of a male and female principle was due to the Semites. Hence it is clear that the system of cosmology embodied in these Creation tablets was of Semitic and not Accadian origin.

The resemblance between the extract from Damascius and the account in the Creation tablet as to the successive stages or forms of the Creation, is striking, and leaves no doubt about the source of the quotation from the Greek writer.

The three next tablets in the Creation series are absent, there being only two doubtful fragments of this part of the story. Judging from the analogy of the Book of Genesis, we may conjecture that this part of the narrative contained the description of the creation of light, of the atmosphere or firmament, of the dry land, and of plants. One fragment which probably belonged to this space is a small portion of the top of a tablet referring to the fixing of the dry land; but it may belong to a later part of the story, since it is part of a speech to one of the gods. This fragment is—

- 1. At that time the foundations of the caverns of rock [thou didst make];

- 2. the foundations of the caverns thou didst call [them] (?)

- 3. the heaven was named ......

- 4. to the face of the heaven ......

- 5. thou didst give ......

- 6. a man ......

There is a second more doubtful fragment which also may come in here, and, like the last, relate to the creation of the dry land. It is, however, given under reserve—

- 1. The god Khir ... si ....

- 2. At that time to the god ....

- 3. So be it, I concealed thee ....

FIGHT BETWEEN MERODACH (BEL) AND THE DRAGON.

- 4. from the day that thou ....

- 5. angry thou didst speak ....

- 6. The god Assur his mouth opened and spake, to the god ....

- 7. Above the deep, the seat of ....

- 8. in front of Bit-Sarra which I have made ...

- 9. below the place I strengthen ....

- 10. Let there be made also Bit-Lusu, the seat ..

- 11. Within it his stronghold may he build and ..

- 12. At that time from the deep he raised ....

- 13. the place .... lifted up I made ....

- 14. above .... heaven ....

- 15. the place .... lifted up thou didst make.

- 16. .... the city of Assur the temples of the great gods ....

- 17. .... his father Anu ....

- 18. the god .... thee and over all which thy hand has made

- 19. .... thee, having, over the earth which thy hand has made

- 20. .... having, Assur which thou hast called its name.

This fragment is both mutilated and obscure, and it is more than doubtful whether it has anything to do with the Creation tablets. It seems rather to be a local legend relating to Assur, the old capital of Assyria, and possibly recording the legend of its foundation. Bit-Sarra or E-Sarra, "the temple of the legions," was dedicated to Ninip, and forms part of the name of Tiglath-Pileser (*Tuculti-pal-esara* "Servant of the son of Bit-Sarra," *i.e.* Ninip). It seems to have denoted the firmament, the "legions" or "hosts" referring to the multitudinous spirits of heaven. The Biblical expression "the Lord of hosts" may be compared.

The next recognizable portion of the Creation legends is the upper part of the fifth tablet, which gives the creation of the heavenly bodies, and runs parallel to the account of the fourth day of creation in Genesis.

This tablet opens as follows:—

Fifth Tablet of Creation Legend.

Obverse.

- 1. (Anu) made suitable the mansions of the (seven) great gods.

- 2. The stars he placed in them, the *lumasi*[8] he fixed.

- 3. He arranged the year according to the bounds (or signs of the Zodiac, Heb. *mazzaroth*) that he defined.

- 4. For each of the twelve months three stars he fixed.

- 5. From the day when the year issues forth unto the close,

- 6. he established the mansion of the god Nibiru, that they might know their laws (or bonds).

- 7. That they might not err or deflect at all,

- 8. the mansion of Bel and Hea he established along with himself.

- 9. He opened also the great gates in the sides of the world;

- 10. the bolts he strengthened on the left hand and on the right.

- 11. In its centre also he made a staircase.

- 12. The moon-god he caused to beautify the thick night.

- 13. He appointed him also to hinder (or balance) the night, that the day may be known,

- 14. (saying): Every month, without break, observe thy circle:

- 15. at the beginning of the month also, when the night is at its height.

- 16. (with) the horns thou announcest that the heaven may be known.

- 17. On the seventh day (thy) circle (begins to) fill,

- 18. but open in darkness will remain the half on the right (?).[9]

- 19. At that time the sun (will be) on the horizon of heaven at thy (rising).

- 20. (Thy form) determine and make a (circle?).

- 21. (From hence) return (and) approach the path of the sun.

- 22. (Then) will the darkness return; the sun will change.

- 23. .... seek its road.

- 24. (Rise and) set, and judge judgment.

All that is left of the reverse is the latter half of the last line of the narrative, and the colophon, which runs thus:—

..... the gods on his hearing.

Fifth tablet of (the series beginning) At that time above.

Property of Assur-bani-pal king of nations king of Assyria.

This fine fragment is a typical specimen of the style of the whole series, and shows a marked stage in the Creation, the appointment of the heavenly orbs. It parallels the fourth day of Creation in the first chapter of Genesis, where we read: "And God said, Let there be lights in the firmament of the heaven to divide the day from the night; and let them be for lights in the firmament of the heaven to divide the day from the night; and let them be for signs, and for seasons, and for days, and years:

"15. And let them be for lights in the firmament of the heaven to give light upon the earth: and it was so.

"16. And God made two great lights; the greater light to rule the day, and the lesser light to rule the night; he made the stars also.

"17. And God set them in the firmament of the heaven to give light upon the earth,

"18. And to rule over the day and over the night, and to divide the light from the darkness: and God saw that it was good.

"19. And the evening and morning were the fourth day."

The fragment of the first tablet of the Creation series was introductory, and dealt with the generation of the gods rather than the creation of the universe, and when we remember that the fifth tablet contains the Creation given in Genesis under the fourth day, while a subsequent tablet, probably the seventh, gives the creation of the animals which, according to Genesis, took place on the sixth day, it would seem that the events of each of the days of Genesis were recorded on a separate tablet, and that the numbers of the tablets generally followed in the same order as the days of Creation in Genesis, thus:

Genesis, Chap. I.

- V. 1 & 2 agree with Tablet 1.

- V. 3 to 5 1st day probably with tablet 2.

- V. 6 to 8 2nd day probably with tablet 3.

- V. 9 to 13 3rd day probably with tablet 4.

- V. 14 to 19 4th day agree with tablet 5.

- V. 20 to 23 5th day probably with tablet 6.

- V. 24 & 25 6th day probably with tablet 7.

- V. 26 and following, 6th and 7th day, probably with tablet 8.

The assertion with which the fifth tablet begins may be compared with the oft-repeated statement of Genesis, after each act of creative power, that "God saw that it was good." In fact, the difference between the expressions used by the Hebrew and Assyrian writers seems greater than it really is, since the word rendered "to make suitable" comes from a root which signifies "pleasant" or "agreeable." It may be noted that the word *yuaddi* "he arranged" or "appointed" in the third line has the same root as the Hebrew *môâdhim*, which is used in the same connection Gen. i. 14 in the sense of "seasons."

We next come to the creation of the heavenly orbs, and just as the book of Genesis says they were set for signs and seasons, for days and years, so the inscription describes that the stars were set in courses to define the year. The twelve constellations or signs of the zodiac, and two other bands of constellations are referred to, corresponding with the two sets of twelve stars, one to the north and the other to the south of the zodiac, which according to Diodorus Siculus played a prominent part in Babylonian astronomy.

The god Nibiru appears in the astronomical tablets as one of the stars. Here, however, in the account of the Creation, he seems to be the deity who specially presided over the signs of the zodiac and the course of the year, and in a hymn to the Creator, which will be translated further on, he takes the place of the classical Fate, and determines the laws of the universe generally, and of the stars in particular. It is evident, from the opening of the inscription on the first tablet of the great Chaldean work on astrology and astronomy, that the functions of the stars were according to the Babylonians to act not only as regulators of the seasons and the year, but to be also used as signs, as in Genesis i. 14, for in those ages it was generally believed that the heavenly bodies gave, by their appearance and positions, signs of events which were coming on the earth.

The passage given in the eighth line of the inscription, to the effect that the God who created the stars fixed places or habitations for Bel and Hea with himself in the heavens, points to the fact that Anu, god of the heavens, was considered to be the creator of the heavenly hosts; for it is he who shares with Bel and Hea the divisions of the face of the sky, which was divided into three zones. Summer was the season of Bel, autumn of Anu, and winter of Hea, the season of spring not being recognized by the Babylonians. The new moon also was called Anu for the first five days, Hea for the next five, and Bel for the third.

The ninth line of the tablet gives us an insight into the philosophical beliefs of the early Babylonians. They evidently considered that the world was drawn together out of the waters, and rested or reposed upon a vast abyss of chaotic ocean which filled the space below the world. This dark infernal lake was shut in by gigantic gates and strong fastenings, which prevented the floods from overwhelming the world. In the centre was a staircase which led from the abyss below to the region of light above.

The account then goes on to describe the creation of the moon for the purpose of beautifying the night and regulating the calendar. The phases of the moon are recorded: its commencing as a thin crescent at evening on the first day of the month, and its gradually increasing and travelling further into the night. It will be noticed that it is regarded as appointed, in the language of the Bible, "to divide the day from the night," and to be for a sign and a season. The expression "judge judgment" may be compared with the expression of Genesis (i. 18.) that the sun and moon were set "to rule over the day and over the night." An account of the creation of the sun probably followed upon that of the creation of the moon.

The creation of the moon, however, is placed first in accordance with the general views of the Babylonians, who, as was natural in a people of astronomers, honoured the moon above the sun, even making the sun-god the son of the moon-god.

The details of the creation of the planets and stars, which would have been very important to us, are unfortunately lost, no further fragment of this tablet having been recovered.

The colophon at the close of the tablet gives us, however, part of the first line of the sixth tablet, but not enough to determine its subject. It is probable that this dealt with the creation of creatures of the water and fowls of the air, and that these were the creation of Bel, the companion deity to Anu.

The next tablet, the seventh in the series, is probably represented by a curious fragment, which was found by Mr. Smith in one of the trenches at Kouyunjik.

This fragment is like some of the others, the upper portion of a tablet much broken, and only valuable from its generally clear meaning. The translation is as follows:

- 1. At that time the gods in their assembly created .....

- 2. They made suitable the strong monsters .....

- 3. They caused to come living creatures .....

- 4. cattle of the field, beasts of the field, and creeping things of the field .....

- 5. They fixed for the living creatures .....

- 6. ..... cattle and creeping things of the city they fixed .....

- 7. ..... the assembly of the creeping things, the whole which were created .....

- 8. ..... which in the assembly of my family ...

- 9. ..... and the god Nin-si-ku (the lord of noble face) joined the two together .....

- 10. ..... to the assembly of the creeping things I gave life .....

- 11. ..... the seed of Lakhamu I destroyed .....

This tablet corresponds with the sixth day of Creation in Genesis (i. 24-25): "And God said, Let the earth bring forth the living creature after his kind, cattle, and creeping thing, and beast of the earth after his kind: and it was so.

"And God made the beast of the earth after his kind, and cattle after their kind, and everything that creepeth upon the earth after his kind: and God saw that it was good."

The Assyrian tablet commences with a statement of the satisfaction a former creation, apparently that of the monsters or whales, had given; here referring to Genesis i. 23. It then goes on to relate the creation of living animals on land, three kinds being distinguished, exactly agreeing with the Genesis account, and then we have in the ninth line a curious reference to the god Nin-si-ku (one of the names of Hea). One of Hea's titles was "the lord of mankind," and Sir Henry Rawlinson has endeavoured to show that Eridu, the city of Hea, was identical with the Biblical Garden of Eden. We may here notice a tablet which refers to the creation of man. In this tablet, K 63, the creation of the human race is given to Hea, and all the references in other inscriptions make this his work. As in Genesis, so in these cuneiform tablets the Creator is made to speak and to address the objects which he calls into existence.

The next fragment was supposed by Mr. Smith to relate to the fall of man and to contain the speech of the deity to the newly-created pair. This, however, is extremely doubtful, as will appear from the revised translation below. The fragment is in so broken a condition that almost anything may be made out of it. It is possible that nothing more is intended by it than instructions as to the construction of an image of a household god or spirit and the correct mode of worshipping it.

K 3364 obverse.

(Many lines lost.)

- 1. The whole day thy god thou shalt approach (or invoke),
- 2. sacrifice, the prayer of the mouth, the image ......
- 3. to thy god a heart engraved ..... thou hast.
- 4. How long to the image of the divinity,
- 5. supplication, humility, and bowing of the face,
- 6. fire (?) dost thou give to him, and bringest tribute,

- 7. and in reverence also with me thou goest straight?

- 8. In thy knowledge (?) also behold; in the tablets (writing)

- 9. worship and blessing thou exaltest.

- 10. Sacrifice and the preservation ...

- 11. and prayer for sin ....

- 12. the fear of the gods deserts thee (?) not ....

- 13. the fear of the Anunnaci thou completest ....

- 14. With friend and comrade speech thou makest ....

- 15. In the under-world speech thou makest to the propitious genii.

- 16. When thou speakest also he will give ....

- 17. When thou trustest also thou ....

- 18. ... a comrade also ....

- 19. .... thou trustest a friend ....

- 20. (In) thy knowledge (?) also

Reverse.

(Many lines lost.)

- 1. in the presence of beauty .... thou didst speak

- 2. thy beauty ....

- 3. beauty also .... the female spirit (?)

- 4. An age thou revolvest .. his enemies?

- 5. his rising (?) he seeks .... the man ....

- 6. with the lord of thy beauty thou makest fat (?)

- 7. to do evil thou shalt not approach him,

- 8. at thy illness .... to him

- 9. at thy distress ....

The next fragment is a small one; it is the lower corner of a tablet with the ends of a few lines. Mr. Smith connected it with the legend of the fall of man, but the mention of the god Sar-tuli-elli, "the king of the illustrious mound," would rather indicate that it has to do with the story of the Tower of Babel. As, however, the fragment is too small and mutilated to decide the question, it has been allowed to remain in the place assigned to it by Mr. Smith, and not transferred to a later chapter.

According to Sir H. Rawlinson, "the holy mound" is now represented by the ruins of Amrán. At any rate, it stood on the site of the Tower of Babel and was dedicated to the god Anu. Along with the adjoining buildings, among which are to be numbered the royal palace and the famous hanging gardens, it formed a particular quarter of Babylon, enclosed within its own wall and known under the name of Su-Anna, the "Valley of Anu," which Sir H. Rawlinson proposes to read Khalannê, and identify with the Calneh of the Old Testament. In support of his reading he refers to the statement of the Septuagint in Isaiah x. 9.: "Have not I taken the region above Babylon and Khalannê, where the tower was built?"

Obverse.

- 1. .... seat her (?)
- 2. .... all the lords
- 3. .... his might
- 4. .... the gods, lord of the mighty hour (?)
- 5. .... lord of the kingdom magnified.
- 6. .... mightily supreme.

Reverse.

- 1. .... Hea called[10] to his men
- 2. .... the path of his greatness
- 3. .... any god
- 4. .... Sar-tuli-elli (the king of the illustrious mound) his knowledge (?)
- 5. .... his illustrious ......
- 6. .... his fear (?) Sar-tuli-elli
- 7. .... his might
- 8. .... to them, in the midst of the sea
- 9. .... thy father battle

We may conclude this chapter with a fragment of some length, which Mr. Smith erroneously supposed to refer to the Fall. His mistake arose from the imperfect state in which the text of it has been preserved, and the consequent obscurity of its reference and meaning. Dr. Oppert has shown that it really contains a hymn to the Creator Hea. Before the commencement of lines 1, 5, 11, 19, 27, and 29 on the obverse, there are glosses stating that the divine titles commencing these lines all apply to the same deity. These explanatory glosses show that even in the Assyrian time the allusions in the original text were not all intelligible without the help of a commentary.

Obverse.

- 1. The god of (propitious) Life ..... (secondly)

- 2. who established light .....

- 3. their precepts .....

- 4. Never may they forsake (their) boundaries ...

- 5. The god of illustrious Life, thirdly, he was called, the director of the bright (firmament),

- 6. the god of good winds, the lord of hearing and obedience,

- 7. the creator of lean (?) and fat, the establisher of fertility,

- 8. who has brought to increase them that were small at the outset.

- 9. In the mighty thickets we have smelt his good wind.

- 10. May he command, may he glorify, may he hearken to his worshippers.

- 11. The god of the illustrious Crown, fourthly, may he quicken the dust!

- 12. Lord of the illustrious charm, who gives life to the dead,

- 13. who to the hostile gods has granted return,

- 14. the homage they rendered he has caused the gods his foes to submit to.

- 15. That they might obey (?) he has created mankind,

- 16. the merciful one with whom is life.

- 17. May he establish, and never may his word be forgotten

- 18. in the mouth of the black-headed race whom his hands created.

- 19. The god of the illustrious incantation, fifthly, may his foes (?) be overthrown (*or* answered) with hostile curse (?)

- 20. He who with his illustrious incantation has removed the curse of the enemy.

- 21. The God the Heart-knower, who knows the hearts of the gods, who fly from the fear of him:

- 22. the doing of evil they caused not to come forth against him.

- 23. He who establishes the assembly of the gods, (who knows) their hearts,

- 24. who subdues the disobedient .....

- 25. who directs justice .....

- 26. who (defends?) sovereignty .....

- 27. The god of prosperous life, (sixthly) .....

- 28. he who cuts off darkness (?) .....

- 29. The god Sukhkhab (?), thirdly, the flock (?) ...

- 30. he who adds unto them .....

Reverse.

- 1. ..... the star .....

- 2. may he seize that which has the head in the tail (? a comet)

- 3. since that in the midst of the sea he passed over .....

- 4. His name accordingly (is) Nibiru (the passer over), the possessor .....

- 5. may he (confirm) the precepts (or laws) of the stars of heaven.

- 6. Like sheep may he feed the gods all of them;

- 7. may he exorcise the sea, its treasures may he hedge in and summon

- 8. among men hereafter through length of days.

- 9. May he also remove mischief; may he overcome it for the future.

- 10. Because (all) places he made, he pierced, he strengthened.

- 11. Lord of the world is his name called, (even) father Bel.

- 12. The names of the angels he gave to them.

- 13. Hea also heard, and his liver (*i. e.* anger) was lulled,

- 14. (saying) "Since that his men he has quickened by his name,

- 15. he like myself has the name of Hea.

- 16. The bond of my command may he bring to them all, and

- 17. all my *tereti* (lots?) may he answer [or throw down]

- 18. by the fifty names of the great gods."

- 19. His fifty names they pronounced; they restored his precepts.

- 20. May they be observed and, as formerly, may he speak.

- 21. Unsearchable, wise, triumphantly may he rule.

- 22. May father to son repeat and exalt (them).

- 23. May he open the ears of shepherd and flocks.

- 24. May (the shepherd) obey Merodach, Bel among the gods.

- 25. May his land be green, may he himself be at peace.

- 26. Established (is) his word, unyielding his command;

- 27. the utterance of his mouth no god has ever despised.

- 28. He was called by name and withdraws not his neck.

- 29. In the abundance of his strength there is no god, that receives for him his crown.

- 30. Far-reaching (is) his heart, an abyss (is) his stomach:

- 31. Sin and cursing before him disappear.

In a second copy which presents several variations lines 14 to 19 are omitted.

It is evident that this hymn to the Creator emanated from what Sir Henry Rawlinson has termed the monotheistic party among the ancient Babylonians, and that the speech of Hea in lines 14 to 19 has been inserted by a poet who did not belong to it. The various deities of the popular faith are all resolved into the one supreme God, the maker of the world and man, who was worshipped at Babylon under the names of Bel, "the Lord," and Merodach the sun-god, at Eridu under that of Hea and at Nipur under that of Anu. The gods of the multitude are said to be only the fifty names of the Creator. To him is ascribed the regulation of the stars, the naming of the angels, and the subjection of the subordinate demi-gods, and marginal notes expressly state that the several titles under which the Creator is addressed on the obverse of the tablets, all belong to one and the same divinity.

In the popular mythology the part of the Creator was usually assigned to Merodach. Thus we find the latter deity addressed as follows in a mutilated bilingual hymn (K 2962 *Obv.*):—

- 1. [King] of the land, lord of the world,

- 2. ... protector of heaven and earth,

- 3. firstborn of the god Hea,

- 4. the restorer of heaven and earth,

- 5. ... mighty lord of mankind, king of the world.

- 6. ... the god of gods,

- 7. (lord) of heaven and earth, who hast no equal,

- 8. companion of Anu and Bel,

- 9. the merciful one among the gods,

- 10. the merciful who raisest the dead to life,

- 11. Merodach, the king of heaven and earth,

- 12. the king of Babylon, the lord of Bit-Saggil,

- 13. the king of Bit-Zida, the lord of the mighty temple of life,

- 14. heaven and earth are thine,

- 15. the circuit of heaven and earth is thine,

- 16. the charm (to produce) life is thine,

- 17. the philtre of life is thine,

- 18. the Illustrious King, the mouth of the Abyss, is thine;

- 19. mankind, (even) the men with the black heads,

- 20. living creatures, as many as are called by a name, as exist in the land,

- 21. the four quarters of the world, as many as there are,

- 22. the angels of the hosts of heaven and earth, as many as there are, (are thine).

In these references to the names of the living creatures made by the Creator at the beginning of the world, we are irresistibly reminded of the passage in Genesis ii. 19., where we read that "out of the ground God formed every beast of the field and every fowl of the air; and brought them to Adam to see what he would call them: and whatsoever Adam called every living creature, that was the name thereof."

One of the most curious statements made in these hymns is that the race of men created by the deity was black-headed. The same race of men is mentioned elsewhere in the ancient literature of the Accadians. Thus in a hymn to the goddess Gula, the goddess is described as "the mother who bore the men of the black heads," and in another hymn the sun-god is declared to "direct the men of the black heads." Sargon of Agané is further described as ruling over "all the men of the black heads," and in imitation of this mode of expression Sennacherib in later days speaks of having overcome "all the black-headed race." The black-headed race of Sennacherib, however, was the Turanian population of Elam and the adjoining districts on the east of Babylonia, whereas it is plain that the Accadian hymns mean by the black-headed race the Accadian people itself. It was over them that Sargon of Agané, the Semite, boasts of having extended his sway, though according to an old geographical list it was Sumer or Shinar rather than Accad, which was inhabited by the people of "the black-face." But after all there is no contradiction between the statements of Sennacherib and of the hymns. The Accadians belonged to the same race as the Turanian inhabitants of Elam, and spoke a similar language to theirs.

Now we shall find in the account of the exploits of Dibbara, which will be translated in a subsequent chapter, that the black race, which is identified with the Accadians, is contrasted with the people of Syria, while in the bilingual tablets, the black race is similarly contrasted with the white race. Hence it is clear that the white race was the same as the Syrians, and since the Syrians were Semites, the white race must have been synonymous in the language of the Accadians with Semitic. As a matter of fact, the Semites belong to the white-skinned division of mankind, and were accordingly painted yellow by the Egyptians. The Accadian population, on the other hand, belonged to the dark-skinned division, though it is not necessary to suppose them to have been as black as the negro or the "blameless Ethiopian." In the bilingual tablets, the black race is rendered in Assyrian by the word *Adamatu* or "red-skins."

A popular etymology connected this word *Adamatu* with the word *Adamu* or *admu*, "man," partly on account of the similarity of sound, partly because in the age of Accadian supremacy and literature, the men *par excellence*, the special human beings made by the Creator, were the dark-skinned race of Accad. The Accadian Adam or "man" was dark; it was only when the culture of the Accadians had been handed on to their Semitic successors that he became fair.

The discovery that the Biblical Adam is identical with the Assyrian *Adamu* or "man," and that the Assyrian *Adamu* goes back to the first-created man of Accadian tradition who belonged to the black, that is, to the Accadian race, is due to Sir Henry Rawlinson. He has also suggested that the contrast between the black and the white races, between the Accadian and the Semite, is indicated in the sixth chapter of Genesis, where a contrast is drawn between the daughters of men, or *Adamu*, and the sons of God. It was owing to the intermarriage of the sons of God with the Adamites that the evils were spread which brought down upon the world the punishment of the Deluge.

It was Sir Henry Rawlinson who further pointed out that the Biblical Gân Eden, or "Garden of Eden," is Gan-Duniyas (also called Gun-duni), a name under which Babylonia is frequently known in the Assyrian inscriptions. Gan-Duniyas signifies "the enclosure" or "fortress of the god Duniyas," a deity whose nature and attributes are still obscure, and who may have been merely a deified monarch of the country. Two of the four rivers of Paradise are the two great rivers that enclose the fruitful plain of Babylonia, the Tigris, and the Euphrates. The Euphrates was called Purrat, or "the curving water" in Accadian from its shape; the Tigris was known under the name of Masgugar, "the current," Tiggar, and Idikna or Idikla, from the latter of which comes the Hiddekhel of Genesis, with prefixed Accadian *hid*, "river." Gihon is identified with the Arakhtu or Araxes, "the river of Babylon," which flowed westward into the desert of Arabia or Cush, though Sir H. Rawlinson suggests its identity with the modern Jukhá, which runs past the site of Eridu, while Sargon calls Elam the country of "the four rivers."[11]

The tree of life was well known to the Accadians and the Assyrians after them, and the bas-reliefs of Nineveh frequently present us with a representation of it, guarded on either side by a winged cherub who has the head sometimes of a man, sometimes of an eagle. The tree always assumes a conventional form, and since it generally bears fir-cones we may infer that the Accadians brought the tradition of it with them from their original seat in the colder mountainous land of Media, where the fir was plentiful, and identified it with the palm-tree only after their settlement in Chaldea. An old name of Babylon, or of a part of Babylon, was Din-Tir, "the life of the forest," which may possibly have some connection with the tree of life. The special spot, however, in which the site of the tree of life was localized was close to the city of Eridu, now represented by Dhib according to Sir H.

Rawlinson, where the solar hero Tammuz was supposed to have received the death-blow which obliged him to spend one half the year in the lower world.

SACRED TREE, OR GROVE, WITH ATTENDANT CHERUBIM, FROM ASSYRIAN CYLINDER.

A fragmentary bilingual hymn speaks thus of the sacred spot, and of the tree of life that grew therein:—

- 1. In Eridu a dark pine grew, in an illustrious place it was planted.

- 2. Its (root) was of white crystal which spread towards the deep.

- 3. The (shrine?) of Hea (was) its pasturage in Eridu, a canal full of (water).

- 4. Its seat (was) the (central) place of this earth.

- 5. Its shrine (was) the couch of mother Zicum, (the mother of gods and men).

- 6. The (roof) of its illustrious temple like a forest spread its shade; there (was) none who within entered.

- 7. (It was the seat) of the mighty mother (Zicum), the begetter of Anu.

Eridu was the special seat of the worship of Hea, and was often known as "the good city."

The flaming sword, which according to Genesis guarded the approach to the tree of life is paralleled by the flaming sword of Merodach, which is explained to be the lightning. It was with this sword which is represented on the monuments as having the form of a sickle like the sword of the Greek hero

Perseus, that Merodach overthrew the dragon and the powers of darkness. A hymn put into the mouth of Merodach, thus speaks of it:—

- The sun of fifty faces, the lofty weapon of my divinity, I bear.

- The hero that striketh the mountains, the propitious sun of the morning, that is mine, I bear.

- My mighty weapon, which like an orb smites in a circle the corpses of the fighters, I bear.

- The striker of mountains, my murderous weapon of Anu, I bear.

- The striker of mountains, the fish with seven tails, that is mine, I bear.

- The terror of battle, the destroyer of rebel lands, that is mine, I bear.

- The defender of conquests, the great sword, the falchion of my divinity, I bear.

- That from whose hand the mountain escapes not, the hand of the hero of battle, which is mine, I bear.

- The delight (?) of heroes, my spear of battle, (I bear).

- My crown which strikes against men, the bow of the lightning, (I bear).

- The crusher of the temples of rebel lands, my club and buckler of battle, (I bear).

- The lightning of battle, my weapon of fifty heads, (I bear).

- The feathered monster of seven heads, like the huge serpent of seven heads, (I bear).

- Like the serpent that beats the sea, (which attacks) the foe in the face,

- the devastator of forceful battle, lord over heaven and earth, the weapon of (seven) heads, (I bear).

- That which maketh the light come forth like day, god of the East, my burning power, (I bear).

- The establisher of heaven and earth, the fire-god, who has not his rival, (I bear).

SACRED TREE, SEATED FIGURE ON EACH SIDE, AND SERPENT IN BACKGROUND, FROM AN EARLY BABYLONIAN CYLINDER.

Allusion is made in this hymn, it will be noticed, to a fabulous serpent with seven heads, which beats the sea into waves. This serpent was originally identical with the dragon of the deep, combated by Merodach, as we shall learn from a fragment to be translated hereafter, that is to say with the principle of chaos and darkness, called Mummu Tiamtu, "the chaos of the deep," in the account of the creation. It is also described as "the serpent of night," "the serpent of darkness," "the wicked serpent," and "the mightily strong serpent," epithets which show that it was on the one hand the embodiment of moral evil, and on the other was primitively nothing more than the darkness destroyed by the sun, the bright power of day. It is difficult not to compare the serpent of Genesis with this serpent of Babylonian mythology. No Chaldean legend of the Fall has as yet been found, but when we remember how few Chaldean legends have been discovered, and that even for these we are dependent on the selection and copies of Assyrian scribes, we need not be surprised that such should be the case. The Babylonian colouring of the history in Genesis, the fact that the rivers of Paradise are Babylonian rivers, and that the tree of life was familiar to Babylonian art and tradition, make it probable that we shall yet discover the Chaldean version of the Fall of Man as soon as the libraries of Babylonia have been explored. Indeed, this is made almost certain by the existence of an early Babylonian seal, now in the British Museum, on which a tree is represented with a human figure seated on either side of it, with the hands stretched out towards the fruit, and a serpent standing erect behind one of them. We know that the devices on these early seals were taken from the popular legends and myths. It must be admitted, however, that the two figures seem both to be males.

But if references to the Fall are few and obscure, there can be no doubt that the Sabbath was an Accadian institution, intimately connected with the worship of the seven planets. The astronomical tablets have shown that the seven-day week was of Accadian origin, each day of it being dedicated to the sun, moon, and five planets, and the word Sabbath itself, under the form of *Sabattu*, was known to the Assyrians, and explained by them as "a day of rest for the heart." A calendar of Saint's days for the month of the intercalary Elul makes the 7th, 14th, 19th, 21st, and 28th days of the lunar month Sabbaths on which no work was allowed to be done. The Accadian words by which the idea of Sabbath is denoted, literally mean, "a day on which work is unlawful," and are interpreted in the bilingual tablets as signifying "a day of peace" or "completion of labours." The calendar lays down the following injunctions to the king for each of these sabbaths:—

A Sabbath: the prince of many nations the flesh of animals and cooked food may not eat.

The garments of his body he may not change. White robes he may not put on.

Sacrifice he may not offer. The king may not ride in his chariot.

In royal fashion he may not legislate. A review of the army the general may not hold.

Medicine for his sickness of body he may not apply.

MERODACH ATTACKING THE SERPENT, ON AN ASSYRIAN CYLINDER, IN THE POSSESSION OF DR. S. WELLS WILLIAMS, NEWHAVEN.

The antiquity of this text is evident not only from the fact that it has been translated from an Accadian original, but also from the word rendered "prince," which literally means "a shepherd," and takes us back to the early times when the Accadian monarchs still remembered that their predecessors had been only shepherd-chieftains.

Before concluding this chapter, it must be noted that the word translated "the sea," in lines three and seven of the reverse of the hymn to the Creator, is Tiamtu, which, as we have seen, was the name applied to the deep, upon which the Babylonians believed that the earth rested, and out of which it had been brought into existence.

Chapter VI.
OTHER BABYLONIAN ACCOUNTS OF THE CREATION.

Cuneiform accounts originally traditions.—Variations.—
Account of Berosus.—Tablet from Cutha.—
Translation.—Composite animals.—Eagle-headed men.—
Seven brothers.—Destruction of men.—Seven wicked
spirits.—Mythical explanation of lunar eclipses.—Hymn
to the God of Fire.—War in heaven.—Tiamat-
Merodach.—The great dragon.—Parallel Biblical account.

THE traditions embodied by Accadians and Assyrians in the literature of which specimens have been given in the preceding chapter, had been handed down by word of mouth through many generations, and committed to writing only at a comparatively late period. When such is the case, traditions are naturally liable to vary, sometimes very widely, according to the period and condition of the country. Thus many different versions of a story arise, and there can be no doubt that this was actually the case with the Creation legends. The account of the Creation in six days was not the only account of the Creation current among the inhabitants of Assyria and Babylonia. It was but one out of many which had slowly grown up among the people, and been finally thrown into a literary form. The story of the Creation transmitted through Berosus (see chapter iii. pp. 34-36), for example, supplies us with an account which differs entirely from the cuneiform account in the last chapter as well as from the Genesis account, and some fragments of tablets from Kouyunjik belonging to the library of Assur-bani-pal give a copy, mutilated as usual, of a third version which has, however, points of agreement with the account of Berosus. This legend, of which the following is a translation, is stated to be copied from a tablet at Cutha.

Legend of Creation from Cutha tablet.

(Many lines lost at commencement.)

- 1. .... his lord, the crown of the gods ....

- 2. the spearmen of his host, the spearmen of (his) host ....

- 3. lord of those above and those below, lord of the angels ....

- 4. who drank turbid waters and pure waters did not drink ....

- 5. who with his flame, as a weapon, that host enclosed,

- 6. has taken, has devoured.

- 7. On a memorial-stone he wrote not, he disclosed not, and bodies and produce

- 8. in the earth he caused not to come forth, and I approached him not.

- 9. Warriors with the bodies of birds of the desert, men

- 10. with the faces of ravens,

- 11. these the great gods created,

- 12. in the earth the gods created their city.

- 13. Tiamtu gave them suck,

- 14. their life (?) the mistress of the gods created.

- 15. In the midst of the earth they grew up and became strong, and

- 16. increased (?) in number,

- 17. Seven kings, brethren, were made to come as begetters;

- 18. six thousand in number were their armies.

- 19. The god Banini their father was king, their mother

- 20. the queen was Melili,

- 21. their eldest brother who went before them, Memangab was his name,

- 22. their second brother Medudu was his name,

- 23. their third brother .... pakh was his name,

- 24. their fourth brother .... dada was his name,

- 25. their fifth brother .... takh was his name,

- 27. their sixth brother .... ruru was his name,

- 28. their seventh brother .... (rara) was his name.

COLUMN II.

(Many lines lost.)

- 1. ..... the evil curse ....

- 2. The man his will turned ....

- 3. on a .... I arranged.

- 4. On a (tablet) the evil curse (which) in blood he raised
- 5. (I wrote and the children of) the generals I urged on.
- 6. Seven (against seven in) breadth I arranged them.
- 7. (I established) the illustrious (ordinances?)
- 8. I prayed to the great gods
- 9. Istar, ..., Zamama, Anunit,
- 10. Nebo .... and Samas the warrior,
- 11. the son of (the moon-god), the gods that go (before me).
- 12. .... he did not give and
- 13. thus I said in my heart,
- 14. that, Here am I and
- 15. may I not go .... (beneath) the ground.
- 16. may I not go ...... may the prayer
- 17. go when .... my heart,
- 18. may I renew, the iron in my hand may I take.
- 19. The first year in the course of it
- 20. one hundred and twenty thousand soldiers I sent out, and among them
- 21. not one returned.
- 22. The second year in the course of it, ninety thousand I sent out, and not one returned.
- 23. The third year in the course of it, sixty thousand seven hundred I sent out, and not one returned.
- 24. They were rooted out, they were smitten with sickness; I ate,
- 25. I rejoiced, I rested.
- 26. Thus I said to my heart that, Here am I and
- 27. for my reign what is left (to rule over)?
- 28. I the king, am not the replenisher of his country,

COLUMN III.

- 1. and (I), the shepherd, am not the replenisher of his people,

- 2. since I established corpses, and a desert is left.

- 3. The whole of the country (and) men with night, death (and) plague I cursed it.

- 4. (I afflicted them) as many as exist.

- 5. ...... there descended

- 6. ...... a whirlwind.

- 7. ...... its whirlwind.

- 8. .... all.

- 9. The foundations (of the earth were shaken?)

- 10. The gods ....

- 11. Thou didst bind and .....

- 12. and they were bound (?) ....

- 13. Thou protectedst .....

- 14. A memorial of ....

- 15. in supplication to Hea ....

- 16. Illustrious memorial sacrifices ....

- 17. Illustrious *tereti* ......

- 18. I collected; the children of the generals (I urged on).

- 19. Seven against seven in breadth I arranged.

- 20. I established the illustrious ordinances (?)

- 21. I prayed to (the great) gods,

- 22. Istar .... (Zamama, Anunit,)

- 23. Nebo ... (and the Sun-god, the warrior,)

- 24. the son (of the Moon-god, the gods who go before me).

COLUMN IV.

(Several lines lost at commencement.)

- 1. Thou O king, viceroy, shepherd, or any one else,

- 2. whom God shall call to rule the kingdom,

- 3. this tablet I made for thee, this record-stone I wrote for thee,

- 4. in the city of Cutha, in the temple of Gallam,

- 5. in the sanctuary of Nergal, I leave for thee;

- 6. this record-stone see, and,

- 7. to the words of this record-stone listen, and

- 8. do not rebel, do not fail,

- 9. do not fear, and do not curse.

- 10. Thy foundation may he establish!

- 11. As for thee, in thy works may he make splendour.

- 12. Thy forts shall be strong,

- 13. thy canals shall be full of water,

- 14. thy papyri, thy corn, thy silver,

- 15. thy furniture, thy goods,

- 16. and thy instruments, shall be multiplied.

- (A few more mutilated lines.)

**SACRED TREE, ATTENDANT FIGURES AND EAGLE-HEADED MEN,
FROM THE SEAL OF A SYRIAN CHIEF, NINTH CENTURY B.C.**

This is a very obscure inscription, the first column, however, forms part of a relation similar to that of Berosus in his history of the Creation; the beings who were killed by the light, and those with men's heads and bird's bodies, and bird's heads and men's bodies, agree with the composite monsters of Berosus, while the goddess of chaos, Tiamtu, who is over them, is the same as the Thalatth of the Greek writer. It may be remarked that the doctrine of the Greek philosopher, Anaximander, that man has developed out of creatures of various shape, and once like the fish was an inhabitant of the water, is but a reminiscence of the old Babylonian legend.

The relation in the third column of the inscription is difficult, and does not correspond with any known incident. The fourth column contains an address to any future king who should read the inscription which was deposited in the temple of Nergal at Cutha.

It is possible that this legend was supposed to be the work of one of the mythical kings of Chaldea, who describes the condition and history of the world before his time.

The war carried on against the monstrous creations of Tiamtu, described in this myth, was but one version of the war waged against Tiamtu, or Chaos, herself by the sun-god Merodach. The most famous form taken by the story of this war was that which described the attack of the seven wicked spirits, or storm-demons, against the moon, and their final discomfiture by the bright power of day. This attack was a primitive attempt to account for lunar eclipses, dressed up in poetry, and may be compared with the Chinese belief that when the moon is eclipsed it has been devoured by the dragon of night. Similarly the Egyptians told how Set or Typhon pursued the moon, the eye of Horus, how it waned week by week as he struck it, and finally passed into eclipse when he blinded it altogether. According to Hindu legend, the immortal head of the serpent-demon Râhu, cut off by Vishnu who had been informed by the sun and moon of his theft of the drink of immortality, incessantly pursues the two informers in order to devour them, and a Scandinavian myth makes the sun and moon to be always pursued by two wolves, Sköll and Hati, the latter of whom, also called Mânagarmr or dog of the moon, will at the end of the times swallow up the chief luminary of night.

Tablet with the story of the Seven Wicked Spirits.

COLUMN I.

- 1. The recurring days[12] are the wicked gods.
- 2. The rebellious spirits, who in the lower part of heaven
- 3. had been created,
- 4. wrought their evil work

- 5. devising with wicked heads (at) sunset;

- 6. (like) a sea-monster to the river (they marched).

- 7. Among the seven of them the first was a scorpion (*or* fiery sting) of rain.

- 8. The second was a thunderbolt which no man could face.

- 9. The third was a leopard ....

- 10. The fourth was a serpent ....

- 11. The fifth was a watch-dog which (rages) against (his foes).

- 12. The sixth was a raging tempest which to god and king submits not.

- 13. The seventh was the messenger of the evil wind which (Anu) made.

- 14. The seven of them (are) messengers of the god Anu their king.

- 15. In city after city they set their returning feet.

- 16. The raging wind which (is) in heaven, fiercely hath been bound to them.

- 17. The fleecy rain-clouds (are they) which in heaven establish cloudy darkness.

- 18. The lightning of the tempest, the raging tempests which in the bright day

- 19. establish gloom, are they.

- 20. With evil tempest, baleful wind, they began:

- 21. the storm of Rimmon, that was their might,

- 22. at the right hand of Rimmon did they march;

- 23. from the foundations of heaven like lightning (they darted),

- 24. (like) a sea-monster to the river in front they marched.

- 25. In the wide heavens the seat of Anu the king

- 26. with evil purpose did they abide, and a rival they had not.

- 27. Then Bel of this matter heard and

- 28. the word sank into his heart.

- 29. With Hea the supreme adviser of the gods he took counsel, and

- 30. Sin (the moon), Samas (the sun), and Istar (Venus) in the lower part of heaven to direct it he had appointed.

- 31. With Anu the lordship of the hosts of heaven he made them share.

- 32. The three of them, those gods his children,

- 33. night and day he had established; that they break not apart,

- 34. he urged them.

- 35. Then those seven, the evil gods,

- 36. in the lower part of heaven commencing,

- 37. before the light of Sin fiercely they came,

- 38. the hero Samas and Rimmon (the god of the atmosphere) the warrior to their quarters returned and

- 39. Istar with Anu the king a noble seat

- 40. chooses and in the government of heaven is glorious.

COLUMN II.

MERODACH DELIVERING THE MOON-GOD FROM THE EVIL SPIRITS; FROM A BABYLONIAN CYLINDER.

The second column, which is much mutilated at the beginning, goes on to describe "the trouble" of the moon-god, how "night and day in eclipse, in the seat of his dominion he sat not." But

- 1. The wicked gods the messengers of Anu their king

- 2. devising with wicked heads assisted one another.

- 3. Evil they plotted together.

- 4. From the midst of heaven like the wind on mankind they swooped.

- 5. Bel the eclipse of the hero Sin

- 6. in heaven saw and

- 7. the god to his messenger the god Nusku (Nebo) said:

- 8. "My messenger, Nebo, my word to the deep carry:

- 9. the news of my son Sin who in heaven is grievously eclipsed

- 10. to the god Hea in the deep repeat." Then

- 11. Nebo the word of his lord obeyed, and

- 12. to Hea in the deep descended and went.

- 13. To the prince, the supreme councillor, the lord, the lord of mankind,

- 14. Nebo the message of his lord in that quarter at once repeated.

- 15. Hea in the deep that message heard, and

- 28. his lips he bit, and with outcry his mouth he filled.

- 29. Hea his son the god Merodach called, and the word he spake:

- 30. "Go, my son Merodach!

- 31. the light of the sky, my son Sin, whom heaven is grievously eclipsed,

- 32. (in) his eclipse from heaven is departing.

- 33. Those seven wicked gods, serpents[13] of death, having no fear,

- 34. those seven wicked gods, who like a whirlwind

- 35. (destroy) the life of mankind,

- 36. against the earth like a storm they come down.

- 37. In front of the bright one Sin fiercely they came,

- 38. the hero Samas and Rimmon the warrior, to their quarters (returned),

- 39. (Istar, with Anu the king, an illustrious seat chooses, and in the dominion of heaven is glorious).

EAGLE-HEADED MAN. FROM NIMROUD SCULPTURE.

Most of the remainder of the legend, consisting of some forty lines, is unfortunately lost, owing to a fracture of the tablet. What is left, however, shows that Merodach, "the brilliance of the sun," for such is the meaning of his name, who always appears in the Accadian hymns as a kind of Babylonian Prometheus and universal benefactor, comes to the help of the "labouring" moon, and "awe" goes before him. Dressed in "glistening armour of unsoiled cloths and broad garments," he enters "the gate of the palace," "a king, the son of his god, who, like the bright one, the moon-god, sustains the life of the land," and there with a helmet of "light like the fire" upon his head, successfully overthrows the seven powers of darkness. The poem concludes with a prayer that they may never descend into the land, and traverse its borders.

In this story, which differs again from all the others, Bel is supposed to place in the heaven the Moon, Sun, and Venus, the representative of the stars. The details have no analogy with the other stories, and this can only be considered a poetical myth of the Creation.

This legend is part of the sixteenth tablet of the series on evil spirits; but the tablet contains other matters as well, the legend apparently being only quoted in it. There is another remarkable legend of the same sort in praise of the fire-god, on another tablet of this series published in "Cuneiform Inscriptions," vol. iv. p. 15. The whole of this series concerns the wanderings of the god Merodach, who goes about the world seeking to remove curses and spells, and in every difficulty applying to his father Hea to learn how to combat the influence of the evil spirits, to whom all misfortunes were attributed.

The seven evil spirits illustrate well the way in which a moral signification may come to be attached to what was originally a purely physical myth. They are frequently mentioned in the literature of ancient Accad. Thus the twenty-third book, on eclipses of the moon, of the great work on astronomy compiled for Sargon of Agané, states that: "When the moon shall describe a section (in) the upper circle (of its revolution), the gods of heaven and earth bring about dearth of men (and) their overthrow; and (there is) eclipse, inundation, sickness, (and) death; the seven great spirits before the moon are broken." Elsewhere, an Accadian hymn, which has an interlinear Assyrian translation attached to it, speaks as follows of these dreaded spirits:—

- 1. Seven (they) are, seven they (are).

- 2. In the abyss of the deep seven they (are).

- 3. The splendours of heaven (are) those seven.

- 4. In the abyss of the deep, (in) a palace, (was) their growth.

- 5. Male they (are) not, female they (are) not. [The Accadian text, in accordance with the respect paid to women in Accad, reverses this order.]

- 6. As for them, the deep (is) their binder.

- 7. Wife they have not, son is not born to them.

- 8. Reverence (and) kindness know they not.

- 9. Prayer and supplication hear they not.

- 10. (Among) the thorns (?) on the mountain (was) their growth.

- 11. To Hea are they foes.

- 12. The throne-bearers of the gods (are) they.

- 13. Destroying the roads on the paths are they set.

- 14. Wicked (are) they, wicked (are) they;

- 15. seven (are) they, seven (are) they, seven twice again (are) they.

Another Accadian poet, who lived at Eridu, the supposed site of Paradise, at the junction of the Tigris and Euphrates, has left another account of the Seven wicked spirits in the hymn to the fire-god mentioned above. He says of them:—

- 1. O god of fire, those seven how were they begotten, how grew they up?

- 2. Those seven in the mountain of the sunset were born;

- 3. those seven in the mountain of the sunrise grew up.

- 4. In the deep places of the earth have they their dwelling.

- 5. In the high places of the earth have they their name.

- 6. As for them, in heaven and earth wide is their habitation.

- 7. Among the gods their couch they have not.

- 8. Their name in heaven (and) earth exists not.

- 9. Seven they (are); in the mountain of the sunset do they rise.

- 10. Seven they (are); in the mountain of the sunrise did they set.

- 11. In the deep places of the earth did they rest their feet.

- 12. On the high places of the earth do they lift up their head.

- 13. As for them, goods they know not, in heaven (and) earth are they not learned.

Merodach is then ordered to fetch "the laurel, the baleful tree that breaks in pieces the incubi, the name whereof Hea remembers in his heart, in the mighty enclosure, the girdle of Eridu," in order that the seven evil spirits may be driven away. Can this laurel-tree be the tree of the knowledge of good and evil? It must be remembered that Hea was "the lord of wisdom," and under the form of a fish as Oannes or *Hea Khan* was supposed to have ascended from the Persian Gulf, and taught the primitive Babylonians the elements of culture and civilization.

At the head of the seven evil spirits stood Tiamtu, the representative of chaos and darkness. One of the most remarkable Babylonian legends yet discovered is one which tells of the primæval struggle between Tiamtu and Merodach, between light and darkness or good and evil, and which does but embody in a new shape the conception which found expression in the myth of the war against the moon. The tablets which contain this legend are unfortunately in a very fragmentary condition.

The first of these is K 4832, too mutilated to translate; it contains speeches of the gods before the war.

The second fragment, K 3473, contains also speeches, and shows the gods preparing for battle. It is so terribly broken that translation is impossible, and all that can be made out is a line here and there.

The third fragment, K 3938, is on the same subject; some lines of this give the following general meaning:—

- 1. winged thunderbolts ....
- 2. fear he made to carry ....
- 3. their sight very great (?) ....
- 4. their bodies may he destroy and ....
- 5. he raised; it was suitable, the strong serpent ....
- 6. Udgallum, Urbat[14] and the god ....
- 7. days arranged, five (?) ....
- 8. carrying weapons unyielding ....
- 9. her breast, her back ....
- 10. flowing (?) and first ....
- 11. among the gods collected ....
- 12. the god Kingu subdued ....
- 13. marching in front before ....
- 14. carrying weapons thou ...
- 15. upon war ....
- 16. his hand appointed ....

There are many more similar broken lines, and on the other side fragments of a speech by some being who desires Tiamtu to make war.

All these fragments are not sufficiently complete to allow us to translate them with certainty, or even to ascertain their order.

The fourth fragment, K 3449, relates to the making of weapons to arm the god who should meet in war the dragon.

This reads with some doubt on account of its mutilation:

- 1. The scimitar he had made the gods saw
- 2. and they saw also the bow how it had been stored up.
- 3. The work he had wrought (on his shoulder)
- 4. he raised and Anu in the assembly of the gods
- 5. kissed the bow; it (he addressed),
- 6. and he spake of the bow thus (and said)
- 7. The illustrious wood I have drawn out once and twice,
- 8. thrice also, her punishment the star of the bow in heaven (shall effect)
- 9. and I have made (it) the protection (of mankind).
- 10. From the choice of ....
- 11. and place his throne ....

BEL ENCOUNTERING THE DRAGON; FROM BABYLONIAN CYLINDER.

The next fragment or collection of fragments gives the final struggle between Tiamtu and Bel Merodach. The *saparu*, or sickle-shaped sword, is always represented both in the sculptures and inscriptions as a weapon of Bel Merodach in this war.

Sixth Fragment.

- 1. .... he fixed it ....
- 2. the weapon with his right hand he took
- 3. .... and the quiver from his hand he hung,
- 4. and he hurled the lightning before him,
- 5. heat filled his body.
- 6. He made also the scimitar (to produce) calm in the midst of the sea (Tiamtu).
- 7. The four winds he imprisoned that they might come forth from its calm,
- 8. the South, the North, the East, and the West winds.
- 9. His hand caused the scimitar to approach the bow of his father Anu.
- 10. He created the evil wind, the hostile wind, the tempest, the storm,
- 11. the four winds, the seven winds, the whirlwind, the unceasing wind.
- 12. He sent forth also the winds he had created, seven of them;
- 13. into the midst of the sea (Tiamtu) they were launched to disturb, they came after him.
- 14. He lifted up the weapon, the thunderbolt, his mighty weapon;
- 15. in a chariot that sweeps away all in front, which gives rest, he rode.
- 16. He fixed it and four yoke-thongs on its pole he hung,
- 17. .... the unyielding, the overwhelming, he that pursues her.
- 18. .... with their sting bringing poison
- 19. .... sweeping away knowledge (?)
- 20. .... destruction and fighting.

(Several other fragmentary lines.)

Reverse.

- 1. Unprevailing (is) thy troop; may thy arms strike their bodies!

- 77 -

- 2. I also stand firm, and with thee make battle.

- 3. Tiamtu (the sea) on hearing this

- 4. as before used spells, she changed her resolution.

- 5. Tiamtu also raised herself; warily she ascended.

- 6. At the roots fully she grounded (her) foundations.

- 7. She told over the spell; she determined return (to chaos),

- 8. and the gods for the war asked for themselves their weapons.

- 9. Then Tiamtu attacked the prince of the gods, Merodach,

- 10. who had made charms as for combat for the conflict in battle.

- 11. Then Bel made sharp his scimitar; he smote her.

- 12. The evil wind that seizes behind from before him fled.

- 13. And Tiamtu opened her mouth to swallow him.

- 14. The evil wind he made to descend so that she could not close her lips;

- 15. the force of the wind her stomach filled, and

- 16. she was sickened in heart, and her mouth it distorted.

- 17. She bit the shaft (of the sword); her stomach failed;[15]

- 18. her inside it cut asunder, it conquered the heart;

- 19. it consumed her, and her life it ended.

- 20. Her death he completed, over her he fixes (it).

- 21. When Tiamat their leader he had conquered,

- 22. her ranks he broke, her assembly was scattered;

- 23. and the gods her helpers who went beside her

- 24. returned in fear, they fled back behind them.

- 25. They fled and feared for their life.

- 26. They are companions in flight, powerless.

- 27. He trampled on them and their weapons he broke.

- 28. Like a scimitar are they laid, and as in darkness they sat.

- 29. (They seek) their quarters, they are full of grief;

- 30. what was left they take away, they pull back like a rope,

MERODACH, OR BEL, ARMED FOR THE CONFLICT WITH THE DRAGON; FROM ASSYRIAN CYLINDER.

- 31. and elevenfold offspring from fear they produce

- 32. (Through) the flood the demons go (all of them?).

- 33. He laid the hostility, his hand ....

- 34. part of their opposition under him ....

- 35. and the god Kingu again ....

Again the main difficulty arises from the fragmentary state of the documents, it being impossible even to decide the order of the fragments. It appears, however, that the gods have fashioned for them a scimitar and a bow to fight the dragon Tiamtu, and Anu proclaims great honour (fourth fragment, lines 7 to 11) to any of the gods who will engage in battle with her. Bel or Merodach volunteers, and goes forth armed with these weapons to fight the dragon. Tiamtu is encouraged by one of the gods who has become her husband, and meets Merodach in battle. The description of the fight and the subsequent triumph of the god are very fine, and remarkably curious in their details, but the connection between the fragments is so uncertain at present that it is better to reserve comment upon them until the text is more complete. The scimitar with which Merodach is armed is shown by the cylinders and bas-reliefs to have been of the shape of a sickle, and is therefore the same as the *harpê* or *khereb* with which the Greek hero Perseus was armed when he went forth to fight against the dragon of the sea at Joppa. The dragon itself, according to the representations of the monuments, was a composite monster, with the tail, horns, claws, and wings of the mediæval devil. The whole war between the powers of good and evil, chaos and order, finds its parallel in the war between Michael and the dragon in Revelation xii. 7 to 9, where the dragon is called "the great dragon, that old serpent, called the devil and Satan, which deceiveth the whole world." This description is strikingly like the impression gathered from the fragments of the cuneiform story; the dragon Tiamtu who fought against the gods, and whose fate it was to be conquered in a celestial war, closely corresponds in all essential points with the dragon conquered by Michael. That the dragon originally symbolized the sea is one proof out of many that the Accadians were a seafaring people, well acquainted with the terrors of the deep, when the waves conspire with the storm-clouds, those seven evil spirits, to throw all nature once more into its primeval anarchy.

FIGHT BETWEEN BEL AND THE DRAGON, FROM BABYLONIAN CYLINDER.

Chapter VII.
THE SIN OF THE GOD ZU.

God Zu.—Obscurity of legend.—Translation.—Sin of
Zu.—Anger of the gods.—Speeches of Anu to
Rimmon.—Rimmon's answer.—Speech of Anu to
Nebo.—Answer of Nebo.—Lugal-turda.—Changes to a
bird.—The Zu bird.—Bird of prey.—Lugal-turda lord of
Amarda.—Prometheus.

AMONG the legends of the gods, companion stories to the accounts of the
Creation and Deluge, one of the most curious is the legend of the sin
committed by the god Zu.

This legend stands quite alone, its incidents and its principal actor being
otherwise almost unknown from cuneiform sources. Only one copy of the
story has at present been detected, and this is in so mutilated a condition that
it cannot be connected with any other of the legends. It belongs to the same
cycle of myths as the myth of the exploits of Dibbara, which will be given in
the next chapter.

The principal actor in the legend is a god named Zu, the name being found
in all the three cases of an Assyrian noun Zu, Za, and Zi. Analogy would lead
us to infer that the name had been borrowed by the Assyrians from the
Accadians, as well as the story with which it is connected.

Mr. Smith compared the legend with that of the mutilation of Uranus by his
son Kronus, and with the history of the outrage of Ham on his father Noah;
but its real analogue is the myth of Prometheus, the benefactor of men, who
stole the fire of heaven for their sake, and brought upon himself the anger
and punishment of Zeus. It contains two difficult words, *partsi* and *tereti*. The
first is ambiguous, meaning either "oracles" or "shrines," but since it is
coupled with *dup-simi*, "tablets of destiny," it is probably to be rendered
"oracles." *Tereti* is very obscure. The sun-god is called "the lord of *tereti*" and
the word occurs in the hymn to the Creator, Rev. 17 (p. 79), where also it is
united with *partsi*, "command" or "oracle." It may signify "lots." The tablets
of destiny, stolen by Zu, for the benefit, apparently, of mankind, formed the
vault of the palace of the under-world. We may compare the books which
are to be opened on the day of judgment in Dan. vii. 10, and Rev. xx. 12.

The tablet containing the account of the sin of Zu, K 3454, in the Museum
collection, originally contained four columns of text, each column having
about sixty lines of writing. The first and fourth columns are almost entirely
lost, there not being enough anywhere to translate from. The mutilation of
the text seriously adds to the difficulties of translation.

The single fragment preserved, belonging to the first column, mentions some being who was the seed or firstborn of Bel, with a number of titles, such as "warrior, soldier of the temple of Bel," and the name of the god Zu occurs, but not so as to prove these titles to be his.

The following is a partial translation of the remains of this tablet:—

K. 3454.

COLUMN I. lost.

COLUMN II.

- 1. .... of the gods all of them he urged on.

- 2. .... the image, Zu grew old (and)

- 3. Zu? like .... Bel seized his heel.

- 4. Three streams? of water in front also

- 5. the work of Bel in .... he dreams of (*or* ponders) in himself.

- 6. The crown of his majesty, the clothing of his divinity,

- 7. the tablets of destiny, himself, Zu, he dreams of, and

- 8. he dreams that he is the father of the gods also, the protector of heaven and earth.

- 9. The desire to be Bel is taken in his heart,

- 10. Zu dreams that he is also the father of the gods, the protector of heaven and earth.

- 11. The desire to be Bel is taken in his heart:

- 12. Let me too seize the tablets of destiny of the gods,

- 13. and the *tereti* of the gods all of them let me kindle,

- 14. may my throne also be established, let me lift up the oracles,

- 15. let me urge on the whole of all of them, even the angels.

- 16. So he lifted up his heart in opposition,

- 17. in the lower part of the forest where he was dreaming he kept his head away from the day.

- 18. When Bel pours out the bright waters,

- 19. spread out also on the throne his crown was placed,

- 20. the tablets of doom his hand took,

- 21. the attributes of Bel he seized, he laid hold of the oracles.

- 22. Zu fled away and a rugged mountain concealed (him).

- 23. He spread darkness, and made a commotion (?).

- 24. The father, their king, the ruler Bel

- 25. ..... outpoured the glory of the gods.

- 26. ....

- 27. Anu his mouth opened, he speaks

- 28. and says to the gods his sons:

- 29. Whoever will, let him slay Zu, and

- 30. among all men may his name be renowned.

- 31. (To Rimmon) the powerful firstborn the son of Anu

- 32. his will also to him he declares:

- 33. To Rimmon the powerful firstborn the son of Anu

- 34. his will to him he declares.

- 35. (O mighty) Rimmon, companion, may thy power of fighting never fail.

- 36. (Slay) Zu with thy weapon.

- 37. (May thy name) be renowned in the assembly of the great gods,

- 38. .... a rival have thy brothers

- 39. may they supply and build of brick (thy) altars,

- 40. in the four regions may they establish thy stronghold.

- 41. May thy stronghold be exalted to become a shrine.

- 42. They shall cry (?) in the presence of the gods and blessed be thy name.

- 43. Rimmon answered the speech,

- 44. to his father Anu a word he speaks;

- 45. My father, to an impenetrable mountain do thou consign (him).

- 46. Let Zu never associate among the gods thy sons.

- 47. The tablets of destiny his hand took;
- 48. the attributes of Bel he seized, laying hold of the oracles,
- 49. Zu fled away and a rugged mountain concealed (him).
- 50. .... the opening of (his) mouth
- 51. .... like mud
- 52. .... the gods sweep away
- 53. .... I will not go he said.

(Sixteen lines lost here, part on this column, part on Column III.)

COLUMN III.

- 1. Zu fled away and a rugged mountain concealed (him).
- 2. .... the opening of his mouth ... the protector of heaven and earth
- 3. .... like mud
- 4. .... the gods sweep away
- 5. .... I will not go he said.

- 6. To Nebo the powerful .... the eldest son of Istar,
- 7. (Anu his will) to him also declares:
- 8. O mighty Nebo, companion, may thy power of fighting never fail!
- 9. (Slay) Zu with thy weapon.
- 10. May (thy name) be renowned in the assembly of the great gods,
- 11. ..... among the gods thy brothers a rival have (?)
- 12. May they supply and build (thy) altars;
- 13. in the four regions may they establish thy stronghold.
- 14. May thy stronghold be exalted to become a shrine.
- 15. They shall cry (?) in the presence of the gods and blessed be thy name.
- 16. Nebo answered the speech,

- 17. to his father Anu a word he speaks:

- 18. My father, to a trackless mountain do thou consign him.

- 19. Let Zu never associate with the gods thy sons.

- 20. The tablets of destiny his hand took,

- 21. the attributes of Bel he seized, laying hold of the oracles.

- 22. Zu fled away and a rugged mountain concealed him.

- 23. .... the opening of his mouth ... the protector of heaven and earth

The rest, including Column IV., is lost.

Such are the fragments of the story so far as they can be translated at present. The divine Zu here mentioned, whose sin is spoken of, is never counted among the gods, and there would be no clue to his nature were it not for a curious tablet printed in "Cuneiform Inscriptions," vol. iv. p. 14, which throws light on his origin and character. This tablet gives the following curious relation:

- 1. The god Lugal-turda (the valiant king) [fled] to the mountains, a place remote;

- 2. in the mountains of Sabu [he dwelt].

- 3. No mother gave him life[16] or (suckled him).

- 4. No father gave him life or with him (associated).

- 5. No noble who knew him (helped him).

- 6. Of the resolution of his heart the resolution he (changed) not.

- 7. In his own heart the resolution (he kept).

- 8. Into the likeness of a bird was he transformed;

- 9. into the likeness of the divine storm bird (or Zu bird) was he transformed.

- 10. The face of his wife who has faced?

- 11. The wife of the Divine Zu bird, the son of the divine Zu bird,

- 12. in companionship he made sit.

- 13. The goddess Enna, the lady of Tigenna,

- 14. in the mountain he brought back.

- 15. A woman fashioned was her mother according to likeness made,

- 16. the goddess of perfumes a woman fashioned was her mother according to likeness made.

- 17. Her hair was white crystal;

- 18. Her navel was pure with silver and gold,

- 19. brightness was fixed in the womb;

- 20. in the womb dwelt perfection (?).

Many lines are lost here, and the story recommences on reverse.

- 1. .... a turban he placed on his head

- 2. (when) from the nest of the god Zu he came.

- ─────────────────────

This Zu bird is plainly the same as the god Zu of the former legend, and his nature is shown by a passage in the annals of Assur-nazir-pal ("Cuneiform Inscriptions," vol. i. p. 22, col. ii. l. 107), who says that his warriors "like the divine Zu bird upon them darted." This bird is called the cloud or storm-bird, the flesh-eating bird, the lion or giant bird, the bird of prey, the bird with sharp beak; and it is not difficult to see what the deified bird really was. It was clearly the storm-cloud, which appears in Aryan folklore under the varying forms of the eagle, the woodpecker, and the robin redbreast, the bird of Thor; while in Chinese mythology the storm-bird is described as "a bird which, in flying, obscures the sun, and of whose quills are made water-tuns." The roc of the "Arabian Nights," with its wings of ten thousand fathoms in width, and its egg, which it was a sin in Aladdin to wish to take from the place where it hung, is but an echo of the Chinese storm-bird; and the identity of the Chaldean Zu with the latter is demonstrated by its Accadian name, which signifies "the bird of the divine storm-cloud." Just as Prometheus brought the lightning from heaven to earth, and suffered the penalty of enchainment to a desert rock, so, too, the storm-bird of Accad stole the secrets of the gods, and was punished by exile from them, and transformation into a bird. When once the storm-cloud had been likened to a bird, it was easy enough to identify it with an actual bird of similar name which swooped upon its prey with sharp beak. That the lightning which darted from the bosom of the black tempest really formed the tablets of destiny was a ready conclusion to a people who read the future in the message sent through the lightning from heaven to earth. Even the Hebrews saw in the thunder "the voice of God." Lugal-turda, it may be added, was the patron of the city of Amarda or Marad, and is said to have been the deity worshipped by Izdubar.

In the story of the offence of Zu there is another instance of the variations which constantly occur in the Assyrian inscriptions with respect to the relationship of the gods. Nebo is usually called son of Merodach, but in this inscription he is called son of Anu. The part that he plays in it is due to the fact that he was identified with the "meridian sun."

Chapter VIII.
THE EXPLOITS OF DIBBARA.

Dibbara.—God of Pestilence.—Itak.—The Plague.—
Seven warrior gods.—Destruction of people.—Anu.—
Goddess of Karrak.—Speech of Bel.—Sin and destruction
of Babylonians.—Samas.—Sin and destruction of
Erech.—Istar.—The great god and Duran.—Cutha.—
Internal wars.—Itak goes to Syria.—Power and glory of
Dibbara.—Song of Dibbara.—Blessings on his worship.—
God Ner.—Prayer to arrest the Plague.—Antiquity of the
legend.—Itak.

THE tablets recording this story are five in number, but a few fragments only of them have as yet been found. From the indications presented by these fragments the first four tablets seem each to have had four columns of writing, while the fifth tablet was a smaller one of two columns containing the remainder of the story.

The god whose exploits are principally recorded was the leader of the plague-demons, and bears the name of Dibbara. He has the title of "the darkening one," which recalls the passage in Psalm xci. 6, "the pestilence that walketh in darkness."

He has a companion deity named Itak who marches before him, and seven gods who follow him in his destructive course. The latter are the seven evil spirits in a new form.

The point of the story in these tablets appears to be, that the people of the world had offended Anu the god of heaven, and accordingly that deity ordered Dibbara to go forth and strike the people with the pest. It is evident here that exactly the same views prevailed in Babylonia as among the Jews, visitations from pestilence or famine being always supposed to be sent by the deity in punishment for some sin. In fact, the account of the pestilence inflicted upon the Israelites on account of David's sin in numbering the people is a striking parallel to the Accadian legend which follows. The angel of the pestilence seen by David, with his sword drawn, may be compared with Dibbara, the Accadian personification of the pest.

The whole of this series of tablets may be described as a poetical picture of the destruction caused by a plague, sweeping over district after district, and destroying everything before it.

The fragment which appears to come first in the series is a very mutilated portion of a tablet, containing parts of three columns of writing. Only a fragment of the first column is perfect enough to translate, and the characters on this are so worn that the translation cannot be other than doubtful. It seems to read

- 1. Against the paling he struck and ....

-

- 2. the fifth time he smote (?) above and below seeking .....

- 3. seven ......

- 4. The words of the account of the seven gods all of them Anu had heard.

- 5. He .... them also to Dibbara the warrior of the gods: May thy hands go

- 5(sic.). whenever the people of the nations their shame [*or* alliance] have destroyed.

- 7. I have set thy heart also to make darkness.

- 8. The people of the black heads to ruin thou shalt strike with the desolation of the god Ner;

- 9. may thy weapons (overthrow) them, and may thy hands go.

- 10. As for them ..... their weapons.

- 11. He said to Dibbara: ......

The speech of Anu which follows is written in characters so broken and indistinct as to make any attempt at translation impossible.

The next fragment is of a different character, but appears from its style to belong to the same series.

- 1. .... he ....

- 2. .. spake to him and he explained (?) ....

- 3. .. spake to him and he learned (?) ....

- 4. Anu at the doing of Hea shouted for joy and ....

- 5. the gods of heaven and earth as many as exist whosoever thus answered;

- 6. his command which was like the command of Anu whosoever appointed

-
- 7. .... extending from the horizon of heaven to the top of heaven
- 8. .... he looked and his fear he saw
- 9. .... Anu who .... over him .... made
- 10. .... of Hea his calamity (?) made
- 11. .... a fierce lord to later days to ....
- 12. .... seed of mankind
- 13. .... triumphantly the net (?) .. he broke
- 14. .... to heaven he had ascended, she thus
- 15. .... 4,021 people he had placed
- 16. .... the illness which was on the body of the people he had placed
- 17. .... the illness the goddess of Karrak made to cease.

The next portion of the legend is a considerable part of one of the tablets, probably the fourth, all four columns of writing being represented. There are many curious points in this tablet, beside the special purpose of the legend, such as the peoples enumerated in the fourth column, the action of the gods of the various cities, &c.

COLUMN I.

- 1. Bel .... his yokes and
- 2. (in his) heart he says:
- 3. Dibbara is crouching at his gate, among the corpses of chiefs and slaves;
- 4. Dibbara is crouching at his gate; thou knowest his seat.
- 5. Babylon their foes besieged, and
-
- 6. their curse art thou.
- 7. To the floor thou didst trample them and thou didst make a passage,
- 8. O warrior Dibbara.
- 9. Thou didst leave the land, thou didst go forth against others;

- 10. the destruction of the nobles wast thou made, and thou didst descend into the palace.

- 11. The people also saw thee; their weapons were shattered.

- 12. The high priest the avenger of Babylon sets his heart,

- 13. when the ranks of the enemies to spoil he urges on his soldiers.

- 14. Before the face of the people they did evil.

- 15. To that city whither I shall send thee, thou a man

- 16. shalt not fear, shalt not respect a man.

- 17. Small and great as one man cast down and

- 18. of that evil race thou shalt not save any one.

- 19. The collection of the goods of Babylon thou spoilest;

- 20. the people of the king (which) is gathered together, and entered into the city,

- 21. shaking the bow, planting the sword (?)

- 22. of the soldiers the help, the transgression (transgressors) against Anu and Dagon,

- 23. their weapons thou plantest,

- 24. their corpses like the pouring down of rain thou dost cast down in the streets of the city,

-

- 25. and their treasures (?) thou openest, and dost sweep into the river.

- 26. The spell Merodach saw and angrily (?) spoke,

- 27. his heart was taken,

- 28. an unsparing curse in his mouth was formed,

- 29. .... the river he did not ....

COLUMN II.

Many lines lost.

- 1. .... that city which the lord of the earth ...

- 2. a whirlwind he did not (make) ....

- 91 -

- 3. without Samas his tower thou crossest, the land thou givest (?)

- 4. of Erech the seat of Anu and Istar,

- 5. the city of (the handmaids) Samkhati and Kharimati, the choirs of

- 6. Istar. Death they fear (and) they are delivered into thy hands (?).

- 7. The Suti (Arab nomads) with the Suti are placed in ....

- 8. they are slain; the temple of Anu the priests, the festival makers,

- 9. who, to make the people of Istar worship, their manhood devoted,

- 10. carrying swords, carrying razors, *dupe*, and knives,

- 11. who to rejoice the glory of Istar trusted,

- 12. O fierce high priest, the bowing-down of the face over them thou hast made.

-

- 13. Their foundations also, their shrines ....

- 14. Istar cried out and was troubled over the city of Erech,

- 15. the enemy she strikes and like corn on the face of the waters she scatters.

- 16. Dwelling in his .... Bit-Parra ....

- 17. ... she rests not from the war.

- 18. The enemy whom thou hast stricken obeys not ....

- 19. The great god answered the speech:

- 20. The city of Duran to streams of blood ....

- 21. the people who dwell in the midst of it like reeds (are trembling);

- 22. .... before the waters their alliance ....

- 23. and ... thou dost not ....

- 24. to the Suti ....

- 25. I in my city Duran judge uprightly

- 26. I do not ....

- 27. evil (?) I do not give and ....

- 28. the upright people I leave ....

- Five other broken lines.

COLUMN III.

Many lines lost.

- 1. .... the house he had built ....

- 2. this he did, and I ....

- 3. the day he brought me my fate I ....

- 4. him, his camp (?) also he caused to destroy ..

- 5. Afterwards may they destroy, and to another

-

- 6. O warrior Dibbara, the established also in Gutium,

- 7. the unestablished also in Gutium,

- 8. who sin against thee also in Gutium,

- 9. who do not sin against thee also in Gutium,

- 10. .... the destroyer (?) of the clothes of the god of Gutium,

- 11. .... the mover of the head of the king.

- Two other mutilated lines.

COLUMN IV.

- 1. May the planet Mercury cause his splendour to wane;

- 2. to his resolutions (?) is he bound:

- 3. he rejoices not the mouth of his (worshippers)

- 4. who the structure ....

- 5. to the seat of the king of the gods may he urge and ....

- 6. The warrior Dibbara heard it also,

- 7. the word (which) the god Itak spake to him ..

- 8. and thus spake the warrior Dibbara:

- 9. Sea against sea, Subartu (Syria) against Subartu, Assyria against Assyria,

- 10. Elam against Elam,

- 11. Kossæan against Kossæan,

- 12. Sutu against Sutu,

- 13. Gutium against Gutium,

- 14. Lullubu against Lullubu,

- 15. country against country, house against house, man against man,

-

- 16. brother against brother also, may they destroy each other,

- 17. and afterwards may Accad come and

- 18. the whole of them destroy, and fight against them.

- 19. The warrior Dibbara to Itak who goes before him a word speaks:

- 20. Go also Itak, in the word thou hast spoken do according to all thy heart.

- 21. Itak against the land of Khikhi (Phœnicia) set his face,

- 22. and the seven warrior gods unequalled

- 23. marched after him.

- 24. To the country of Khikhi to the mountains the warrior went,

- 25. his hand he also lifted and destroyed the land,

- 26. the land of Khikhi he counted as his own country.

The next fragments of the story are on a mutilated copy of the last tablet, K. 1282. This tablet, as has been before stated, is only a smaller supplemental one to include the end of the story, which could not be written on the fourth tablet.

K. 1282.

Obverse.

- 1. From Dibbara ....

- 2. the gods all of them ....

- 3. the angels and spirits all ....

- 4. Dibbara his mouth opened and ....

-
- 5. a voice also the whole of you ....
- 6. I also in the first sin ....
- 7. in heart I cried out and ....
- 8. like a flock of sheep may ....
- 9. without the planting of boundaries against ...
- 10. like the spoiling of the country steadfast and ..
- 11. in the mouth of the high noble ....
- 12. and the place ....
- Fifteen lines much broken here.
- 28. .... the land of Accad its strength ....
- 29. May one slay seven like ....
- 30. his cities to ruins and mounds thou dost reduce ....
- 31. his great spoil thou dost spoil, to the midst of ....
- 32. the gods of the country .... thou removest afar off ....
- 33. the god Ner and the God Serakh thou directedst ....
- 34. the countries their productions, the sea thou ..
- 35. its interior they destroyed ....
- Four mutilated lines here.

Reverse.

- 1. For years untold the glory of the great lord the god ....
- 2. When Dibbara had cried out and to sweep the countries ....
- 3. had set his face
- 4. Itak his adviser had quieted him and stayed ...
-
- 5. gathering together his forces to the glorious one of the gods, Merodach the son of (Hea).
- 6. In the hour of night he sent him, and when in the year ....
- 7. Not any one ....

- 8. .... and sent not down against ....

- 9. his .... also Dibbara received before ....

- 10. .... Itak who goes before him, the illustrious god ....

- 11. are all of them laid with him.

- 12. Any one who speaks of the warrior Dibbara

- 13. and that song shall glorify, in his place thou wilt keep (his) canals,

- 14. .... never may he fall (?) ....

- 15. the heavens have caused the borders of (his) regions to increase.

- 16. Whoever the glory of my heroism shall recount,

- 17. an adversary never may he have.

- 18. The musician who shall sing, shall not die by the chastisement;

- 19. higher than king and prince may that man ascend.

- 20. The tablet writer who studies it (and) flees from the hostile, shall be great in the land.

- 21. If in the places of the people, the established place, my name they proclaim,

- 22. their ears I open.

- 23. In the house, the place where their goods are placed, if I Dibbara am angry

- 24. may the seven gods turn him aside,

-

- 25. may the chastising sword not touch him whose face thou establishest.

- 26. That song for ever may they establish and may they fix the part ....

- 27. may all the world hear, and glorify my heroism;

- 28. may the men of all nations see, and exalt my name.

- Fifth tablet of the exploits of the god (Dibbara).

Here we see a picture of Oriental feeling with reference to natural phenomenon or disaster to mankind. It is supposed that some deity or angel stands with a sword over the devoted people and sweeps them into eternity.

The first fragment shows the anger of Anu at the sin of some doomed race, and his command to Dibbara to take his weapon, slay the people, and desolate the land like the god Ner. This god Ner was one of the mythical kings of Babylon who reigned after the flood, and is mentioned as having a terrible name and being with Etana a dweller in Hades. The allusion to him in this passage seems to imply that he was believed to have once rescued Babylon from a hostile attack.

The next fragment exhibits the goddess of Karrak as healing the illness of some of the people, 4,102 being mentioned as struck with disease.

In the next and largest fragment the story becomes a little more connected; it commences with a description of preparation for battle, and goes on through speeches and actions to describe the course of Dibbara and his plague that he inflicts upon Babylon, and its besiegers where he spares neither chief nor slave, and enters even the palace. It would seem that the sin of the Babylonians arose from the chief priest or governor of the city arming the troops and sending them out to plunder the enemy. For this the plague is sent, and its progress is graphically described. Merodach the special protector of Babylon at last interferes, and the god of pestilence is checked in his course. The next city visited belongs to Samas, being either Larsa, or Sippara, and then the plague reaches Erech. The character of this city is described, the worship of Venus, with her handmaids Samkhati and Kharimati, or "Joy" and "Seduction," the priests and ceremonies, and the progress of the plague over the place. Then the great god the deity of Duran comes forward and pleads for his city, calling to mind its uprightness and justice, and praying for its exemption from the plague.

In the third column mention is made of Gutium, under which name the Accadians designated the whole tract of country which extended from the Tigris to the eastern borders of Media, including the district afterwards known as Assyria. The land of Nizir, in which rose the mountain of Elwend, on the top of which the Accadians supposed the ark to have rested, also formed part of this vast tract. Sir Henry Rawlinson long ago pointed out that Gutium must be the Goyim of the 14th chapter of Genesis, ruled by Tidal, or rather, according to the reading of the Septuagint, Tur-gal "the great Son."

The fourth column next describes a prophecy of Dibbara that there should be internal war among the peoples of the Persian Gulf, of Syria, Assyria, Elam, Gutium, Lullubu and the Kossæans, from all which troubles benefit should come to the Accadians or northern Babylonians. The Kossæans or Cassi inhabited the northern part of Elam, and under Khammuragas conquered Babylonia and founded there a dynasty which lasted a long time. Lullubu lay northward of Mesopotamia and Nizir.

Then according to his wish Dibbara sends the god Itak his servant, with the seven warrior gods, to devastate, and Itak sweeps over the country and destroys it.[17]

The last tablet deals in generalities pointing out the action of Dibbara when his praise was neglected, and telling all the glories and good that should come to those who should celebrate this deity in song. On the spread of a plague it is evident that the Babylonians had no better means of arresting it than to pray and praise the supposed terrible deity of the scourge, that he might sheathe his sword of anger.

The antiquity of the legend is evident from the geographical names which occur in it. A geographical list which seems based on an Accadian original is the only other document which speaks of Phœnicia, or rather a part of Phœnicia, under the name of Khikhi; and the fact that no reference is made to the Hittites shows that the poem is earlier than the sixteenth century B.C., when the Hittites first rose into power in western Asia. Subartu is derived from the Accadian *subar* "high," applied by the Accadians to the highlands of Aram or Syria.

Chapter IX.
BABYLONIAN FABLES.

Fables.—Common in the East.—Description.—Power of speech in animals.—Story of the eagle.—Serpent.—Samas.—The eagle caught.—Eats the serpent.—Anger of Birds.—Etana.—Seven gods.—Third tablet.—Speech of eagle.—Story of the fox.—His cunn

ing.—Judgment of Samas.—His show of sorrow.—His punishment.—Speech of fox.—Fable of the horse and ox.—They consort together.—Speech of the ox.—His good fortune.—Contrast with the horse.—Hunting the ox.—Speech of the horse.—Offers to recount story.—Story of Istar.—Further tablets.

COMBINED with these stories of the gods, traditions of the early history of man, and accounts of the Creation, are fragments of a series in which various animals speak and act. As these resemble the beast-fables of other races, more especially the African, they may be conveniently classed under the general heading of "Fables." The idea that animals can speak, or have spoken in some former age of the world, even occurs in Genesis, where we have a speaking serpent; in Numbers, where Balaam's ass reproves his master; and in the stories of Jotham and Joash, where the trees are made to talk; as also in the Izdubar legends, where the trees answer Hea-bani.

Four fables have been preserved among the fragmentary records of Assur-bani-pal's library.

The first contained at least four tablets each having four columns of writing. Two of the acting animals in it are the eagle and the serpent.

The second is similar in character, the leading animal being the fox or jackal, but there are only four fragments of it; it may belong to the same series as the fable of the eagle.

The third is a single tablet with two columns of writing, and contains a discussion between the horse and ox.

The fourth is a single fragment in which a calf speaks, but there is nothing to show the nature of the story.

I. THE STORY OF THE EAGLE.

This story appears to be the longest and most curious of the fables, but the very mutilated condition of the various fragments gives as usual considerable difficulty in attempting a translation of it. One of the actors in the story is an ancient monarch named Etana, who, like Ner, ruled over Babylon in the mythical period that followed the Deluge, and whose phantom was believed to sit, crowned, on a throne in Hades along with the shades of the other heroes of old time. The story of Etana was supposed to have been written by an early poet named Nis-Sin.

It is impossible to determine the proper order of the fragments of the story owing to their mutilated condition; they must therefore be translated as they come.

K 2527.

Many lines lost at the commencement.

- 1. The serpent in ...
- 2. I gave a command (?) .....
- 3. to the eagle .....
- 4. Again the nest .....
- 5. my nest I have left in .....
- 6. the assembly? of my people .....
- 7. I went down and entered:
- 8. the sentence which Samas has pronounced on me .....
- 9. the ear of corn (?) which Samas thy field the earth ....
- 10. this thy fruit ....
- 11. in thy field let me not ....
- 12. the doing of evil the goddess Bahu (Gula) ....
- 13. The sorrow of the serpent [Samas saw and]
- 14. Samas opened his mouth and a word he spoke:
- 15. Go, along the way pass ....
- 16. he covered thee ....

- 17. open also his heart ....
- 18. .... he placed (?) ....
- 19. .... birds of heaven ....

Reverse.

- 1. The eagle with them ....
- 2. the god? had known ....
- 3. he descended, the flesh he ....
-
- 4. to cover the ....
- 5. to the midst at his entering ....
- 6. the cutting off of the feathers of his wings ....
- 7. his claws? and his pinions to ....
- 8. death by hunger and thirst ....
- 9. for the work of Samas the warrior, the serpent ....
- 10. he took also the serpent ....
- 11. he opened also his heart ....
- 12. seat he placed ....
- 13. peace the birds of heaven ....
- 14. May the eagle ....
- 15. with the young of the birds ....
- 16. The eagle opened his mouth ....
- Five other mutilated lines.

On another fragment are the following few words:—

Obverse.

- 1. .... fierce to him also ....
- 2. .... the god (?) my father ....
- 3. like Etana thy death ....
- 4. like thee ....

- 5. the god Etana the king ....
- 6. they stripped him in ....

Reverse.

- 1. Within the gate of Anu, Bel (and Hea)
- 2. they are established ....
- 3. within the gate of Sin, Samas, Rimmon, and ....
- 4. .... I opened ....
-
- 5. its ... I devastated ....
- 6. .... in the midst ....
- 7. the king ....
- 8. the god also ....
- 9. I overshadowed the throne ....
- 10. I took (?) also ....
- 11. to the great one also I have explained (?) ....
- 12. The eagle to him also even to Etana ....
- 13. his .... the mouth ....
- 14. may thy city submit ....

The next fragment, K 2606, is curious, as containing an account of some early legendary story in Babylonian history. This tablet formed the third in the series, and from it we gain part of the title of the tablets.

K 2606.

- 1. .... the god had placed ....
- 2. of the city he had fixed its brickwork ....
- 3. he had shepherded them ....
- 4. Etana gave them ....
- 5. .... corn ....
- 6. the seven spirits of earth ....
- 7. .... they took their counsel ....

- 8. .... the world ....
- 9. .... all of them the angels ....
- 10. .... they ....
- 11. In those days also ....
- 12. and a sceptre of crystal ....
- 13. the bowing down of the world ....
-
- 14. the seven gods over the people raised ....
- 15. over the men they raised ....
- 16. the city of the angels Surippak
- 17. Istar the streets ....
- 18. and the king flew ....
- 19. the god Inninna the streets ....
- 20. and the king flew ....
- 21. Bel encircled (?) the sanctuary of the god ....
- 22. he worshipped also ....
- 23. in the wide country ....
- 24. the kingdom ....
- 25. he brought and ....
- 26. the gods of the country ....

Reverse.

Many lines lost.

- 1. from of old he caused him to wait ....

- 2. Third tablet of "The city he left (?) ...."

- 3. The eagle his mouth opened and to Samas his lord he spake.

The next fragment is a small portion probably of the fourth tablet.

- 1. The eagle his mouth (opened) ....

- 2. ....

- 3. the people of the birds ....

- 4. ....

- 5. peace he speaks ....

- 6. peace I speak ....

- 7. in the mouth of Samas the warrior ....

-

- 8. the people of the birds ....

- 9. The eagle his mouth opened and ....

- 10. Why do I go ....

- 11. the god Etana his mouth opened and ....

Such are the principal fragments of this curious legend. According to the fragment K 2527, the serpent had committed some sin for which it was condemned by the god Samas to be eaten by the eagle; but the eagle declined the repast.

After this, some one, whose name is lost, baits a trap for the eagle, and the bird going to get the meat, falls into the trap and is caught. Now the eagle is left, until dying for want of food it is glad to eat the serpent, which it takes and tears open. The other birds then interfere, but the tablet is too mutilated to allow us to discover for what purpose.

The other fragments concern the building of some city, Etana being king, and in these relations the eagle again appears; there are seven spirits or angels principal actors in the matter, but the whole story is obscure at present, and a connected plot cannot be made out.

This fable has evidently some direct connection with the mythical history of Babylonia, for Etana is mentioned as an ancient Babylonian monarch in the Izdubar legends. He seems to be the Titan of the Greek writers, who lived after the Deluge and made war against Kronos or Hea shortly after the confusion of tongues. The city built by Etana may be the city mentioned in Gen. xi. 4 as built at the same time as the Tower of Babel. If the Sibyl can be trusted Titan was a contemporary of Prometheus, in whom we may perhaps see the Inninna of the cuneiform inscription. That Etana was closely associated with the story of the Deluge appears plain from the fact that he ruled at Surippak, the home and kingdom of the Chaldean Noah. The legend of Etana seems in the fable to be put into the mouth of the eagle.

II. STORY OF THE FOX.

The next fable, that of the fox, was ascribed to an author called Lal-Merodach, the son of Eri-Turnunna, but the fragments are so disconnected that they must be given without any attempt at arrangement.

K 3641.

COLUMN I.

- 1. he had raised life ....

- 2. thou in that day also didst establish ....

- 3. thou knowest plots (and) the making of snares ....

- 4. of .... chains, his command he ....

- 5. from the time the fox approaches he urged me; let not ....

- 6. in treading down .... he had established on my feet,

- 7. again by command is the fecundity of life.

- 8. Samas by thy judgment is ruler; never may he go forth;

-

- 9. if need be, with the making of snares let them put to death the fox.

- 10. The fox on hearing this, raised his head in the presence of Samas and weeps.

- 11. To the presence of the splendour of Samas his tears went:

- 12. by this judgment O Samas thou dost not make me fecund.

(Columns II. and III. lost.)

COLUMN IV.

- 1. I went to my forest, I turned not back after him

- 2. and in peace I came not forth, and the sun sees not.

- 3. As for thee, never may man imprison (thee),

- 4. since in the pride of my heart and the strength of my face thou goest straight before (me).

- 5. May I confine thee and not send (thee) away.

- 6. May I take hold of thee and thou lacerate not ....

- 7. May I seize thee and not tear (thee) to pieces.
- 8. May I tear thy limbs to pieces and (not) ....
- 9. The fox weeps ....
- 10. he bowed his face ....
- 11. I went and ....
- Five other mutilated lines.

The next fragment has lost the commencements and ends of all the lines.

- 1. .... he carries (?) in the mouth ....
- 2. .... the face of his ....
- 3. .... thou knowest wisdom all ....
- 4. .... in the pathway the fox they are ....
- 5. .... in the field the fox a combatant ....
- 6. .... was decided under the ruler ....
- 7. .... all (?), the lying down of his feet at dawn ....
- 8. .... a sign he set up and he fled ....
- 9. .... no one ....
- 10. .... may it become old to thee .... and take ....
- 11. .... in those days also the fox carried ....
- 12. .... to the people he spoke. Why ....
- 13. .... the dog is removed and ....

The following fragment is in a similar condition.

- 1. .... The limbs I did not ....
- 2. .... I did not weave and against the unclothed (?) I did not ....
- 3. .... a stranger I cover ....
- 4. .... I caught and I surrounded (?) ....
- 5. .... from of old also the dog was my brother ....
- 6. .... he begot me, a firm place ....

- 7. .... of the city of Nisin; I of Bel ....
- 8. .... limbs and the bodies did not stand ...
- 9. .... life I did not end (?) ....
- •

The fourth fragment contains only five legible lines.

- 1. .... was placed also right (and left) ....
- 2. .... their shepherd was prostrate ....
- 3. .... let it not be ....
- 4. .... they guarded and did not throw down his spoil ...

- 5. ...... the fox in the trap (?) ....

The last fragment is a small scrap, at the end of which the fox petitions Samas to spare him.

The incidental allusions in these fragments show that the fox was even then considered cunning, and the animal in the story was evidently a watery specimen, as he brings tears to his assistance whenever anything is to be gained by it. He had offended Samas by some means and the god sentenced him to death, a sentence which he escaped through powerful pleading on his own behalf.

III. FABLE OF THE HORSE AND OX.

The next fable, that of the horse and the ox, is a single tablet with only two columns of text. The date of the tablet is in the reign of Assur-bani-pal, and there is no statement that it is copied from an earlier text. There are altogether four portions of the text, but only one is perfect enough to be worth translating. This largest fragment, K 3456, contains about one-third of the story.

K 3456.

(Several lines are lost at the commencement.)

- 1. ..... the river ....
- 2. of food (?) .... rest ....
- 3. full flood .... the Tigris ....
- 4. they restrained .... they had the face ...

- 5. the water-lily .... not in the neighbourhood

- 6. the high place .... appearance

- 7. the valley .... the mountain (was perishing),

- 8. at the appearance .... the timid fled (not),

- 9. a boundless place .... he turned

- 10. in the side ....

- 11. of the waste .... earth was free within it;

- 12. the tribes of cattle rejoiced in companionship and friendship,

- 13. the ox and the horse made friendship,

- 14. their maw rejoiced when to friendship

- 15. it inclined, and their heart was glad; they made agreement together.

- 16. The ox opened his mouth, and speaks; he says to the horse glorious in war:

- 17. I am pondering now upon the good fortune at my hand.

- 18. At the beginning of the year and the end of the year I dream (*or* ponder) of fodder.

-

- 19. The abundant floods had been dried up, the waters of the canals were reduced,

- 20. the water-lily had drooped, it was suffering the summer-heat,

- 21. the valleys were stony, my mountain was perishing,

- 22. the high places had perished, the *zambatu* languished,

- 23. at the sight of my horn the timid fled not.

- 24. A boundless place is portioned for his ....

- 25. the man .... who knew ceased ....

- 26. he smote the ropes (?) and waited ....

- 27. and the horse ....

- 28. cut off thyself thy ....

- 29. he ascends also ....

Here the ox describes the state of the country during the drought of summer, and makes a league with the horse, apparently for the purpose of sharing with him the same pastures. Most of the speeches, however, made by the two animals are lost or only present in small fragments, and the story recommences on the reverse with the end of a speech from the horse.

- 1. fate ....

- 2. strong brass? ....

- 3. as with a cloak I am clothed ....

- 4. over me a child not suited ....

- 5. king, high priest, lord and prince do not seek the plain ....

- 6. The ox opened his mouth and spake and says to the horse glorious (in war):

- 7. Thee they strike and thou alliest ....

- 8. in thy fighting why ....

- 9. the lord of the chariot ....

- 10. in my body firmness ....

- 11. in my inside firmness ....

- 12. the warrior draws out the quiver ....

- 13. strength carries a curse ....

- 14. the weapon (?) of thy masters over ....

- 15. he causes to see servitude like ....

- 16. shudder and in thee is not ....

- 17. he causes to go on the path over (the marsh) ..

- 18. The horse opened his mouth and spake (and said to the ox) ....

- 19. In my hearing ....

- 20. the weapon (?) ....

- 21. the swords ....

- 22. ......

- 23. strength? of the heart which ....

- 24. in crossing that river ....

- 25. in the path of thy mountains ....

- 26. I reveal? and the ox the story ....

- 27. in thy appearance, it is not ....

- 28. thy offspring is subdued? ....

- 29. when thou runnest, O horse ....

- 30. The ox opened his mouth and spake and says to (the horse glorious in war) ....

- 31. In addition to the stories which thou hast told

- 32. open first (that of) "Behold Istar the noble ...." (Colophon)

- Palace of Assur-bani-pal, king of nations, king (of Assyria).

It appears from these fragments that the story described a time when the animals associated together, and the ox and horse fell into a friendly conversation. The ox, commencing the discussion, praised himself; the answer of the horse is lost, but where the story recommences it appears that the ox objects to the horse drawing the chariot from which he himself is hunted, and the horse ultimately offers to tell the ox a story, the ox choosing the story called "Behold Istar," probably some story of the same character as that of Istar's descent into Hades.

It is uncertain if any other tablet followed this; it is, however, probable that there was one containing the story told by the horse. Although there is no indication to show the date of this fable, the fact that it is not stated to have been copied from an older document seems to show that it is not earlier than the time of Assur-bani-pal. The loss of the tablet containing the story of Istar, told by the horse to the ox, is unfortunate. The last fable is a mere fragment similar to the others, containing a story in which the calf speaks. There is not enough of it to make it worth translation.

Chapter X.
FRAGMENTS OF MISCELLANEOUS TEXTS.

Atarpi.—Punishment of world.—Riddle of wise man.—
Nature and universal presence of air.—Sinuri.—Divining
by fracture of reed.—The foundling.—Tower of Babel.—
Obscurity of legend.—Not noticed by Berosus.—
Fragmentary tablet.—Destruction of Tower.—
Dispersion.—Site of the Tower.—Meaning of Babel.—
Chedor-laomer.—The destruction of Sodom and
Gomorrah.

A NUMBER of stories of a similar character to those of Genesis, though not directly connected with the latter, have been included in this chapter, together with two fragments which probably relate, the one to the Tower of Babel, the other to the destruction of the cities of the Plain. The first and principal text is the story of Atarpi, or Atarpi nisu, "Atarpi the man." This story is on a tablet in six columns, and there is only one copy of it. It is terribly mutilated, very little being preserved except Column III., but there are numerous repetitions throughout the text. The inscription has originally been a long one, probably extending to about 400 lines of writing, and the text differs from the generality of these inscriptions, being very obscure and difficult. In consequence of this and other reasons, only an outline of most of the story is given here.

We are first told of a quarrel between a mother named Zibanit and her daughter, and that the mother shuts the door of the house, and turns her daughter adrift, the words of the original being "the mother to the daughter opens not her door." The doings of a man named Zamu have some connection with the affair, his "descending into the street on getting" something being mentioned immediately before the expulsion of the daughter; and at the close we are told of Atarpi, sometimes called Atarpi-nisu, or Atarpi the "man" who had his couch beside the river of the north, and was pious to the gods, but took no notice of these things. When the story next opens, we find the god Bel calling together an assembly of the gods his sons, and relating to them that he is angry at the sin of the world, stating also that he will bring down upon it disease, tempest, distress, madness, burning and sickness. This is followed by the statement that these things came to pass, and Atarpi then invoked his god Hea to remove these evils. For a whole year, it would seem, he interceded for the people, and at last Hea answered, and announced his resolve to destroy the people. After this the story reads:

- 1. (Hea called) his assembly (by the river) of the north; he said to the gods his sons:

- 2. ...... I made them

- 3. .... shall not stretch until before he turns.

- 4. Their famine I observe,

- 5. their shame the woman takes not;

- 6. I will look to judge the people?

- 7. in their stomach let famine dwell,

- 8. above let Rimmon drink up his rain,

- 9. let him drink up below, let not the flood be carried in the canals,

- 10. let it remove from the field its inundations,

- 11. let the corn-god give over increase, let blackness overspread the corn,

- 12. let the plowed fields bring forth thorns,

- 13. let the growth of their fruit perish, let food not come forth from it, let bread not be produced,

- 14. let distress also be spread over the people,

- 15. may favour be shut up, and good not be given.

- 16. He looked also to judge the people,

- 17. in their stomach dwelt famine,

- 18. above Rimmon drank up his rain,

- 19. he drank it up below, the flood was not carried in the canals,

- 20. it removed from the field its inundations,

- 21. the corn-god gave over increase, blackness spread over the corn,

- 22. the plowed fields brought forth thorns, the growth of their fruit perished,

- 23. food came not forth from it, bread was not produced,

- 24. distress was spread over the people,

-
- 25. favour was shut up, good was not given.

This will serve to show the style of the tablet. The instrument of punishment was apparently famine from want of rain.

Here the story is again lost, and where it recommences Hea is making a speech, directing another person to cut something into portions, and place seven on each side, and then to build brickwork round them. After this comes a single fragment, the connection of which with the former part is obscure.

- 1. Seated was the goddess ....
- 2. to her face also he gave ....

- 3. Anu opened his mouth and speaks; he said to (Nusku);
- 4. Nusku open thy gate; thy weapons (take)
- 5. in the assembly of the great gods when ....
- 6. their speech? ....
- 7. Anu sent m ....
- 8. your king sent ....

At present no satisfactory story can be made out of the detached fragments of this tablet, but it evidently belongs to the mythical portion of Babylonian history, and it is impossible not to compare the unsuccessful intercession of the righteous man Atarpi with the pleadings of Abraham on behalf of the cities of the plain.

The next text is a single fragment, K 2407, belonging to a curious story of a wise man who puts a riddle to the gods.

K 2407.

(Many lines lost.)

- 1. The clothing of the god ....
- 2. What in the house is (fixed) ....
- 3. What in the secret place is ....
- 4. what is in the foundation of the house ....
- 5. what on the floor of the house is fixed, what ...

- 6. what the lower part ....

- 7. what by the sides of the house goes down ....

- 8. what in the ditch of the house broad *nigitstsi* ....

- 9. what roars like a bull, what brays like an ass,

- 10. what flutters like a sail, what bleats like a sheep,

- 11. what barks like a dog,

- 12. what growls like a bear,

- 13. what into the fundament of a man enters, what into the fundament of a woman enters.

- 14. Then Lugal-girra (Nergal) heard the wise word the son of the people

- 15. asked, and all the gods he urged (to solve it):

- 16. Let your solution be produced, that I may bring back your answer.

After this there is a mutilated passage containing the names, titles, and actions of the gods who consider the riddle. It is evident that it is air or wind which the wise man means in his riddle, for this is everywhere, and in its sounds imitates the cries of animals.

Next we have another single fragment about a person named Sinuri, who uses a divining rod to ascertain the meaning of a dream.

- 1. Sinuri with the cut reed pondered ....

- 2. with his right hand he broke it, and Sinuri speaks and thus says:

- 3. Now the plant of Nusku, the shrub? of Samas art thou.

- 4. Judge, thou judgest (*or* divinest), divine concerning this dream,

- 5. which in the evening, at midnight, or in the morning,

- 6. has come, which thou knowest, but I do not know.

- 7. If it be good may its good not be lost to me,

- 8. if it be evil may its evil not happen to me.

There are some more obscure and broken lines, but no indication as to the story to which it belongs.

A specimen of early Babylonian folklore may fitly be added here. It is a bilingual fragment which treats of a foundling who was picked up in the streets and finally became a great scholar. Unfortunately both the beginning and the end of the story are wanting.

- 1. He who father and mother had not,

- 2. who his father (and) his mother knew not,

- 3. in the gutter (was) his going, in the street (his) entering.

-

- 4. From the mouth of the dogs one took him,

- 5. from the mouth of the ravens one put him away.

- 6. In the presence of the soothsayer the .... of his mouth one took.

- 7. The sole of his feet with the seal the soothsayer has marked.

- 8. To a nurse he gave him.

- 9. To his nurse for three years, corn, a cradle (?)

- 10. (and) clothing he guaranteed.

- 11. Then and ever he hid from him how he was taken (from the streets).

- 12. His rearer he rooted out (?).

- 13. The ..... of the milk of mankind he gave him, and

- 14. as his own son he made him.

- 15. As his own son he inscribed him.

- 16. A knowledge of writing he made him possess.

- 17. For his education (he cared).

One of the most obscure incidents in the Book of Genesis is undoubtedly the building of the Tower of Babel. So far as we can judge from the fragments of his copyists, there was no reference to it in the work of Berosus, and early writers had to quote from writers of more than doubtful authority in order to confirm it.

MEN ENGAGED IN BUILDING COLUMNS; FROM BABYLONIAN CYLINDER.

There is also no representation on any of the Babylonian gems which can with any certainty be described as belonging to this story. Mr. Smith, however, picked out three from a series of these carvings which he thought might be distorted representations of the event. In these and some others of the same character, figures have their hands on tall piles, as if erecting them;

and there is a god always represented near in much the same attitude. There is no proper proportion between the supposed structure and the men, and no stress can consequently be laid on the representations. The Babylonian origin of the story is, however, self-evident. According to Genesis, mankind after the flood travelled from the east, that is from Kharsak-kurra, "the mountain of the East," now Elwend, where the Accadians believed the ark to have rested, to the plain of Shinar or Sumir. Both Alexander Polyhistor and Abydenus state that the building of the Tower of Babel was known to Babylonian history, Babel, in fact, being the native form of the name which the Greeks changed into Babylon. The legend of Etana given in the last chapter seems to imply that the Tower was supposed to have been built under the superintendence of this mythical hero. However that may be, a fragment of the native story of its construction was discovered by Mr. Smith, and though shockingly mutilated, is sufficient to show what the Babylonians themselves believed on the matter.

It is evident from the wording of the fragment that it was preceded by at least one tablet, describing the sin of the people in building the tower. The fragment preserved belongs to a tablet containing from four to six columns of writing, of which portions of four remain. The principal part is the beginning of Column I.

COLUMN I.

- 1. .... them the father ....
- 2. the thought of his heart was evil,
-
- 3. .... he the father of all the gods had repudiated;
- 4. the thought of his heart was evil,
- 5. .... of Babylon he hastens to the submission (?),
- 6. [small] and great he confounded (on) the mound.
- 7. .... of Babylon he hastens to the submission,
- 8. [small] and great he confounded (on) the mound.
- 9. Their walls all the day he founded;
- 10. for their destruction (punishment) in the night
- 11. .... he did not leave a remainder.
- 12. In his anger also (his) secret counsel he pours out:
- 13. [to] confound (their) speeches he set his face.

- 14. He gave the command, he made strange their counsel

- 15. .... the going he inspected it.

- 16. .... he took (selected) a shrine.

There is a small fragment of Column II., but the connection with Column I. is not apparent.

COLUMN II.

- 1. Sar-tuli-elli (the king of the illustrious mound, *i.e.* Anu) destroys (*or* punishes).

- 2. In front had Anu lifted up ....

- 3. to Bel-esir his father ....

-

- 4. Since his heart also ....

- 5. who carried the command ....

- 6. In those days also ....

- 7. he lifted him up ....

- 8. The goddess Dav-kina ....

- 9. My son I rise and ....

- 10. his number(?) ....

- 11. he did not ....

There is a third portion on the same tablet belonging to a column on the other side, either the third or the fifth.

REVERSE COLUMN III. OR V.

- 1. In ....

- 2. they blew and ....

- 3. for future times ....

- 4. The god of no government went ....

- 5. He said, like heaven and earth ....

- 6. his path they went ....

- 7. fiercely they fronted his presence ....

- 8. He saw them and the earth ....

- 9. Since a stop they did not (make) ....

- 10. of the gods ....

- 11. the gods they revolted against ....

- 12. offspring ....

- 13. They weep hot tears for Babylon;

- 14. bitterly they wept (for Babylon);

- 15. their heart also ....

These fragments are so remarkable that it is most unfortunate we have not the remainder of the tablet.

In the first part we have the anger of Bel, the father of the gods, at the sin of those who were building the walls of Babylon and the mound of tower or palace. This mound is termed "the illustrious," and the god Anu who destroyed the builders is accordingly called *Sar-tuli-elli*, "the king of the illustrious mound." Since the Accadian name of the month Tisri, our October, was "the month of the illustrious mound," it would appear that the construction of it was believed to have taken place at the time of the autumnal equinox. The builders were punished by the deity, and the walls that had been set up in the day were destroyed at night. Prof. Delitzsch has drawn attention to a possible reference to this legend in an Accadian hymn in which the poet says to Merodach, "found during the day, destroy during the night." It is plain from the first lines that the whole attempt was directed against the gods; in fact, that like the giants and Titans in Greek mythology, whose assault on Zeus is probably but an echo of the old Babylonian tale, conveyed to Greece through the hands of the Phœnicians, the builders of the Tower of Babylon intended to scale the sky. They were, however, confounded on the mound, as well as their speech (*tammaslè*). It is interesting to find the very same word signifying "to confound" used in the Babylonian as in the Hebrew account, namely *bâlal*, or rather *bâlâh*. We may also notice that the Hebrew writer once (Gen. xi. 7.) adopts the polytheistic language of the Accadian scribe; the Lord being made to say "Let *us* go down, and there confound their language."

VIEW OF THE BIRS NIMRUD, THE SUPPOSED SITE OF THE TOWER OF BABEL.

The last column shows that the winds finally destroyed the impious work of the Babylonians. This fully accords with the legend reported by Alexander Polyhistor. For a time Babylon was given over to the god of lawlessness; but at last the gods repented of the evil they had done, and order was once more restored. The shrine mentioned in the sixteenth line of the first column may receive some light from the fact that the Accadian name of Nisan or March was "the month of the upright altar," or "of the altar of Bel," and that Nisan corresponded with the vernal equinox just as Tisri did with the autumnal equinox.

VIEW OF THE BABIL MOUND AT BABYLON, THE SITE OF THE TEMPLE OF BEL.

The etymology of the name of Babel from *balbel*, "to confound," suggested in Genesis is one of those "popular etymologies" or plays on words of which the Old Testament writers are so fond. Thus, for instance, the name of Joseph is connected first with *'âsaph* "to take away," and then with *yâsaph* "to add" (Gen. xxx. 23, 24.), and the name of the Moabite city Dibon is changed into Dimon by Isaiah (xv. 9) to indicate that its "waters shall be full of blood," Hebrew *dâm*. Babel is the Assyrian *Bab-ili* "the gate of God" (or, as it is occasionally written in the plural, *Bab-ili* "Gate of the gods"), which was the Semitic translation of the old Accadian name of the town Ca-dimirra with the same meaning. This is not the only instance in which the original Accadian names of Babylonian cities were literally translated into Semitic Babylonian after the Semitic conquest of the country. It is possible that the name had some reference to the building of the Tower. Babylon was first made a capital by Khammuragas, the leader of the Cossæan dynasty, a position which it never afterwards lost; but the first antediluvian king of Chaldea, Alorus, according to Barosus, was a native of the place.

TOWER IN STAGES, FROM AN ASSYRIAN BAS-RELIEF.

The actual site of the Tower of Babel, beyond the mere fact that it was somewhere in Babylon, has not yet been settled. It is generally considered to be represented by the great pile of Birs Nimrud, which stood in Borsippa, the suburb of Babylon, and was dedicated to Nebo and called "the Temple of the Seven Lights" or planets. This ruin has been examined by Sir Henry Rawlinson; details of his operations here are given in the "Journal of the Royal Asiatic Society," vol. xviii., and Rawlinson's "Ancient Monarchies," p. 544. Sir Henry discovered by excavation that the tower consisted of seven stages of brickwork on an earthen platform, each stage being of a different colour. This is explained by the fact that it was devoted to the seven planets. The height of the earthen platform was not ascertained, but the first stage, which was an exact square, was 272 feet each way, and 26 feet high, the bricks being blackened with bitumen; this stage is supposed to have been dedicated to the planet Saturn. The second stage was a square of 230 feet, 26 feet high, faced with orange-coloured bricks; supposed to have been dedicated to Jupiter. The third stage, 188 feet square, and 26 feet high, faced with red bricks, was probably dedicated to Mars. The fourth stage, 146 feet square, and 15 feet high, was probably dedicated to the Sun, and is thought by Sir H. Rawlinson to have been originally plated with gold. The fifth stage is supposed to have been 104, the sixth 62, and the seventh 20 feet square, but the top was too ruinous to decide these measurements. These stages were probably dedicated to Venus, Mercury, and the Moon. Each stage of the building was not set in the centre of the stage on which it rested, but was placed 30 feet from the front, and 12 feet from the back. The ruin at present rises 154 feet above the level of the plain, and is the most imposing pile in the whole country. According to Nebuchadnezzar it had been built to the height of 42 cubits by "a former king," who however had not completed its summit, and it had long been in a ruinous condition when Nebuchadnezzar undertook to restore and finish it. Prof. Schrader imagines that the long period during which it had remained an unfinished ruin caused the growth of the legend which saw in it a monument of the overthrow of human presumption, the diversity of languages in Babylonia being sufficient to account for the localization of the confusion of tongues in the country.

Sir Henry Rawlinson now proposes to place the Tower or *tul ellu* at the ruins now called Amrán, within the city of Babylon itself. Here he thinks were the temple of Anu, on the site of the ruined Tower, a chapel dedicated to Nebo, an altar of Merodach, the royal palace (now represented by the mound of the Kasr), and the hanging gardens, all enclosed by a common wall. The quarter of Babylon thus enclosed he would identify with the Calneh of the Bible, principally on the ground that the Septuagint rendering of Isaiah x. 9 is, "Have I not taken the region above Babylon and Chalanne where the tower was built?"

A third site has been claimed for the Tower on the Babil or Mujellibeh mound on the north side of Babylon. This represents the famous temple of Belus or Bel, whose great festival marked the beginning of the year and the vernal equinox. But there is no evidence to support this third opinion.

In the Babylonian and Assyrian sculptures there are occasionally representations of towers similar in style to the supposed Tower of Babel; one of these is given on the stone of Merodach Baladan I., opposite p. 236 of Mr. Smith's "Assyrian Discoveries;" another occurs on the sculptures at Nineveh, representing the city of Babylon; this tower, however, cannot represent the Borsippa pile, since it consists of only five stages.

Besides the Tower of Babel, the destruction of Sodom and Gomorrah by fire from heaven may also have been known to the Accadians. We learn from Genesis xiv. that the cities of the plain were among the conquests of Chedor-laomer and his allies, and there is some reason for thinking that the history of Chedor-laomer's campaign may have been derived from the Babylonian state archives. At all events Amraphel or Amarpel, the king of Sumir, is mentioned first, although Chedor-laomer was the paramount sovereign and the leader of the expedition. The expedition must have taken place during the period when, as we learn from the inscriptions, Babylonia was subject to the monarchs of Elam, though subordinate princes were ruling over the states into which it was divided at the time. Though the name of Chedor-laomer has not been found, Laomer or Lagamar appears as an Elamite god, and several of the Elamite kings bore names compounded with Kudur "a servant," as Kudur-Nankhunte, "the servant of the god Nankhunte," Kudur-Mabug, "the servant of Mabug," and the like. Arioch, king of Ellasar, which probably stands for al Larsa, "the city of Larsa," has the same name as Eri-Acu ("the servant of the moon-god"), the son of the Elamite monarch Kudur-Mabug, who reigned over Larsa during his father's lifetime, and was eventually overthrown by the Cossæan conqueror Khammuragas.

The text which perhaps relates to the destruction of the guilty cities is a bilingual one, much mutilated, and runs as follows:—

- 1. An overthrow came from the midst of the deep (the waters above the firmament).

- 2. The fated punishment from the midst of heaven descended.

- 3. A storm like a plummet the earth (overwhelmed).

- 4. Towards the four winds the destroying flood like fire burnt.

- 5. The inhabitants of the city it had caused to be tormented; their bodies it consumed.

- 6. In city and country it spread death, and the flames as they rose overthrew.

- 7. Freeman and slave were equal, and the high places it filled.

- 8. In heaven and earth like a thunderstorm it had rained; a prey it made.

- 9. To a place of refuge the gods hastened, and in a throng collected.

- 10. Its mighty (onset) they fled from, and like a garment it concealed (the guilty).

- 11. They (feared), and death (overtook them).

-

- 12. (Their) feet and hands (it embraced).

- 13. ....

- 14. Their body it consumed.

- 15. ..... as for the city, its foundations it defiled.

- 16. .... with (glory?) and breadth his mouth he filled.

- 17. This man the voice (of the thunder) called; the thunderbolt descended;

- 18. during the day it flashed; grievously (it fell).

Here the fragment breaks off. It is possible that the person referred to in line 17 was the pious man who like Lot escaped the destruction that befell his neighbours.

IZDUBAR STRANGLING A LION. FROM KHORSABAD SCULPTURE.

Chapter XI.
THE IZDUBAR LEGENDS.

Izdubar.—Meaning of the name.—A solar hero.—
Prototype of Herakles.—Age of Legends.—Babylonian
cylinders.—Notices of Izdubar.—Surippak.—Ark City.—
Twelve tablets.—Extent of Legends.—Description.—
Introduction.—Meeting of Hea-bani and Izdubar.—
Destruction of tyrant Khumbaba.—Adventures of Istar.—
Illness and wanderings of Izdubar.—Description of
Deluge and conclusion.—First Tablet.—Kingdom of
Nimrod.—Traditions.—Identifications.—Translation.—
Elamite conquest—Dates.

WE now come to the great Epic of early Chaldea, first discovered by Mr.
Smith in 1872. The hero of this Epic is provisionally called Izdubar, though
this is certainly not the right reading of his name. The first and last characters
which compose it together form a compound ideograph signifying "fire,"
and pronounced *gibil* in Accadian, *isatu* in Assyrian, while the middle
character, *dhu* or *dhun*, meant "a mass" or "a going." "A mass of fire" would
have been by no means an inappropriate name for a hero, who, as we shall
see, was originally the Accadian fire-god, and then a personified form of the
sun-god. The two last characters of the name, however, when used as a
compound ideograph, denoted "the under-lip," and the first character
symbolizes "wood."

Mr. Smith believed that Izdubar was the Biblical Nimrod, and was almost
inclined to think that this was the way in which the name ought to be
phonetically rendered. One passage, however, in which the last syllable is
followed by the syllable *ra* seems to imply that the final letter was *r*.

The originally solar character of the hero was still remembered at the time
when the great Epic of the Accadians was put together. As was pointed out
by Sir Henry Rawlinson shortly after Mr. Smith's first discovery of it, it is
arranged upon an astronomical principle, its twelve books or tablets
corresponding with the twelve signs of the Zodiac, through which the sun
passes in his yearly course. Thus the eleventh tablet, which contains the
episode of the Deluge, answers to Aquarius the eleventh sign of the Zodiac,
and the eleventh month of the Accadian year called "the rainy;" and the sixth
tablet, describing his courtship by Istar, answers to Virgo the sixth sign of
the Zodiac, and the sixth Accadian month called that "of the errand of Istar."
It is in the second month, that of "the directing bull," and under the sign of
Taurus, that Hea-bani, half-man, half-bull, is brought to Izdubar in the

second tablet; the lion is slain by Izdubar under the Zodiacal Leo, and the lamentation he makes over the corpse of his friend and seer Hea-bani is made in "the dark month" of Adar, as it was termed, at the end of the year. Like the autumnal sun, too, Izdubar sickens in the eighth book corresponding with the month of October, and only recovers his health and brilliance after bathing in the waters of the eastern ocean at the beginning of the new year.

If anything were needed to confirm the solar character of Izdubar and his history, it would be afforded by a comparison with the legends of the Greek solar hero, Herakles. Like much else of Greek mythology, the twelve adventures of Herakles were brought to Greece from Babylonia through the hands of the Phœnicians, and it has long been recognized that Herakles is but a form of Baal Melkarth, the sun-god of Tyre. Hea-bani reappears in Cheiron, the centaur, the friend and instructor of Herakles, and just as Hea-bani was created by Hea, Cheiron was said to be the son of Kronos, who is identified by Berosus with Hea in the account of the Deluge. The lion slain by Izdubar is the lion of Nemea slain by Herakles; the winged bull made by Anu is the famous bull of Krete; the tyrant Khumbaba is the tyrant Geryon; the gems borne by the trees of the forest beyond the gateway of the sun are the apples of the Hesperides; and the deadly sickness of Izdubar himself is but the fever of Herakles, caused by the poisoned tunic of Nessus.

A very slight inspection of the Epic is sufficient to show that it has been pieced together out of a number of previously existing and independent materials. Thus the history of the Deluge, which is itself but an episode somewhat violently foisted into the legend of Izdubar in order to preserve the astronomical arrangement of the Epic, may be shown to have consisted of at least two older poems on the subject; and a careful examination of other portions of the Epic brings the same fact to light elsewhere.

As, however, there is clear proof that the Epic was originally composed in Accadian, our present text being merely the Semitic translation of the Accadian original, it must have existed in the form in which we now have it before the age of Sargon and the extinction of the Accadian language in Chaldea. We shall not be far wrong, therefore, in ascribing its composition to about B.C. 2000, or a little earlier. The older lays or poems out of which it was formed must therefore date before this period. There seems to have been a considerable number of them, each incident in the cycle of ancient Accadian mythology having been the subject of various poems. Many of these originated in different parts of the country, so that a long period of time must be allowed for their growth and subsequent reduction to a literary form. But as the legends they celebrated were traditions in the country before they were embodied in poems and committed to writing, we must go back to quite a remote epoch for their first starting-point.

The earliest evidence we have of them is in the carvings on early Babylonian cylindrical seals. Among the earliest known devices on these seals we have scenes from the legends of Izdubar, and from the story of the Creation. The seals mostly belong to the age of the kings of Ur, and some of them are a good deal older than B.C. 2000. The principal incidents represented on them are the struggles of Izdubar and his companion Hea-bani with the lion and the bull, the journey of Izdubar in search of Xisuthrus, Noah or Xisuthrus in his ark, and the war between Tiamtu the sea-dragon and the god Merodach. There is a fragment of a document in the British Museum which claims to be copied from an omen tablet belonging to the time of Izdubar himself, but it is probably not earlier than B.C. 1600, when many similar tablets were written.

There is an incidental notice of the ship or ark of "the god Izdubar" in a tablet printed in "Cuneiform Inscriptions," vol. ii. p. 46. He is here called "the king who bears the sceptre." This tablet, which contains lists of wooden objects, was written in the time of Assur-bani-pal, but is copied from an original, which must have been written at least eighteen hundred years before the Christian era. The geographical notices on this tablet suit the period before the rise of Babylon. Surippak is called in it the ship or ark city, this name forming another reference to the Flood legends. Izdubar is also mentioned in a series of tablets relating to witchcraft, and on a tablet containing prayers to him as a god; this last showing that he was deified, which, however, was an honour also given to several Babylonian kings.

As already stated, the legends of Izdubar are inscribed on twelve tablets, of which there are remains of at least four editions. All the tablets are in fragments, and none of them are complete; but it is a fortunate circumstance that the most perfect tablet is the eleventh, which describes the Deluge, this being the most important of the series. In the first chapter the successive steps in the discovery of these legends have been already described, and we may now therefore pass on to the description and translation of the various fragments. All the fragments of our present copies belong to the reign of Assur-bani-pal, king of Assyria, in the seventh century B.C. From the mutilated condition of many of them it is impossible at present to gain an accurate idea of the whole scope of the legends, and many parts which are lost have to be supplied by conjecture; the order even of some of the tablets cannot be determined, and it is uncertain if we have fragments of the whole twelve in what follows. Mr. Smith has, however, conjecturally divided the fragments into groups corresponding roughly with the subjects of the tablets. Each tablet when complete contained six columns of writing, and each column had generally from forty to fifty lines of writing, there being in all about 3,000 lines of cuneiform text. The divisions adopted by Mr. Smith will be seen by the following summary, which exhibits our present knowledge of the fragments.

Part I.—Introduction.

Tablet I.—Number of lines uncertain, probably about 240. First column initial line preserved, second column lost, third column twenty-six lines preserved, fourth column doubtful fragment inserted, fifth and sixth columns lost.

Probable subjects: conquest of Babylonia by the Elamites, birth and parentage of Izdubar.

Part II.—Meeting of Hea-bani and Izdubar.

Tablet II.—Number of lines uncertain, probably about 240. First and second columns lost, third and fourth columns about half-preserved, fifth and sixth columns lost.

Tablet III.—Number of lines about 270. First column fourteen lines preserved, second, third, fourth, and fifth columns nearly perfect, sixth column a fragment.

Probable subjects: dream of Izdubar, Hea-bani invited comes to Erech, and explains the dream.

Part III.—Destruction of the tyrant Khumbaba.

Tablet IV.—Number of lines probably about 260. About one-third of first, second, and third columns, doubtful fragments of fourth, fifth, and sixth columns.

Tablet V.—Number of lines about 260. Most of first column, and part of second column preserved, third, fourth, and fifth columns lost, fragment of sixth column.

Probable subjects: contests with wild animals, Izdubar and Hea-bani slay the tyrant Khumbaba.

Part IV.—Adventures of Istar.

Tablet VI.—Number of lines about 210. Most of first column preserved, second column nearly perfect, third and fourth columns partly preserved, fifth and sixth columns nearly perfect.

Tablet VII.—Number of lines probably about 240. First line of first column preserved, second column lost, third and fourth column partly preserved, fifth and sixth columns conjecturally restored from tablet of descent of Istar into Hades.

Probable subjects: Istar loves Izdubar, her amours, her ascent to heaven, destruction of her bull, her descent to Hades.

Part V.—*Illness and wanderings of Izdubar.*

Tablet VIII.—Number of lines probably about 270. Conjectured fragments of first, second, and third columns, fourth and fifth columns lost, conjectured fragments of sixth column.

Tablet IX.—Number of lines about 190. Portions of all six columns preserved.

Tablet X.—Number of lines about 270. Portions of all six columns preserved.

Probable subjects: discourse to trees, dreams, illness of Izdubar, death of Hea-bani, wanderings of Izdubar in search of the hero of the Deluge.

Part VI.—*Description of Deluge, and conclusion.*

Tablet XI.—Number of lines 294. All six columns nearly perfect.

Tablet XII.—Number of lines about 200. Portions of first four columns preserved, two lines of fifth column, sixth column perfect.

Probable subjects: description of Deluge, cure of Izdubar, his lamentation over Hea-bani.

TABLET I.

The opening words of the first tablet are preserved, and form as usual the title of the series, but the expressions used are obscure from want of any context to explain them. There are two principal or key-words, *naqbi* and *kugar*; the first of which means "a channel," and is more particularly applied to the canals with which Babylonia was intersected and watered, while the second is the compound ideograph which literally signifies "minister" or "servant of work." It was the special title of Izdubar, who, like his Greek double Herakles, was celebrated for 'the twelve labours' he successfully undertook. The title had no doubt been originally given to the fire-god, in whom primitive man sees his most useful servant and workman. The first line of the Epic would consequently have run: "The canals, the toiling hero, the god Izdubar, had seen." Elsewhere, however, the title of Izdubar is written *Zicar*, that is, "the male" or "hero."

After the heading and opening line there is a considerable blank in the story, two columns of writing being entirely lost. It is probable that this part contained the account of the parentage and previous history of Izdubar, forming the introduction to the story. In the subsequent portions of the history there is very little information to supply the loss of this part of the inscription; but it appears that the mother of Izdubar was named Dannat, which signifies "the powerful lady." His father is not named in any of our present fragments, but he is referred to in the third tablet. He was no doubt a deity, possibly the Sun-god, who is supposed to interfere very much in his behalf. When Izdubar, the old god of fire, after first becoming a form of the solar deity, was finally personified and regarded as a mighty leader, strong in war and hunting, he was turned into a giant, one of the mythical monarchs who had ruled in Babylonia in long-past days, and had subdued the many petty kingdoms into which the valley of the Euphrates was then divided.

The centre of the empire of Izdubar is laid in the region of Shinar, or Sumir, Erech "the lofty" being the chief seat of his power, and thus agrees with the site of the kingdom of Nimrod, according to Genesis x. 8, 9, 10, where we read: "And Cush begat Nimrod: he began to be a mighty one in the earth. He was a mighty hunter before the Lord: wherefore it is said, even as Nimrod the mighty hunter before the Lord. And the beginning of his kingdom was Babel, and Erech, and Accad, and Calneh, in the land of Shinar." We cannot overlook the fact that the character of Izdubar as hunter, leader, and king, corresponds with that of Nimrod. Cush, the father of Nimrod, may be identified with Cusu, Cusi or Cus, the Accadian deity of sunset and night. The word in Accadian signified "rest" and "darkness," and is translated by the Assyrian *nakhu* "to rest," and *nukhu* or *nukh* "rest." This latter word is identical with the Biblical Noah. It is very possible, therefore, that Cush, the father of Nimrod, has nothing to do with Cush or Ethiopia, the son of Ham, the two being set side by side in Genesis merely on account of the similarity of their names. In this case all the ethnological difficulties occasioned by the belief that the Accadians of Babylonia were Cushites, and connected with Egypt or Ethiopia, will be avoided. It is curious to find the Christian writers identifying Nimrod with Evechous, the first king of Babylon, according to Berosus, after the flood.

The next passage in Genesis after the one describing Nimrod's dominion may also refer to Nimrod, if we read with the margin, "Out of that land he went forth to Assyria," instead of "Out of that land went forth Assur." These verses will then read (Genesis x. 11, 12): "Out of that land he went forth to Assyria, and builded Nineveh, and the suburbs of the city, and Calah, and Resen, between Nineveh and Calah: the same is a great city." It must be remembered, however, that Assur was regarded by the Assyrians as their supreme god and eponymous founder, and that in Micah v. 6, "the land of Assur" and "the land of Nimrod" seem to be contrasted with one another. But it is possible to consider the two expressions in the latter passage to be both applied to the same country.

After the date of the later books of the Old Testament we know nothing of Nimrod for some time; it is probable that he was fully mentioned by Berosus in his history, but his account of the giant hunter has been lost. The reason of this appears to be, that a belief had grown up among early Christian writers that the Biblical Nimrod was the first king of Babylonia after the Flood, and looking at the list of Berosus they found that after the Flood according to him Evechous first reigned in Babylonia, and at once assumed that the Evechous of Berosus was the Nimrod of the Bible; but as Evechous has given to him the extravagant reign of four ners or 2,400 years, and his son and successor, Chomasbelus, four ners and five sosses, or 2,700 years, this identification gives little hope of our finding an historical Nimrod.

It is possible that this identification of Nimrod with Evechous, made by the early chronologists, has caused them to overlook his name and true epoch in the list of Berosus, and has thus lost to us his position in the series of Babylonian sovereigns.

Belonging to the first centuries of the Christian era are the works of various Jewish and Christian writers, who have made us familiar with a number of later traditions concerning Nimrod. Josephus declares that he was a prime mover in building the Tower of Babel, an enemy of God, and that he reigned at Babylon during the dispersion. Later writers make him a contemporary with Abraham, the inventor of idol worship, and a furious worshipper of fire. At the city of Orfa, in Syria, he is said to have cast Abraham into a burning fiery furnace because he would not bow down to his idols. These legends have been taken up by the Arabs, and although his history has been lost and replaced by absurd and worthless stories, Nimrod still remains the most prominent name in the traditions of the country; everything good or evil is attributed to him, and the most important ruins are even now called after his name. From the time of the early Christian writers down to to-day, men have been busy framing systems of general chronology, and since Nimrod was always known as a famous sovereign it was necessary to find a definite place for him in each chronological scheme. Africanus and Eusebius held that he was the Evechous of Berosus, and reigned first after the Flood. Moses of Khorene identified him with Bel, the great god of Babylon; and he is said to have extended his dominions to the foot of the Armenian mountains, falling in battle there when attempting to enforce his authority over Haic, king of Armenia. Other writers identified Nimrod with Ninus, the mythical founder of the city of Nineveh. These remained the principal identifications before modern research took up the matter; but so wide a door was open to conjecture, that one writer actually identified Nimrod with the Alorus of Berosus, the first king of Babylonia *before* the Flood.

One of the most curious theories about Nimrod, suggested in modern times, was grounded on the "Book of Nabatean Agriculture." This work is a comparatively modern forgery, pretending to be a literary production of the early Chaldean period. In this work Nimrod heads a list of Babylonian kings called *Canaanite*, and a writer in the "Journal of Sacred Literature" has argued with considerable force in favour of these Canaanites being the Arabs of Berosus, who reigned about B.C. 1550 to 1300. The southern half of Arabia is known as Cush in the Old Testament like the opposite coast of Africa, and, as Nimrod is called a Cushite in Genesis, there was a great temptation to identify him with the leader of the Arab dynasty. This idea, however, gained little favour, and has not been held by any section of inquirers as fixing the position of Nimrod. The discovery of the cuneiform inscriptions threw a new light on the subject of Babylonian history, and soon after the decipherment of the inscriptions attention was directed to the question of the identity and age of Nimrod. Sir Henry Rawlinson, the father of Assyrian discovery, first seriously attempted to fix the name of Nimrod in the cuneiform inscriptions, and he endeavoured to find the name in that of the second god of the great Chaldean triad. (See Rawlinson's "Ancient Monarchies," vol. i. p. 117.) The names of this deity are really Enu, Elum, and Bel, and he was evidently worshipped at the dawn of Babylonian history, and is in fact represented as one of the creators of the world; time, moreover, has shown that the cuneiform characters on which the identification was grounded do not bear the phonetic values then supposed.

Sir Henry Rawlinson also suggested ("Ancient Monarchies," p. 136) that the god Nergal was a deification of Nimrod. Nergal, however, which means literally "the illuminator of Hades," was a god of the lower world, and even if Nimrod was deified under the name of Nergal this does not explain his position or epoch.

Canon Rawlinson, brother of Sir Henry, in the first volume of his "Ancient Monarchies," p. 153, and following, makes some judicious remarks on the chronological position of Nimrod, and suggests that he may have reigned a century or two before B.C. 2286; he asserts the historical character of his reign, and supposes him to have founded the Babylonian monarchy, but does not himself identify him with any king known from the inscriptions. At the time when this was written (1871), the conclusions of Canon Rawlinson were the most satisfactory that had been advanced since the discovery of the cuneiform inscriptions. Since this time, however, some new theories have been started, with the idea of identifying Nimrod; one of these, brought forward by Professor Oppert, makes the word a geographical term, but such an explanation is evidently quite insufficient to account for the traditions attached to the name.

Another theory brought forward by the Rev. A. H. Sayce and Josef Grivel, "Transactions of Society of Biblical Archæology," vol. ii. part 2, p. 243, and vol. iii. part 1, p. 136, identifies Nimrod with Merodach, the god of Babylon; partly on the ground of the similarity of name, Merodach being Amar-utuci or Amar-ud in Accadian, partly because Merodach the patron-deity of Babylon stood in the same relation to that city that Asshur did to Assyria (see Micah v. 6), and partly since we find Merodach called "a hero" like Nimrod in Genesis, and assigned "four divine dogs" as though he were a hunter. These dogs are Uccumu "the despoiler," Acculu "the devourer," Icsuda "the capturer," and Iltebu "the carrier away." Merodach, it must be remembered, is always represented as a man, and is armed with weapons of war.

Mr. Smith first fancied that Nimrod might be Khammuragas, whom he identified with the first Arab king of Berosus, as this line of kings appeared to be connected with the Cossæans. This identification failing, after the discovery of the Deluge tablet in 1872, he conjectured that the hero whose name is provisionally read Izdubar is the Nimrod of the Bible, a conjecture which has since been adopted by several other scholars.

The supposition that Nimrod was an ethnic or geographical name, which was at one time favoured by Sir Henry Rawlinson, and has since been urged by Professor Oppert, is quite untenable, for it would be impossible on this theory to account for certain features in what we are told of the hero.

Mr. Smith's opinion that he was the hero of the Izdubar Epic was first founded on the discovery that the latter formed the centre of the national historical poetry, and was the hero of Babylonian legend—in fact, occupies much the same place as Nimrod in later Arab tradition.

Izdubar, moreover, agrees *exactly* in character with Nimrod; he was a hunter, according to the cuneiform legends, who contended with and destroyed the lion, tiger, leopard, and wild bull or buffalo, animals the most formidable in the chase in any country. He ruled first in Babylonia over the region which from other sources we know to have been the centre of Nimrod's kingdom. The principal scene, too, of his exploits and triumphs was the city of Erech, which, according to Genesis, was the second capital of Nimrod.

There remains the fact that the cuneiform name of this hero is undeciphered, the name Izdubar being a mere makeshift. It is possible that when the phonetic reading of the characters is found it will turn out to correspond with the name Nimrod. At all events it is noteworthy that Izdubar seems to have been specially connected with the town of Marad, the original Accadian name of which was Amarda, and that the Accadian *an Amarda* or "god of Amarda," closely corresponds with the Biblical name of Nimrod. The translations and notes given in this book will lead, perhaps, to the general admission of the identity of the hero Izdubar with the traditional Nimrod;

but this result can be firmly established only when more evidence is before us than that which we have at present.

At the time of the opening of the Epic, the great city of the south of Babylonia, and the capital of this part of the country, was Uruk, called in Genesis, Erech. Erech was devoted to the worship of Anu, the god of heaven, and his wife, the goddess Anatu, as well as of Istar, the Phœnician Ashtoreth, or Astarte, the myth of whose love for the Sun-god Dumuzi or Tammuz, the Adonis of Greek story, is alluded to in the course of the poem. The worship of Anatu, however, was subsequent to the Semitic occupation of the country, since the necessity of providing a female deity by the side of every male one was not felt until the Accadians, whose language was unacquainted with genders, were succeeded by the Semites with their nouns either masculine or feminine.

Here may provisionally be placed the first fragment of the Izdubar legends, K 3200. This fragment consists of part of the third column of a tablet, which is probably the first; and it gives an account of a conquest of Erech by its enemies. The fragment reads:—

- 1. his ..... he left
- 2. .... and he goes down to the river,
- 3. .... in the river his ship is made good.
- 4. ..... he is .... and he weeps bitterly
-
- 5. .... placed, the city of Ganganna which had (suffered) destruction.
- 6. .... their *samuri* (were) she asses
- 7. .... their *raburi* (were) great wild bulls.
- 8. Like cattle the people fears,
- 9. like doves the slaves mourn.
- 10. The gods of Erech the lofty
- 11. turned to flies and brood in swarms.
- 12. The spirits (*sedu*) of Erech the lofty
- 13. turned to cocks and went forth in outposts.
- 14. For three years the city of Erech does the enemy besiege,
- 15. the great gates were thrown down and trampled upon,

- 16. the goddess Istar before its enemies could not lift her head.

- 17. Bel his mouth opened and speaks,

- 18. to Istar the queen a speech he makes:

- 19. ..... in the midst of Nipur my hands have placed,

- 20. .... my country? Babylon (Din-tir) the house of my delight,

- 21. my .... I gave my hands.

- 22. ..... he was favourable to the sanctuaries

- 23. ..... in the day ....

- 24. ..... the great gods. ....

Here we have a graphic account of the condition of Erech, when the enemy overran the country, and the first question which occurs is, who were these conquerors? Conjecture is idle in the want of evidence. They may have been the Semitic successors of the Accadians, they may have been the Medes of Berosus, or they may have been tribes who belong only to the realm of mythology. Mr. Smith believed that they were the subjects of Khumbaba, the tyrant whose death is related in the fourth book of the Epic, and who ruled over the land of Elam.

The name of Khumbaba, or Khubaba, as it is occasionally written, is probably a compound of "Khumba," or "Khumbume," the name of one of the chief Elamite gods. Many other Elamite names compounded with Khumba are mentioned in the inscriptions: Khumba-sidir, an early chief; Khumba-undasa, an Elamite general opposed to Sennacherib; Khumba-nigas, an Elamite monarch opposed to Sargon; Tul-khumba, an Elamite city, &c.

The notice of foreign dominion, and particularly of Elamite supremacy at this time, may, perhaps, form a clue from which to ascertain the approximate age of the poems as we have them. We know that myths are localized in the country of those who hand them down to posterity, and assigned to an age which has made an impression on their narrators. There must have been some reason for the legendary siege and capture of Erech, some actual event around which the story of Izdubar has entwined itself.

Looking at the fragments of Berosus and the notices of Greek and Roman authors, we may ask whether there is any epoch of conquest and foreign dominion which can be fixed upon as representing such an actual event? Let us glance for a moment at the earlier history of Babylonia so far as it is known to us.

The earlier part of the list of dynasties quoted from Berosus gives the following periods from the Flood downwards:—

86 Chaldean kings from the Flood down to the Median conquest, reigning for 34,080 or 33,091 years.

8 Median kings who conquered and held Babylon, 234, or 224, or 190 years.

11 other kings, race and duration unknown.

49 Chaldean kings, for 458 years.

The last of these dynasties preceded a dynasty of kings called Arabian by the copyists of Berosus, and though neither the number of the reigns nor the length of time assigned to the dynasty agrees with what the monuments tell us of the Cassite or Cossæan line of kings, there is no other line which can in any way be identified with the Arabians of the Babylonian historian. The 49 Chaldean kings must, therefore, have reigned before Khammuragas, that is before B.C. 2000-1750. Now an inscription of Nabonidus informs us that Lig-bagas, the first monarch of all Chaldea of whom we know, flourished 700 years anterior to the reign of Khammuragas; he would, therefore, come among the 11 nameless kings of Berosus, supposing any reliance can be placed on the statements of the latter, and about 250 years before the accession of the Chaldean dynasty. But the engraved cylinders and seals of the age of Lig-bagas show that the legend of Izdubar was already popular, and we must accordingly seek a still older period in which to place its origin and attachment to a particular historical event. Hence it may well be that the siege of Erech, the memory of which is preserved in the first book of the Izdubar Epic, was the work of those foreign invaders whom the Babylonian historian has termed Median.

Now it is not improbable that the Median dynasty was really Elamite; or at all events belonged to the same race as the primitive inhabitants of Elam. This race was closely allied to the Accadians; and it was spread over the whole range of country which stretched from the southern shores of the Caspian to the Persian Gulf. The Protomedes, as they are sometimes called, were not conquered and supplanted by Aryan invaders from the east till the ninth century B.C. It was in their country that Kharsak-kurra, "the Mountain of the East," was localized whereon the Accadians and their kinsfolk in Elam and Media believed the ark to have rested after the Flood, and which they regarded as the cradle of their race. It was therefore pre-eminently "the land," *mada* in Accadian, and from this *mada* there is every reason to think the name of Media has been derived. Consequently, the Medians of Berosus, the inhabitants of *mada* "the land" of the east, need not have been more than one of the many Elamite swarms that from time to time descended into the fertile plains of Babylonia, and not unfrequently obtained a settlement there. Such were the Accadians, or "Highlanders" themselves; such, too, the two Cassite or Cossæan dynasties which we learn from the monuments long held sway over Chaldea.

MIGRATION OF EASTERN TRIBE; FROM EARLY BABYLONIAN CYLINDER.

An early Babylonian cylinder, which came from Erech and originally belonged to a member of the royal family of that city, presents us with a curious picture of a rude nomad tribe apparently arriving in Babylonia. The chief marches in front armed with bow and arrows, and wearing the same kind of boots with turned-up ends as distinguished the Hittites in ancient times and are still worn in Asia Minor and Greece. They indicate that the wearer came from a cold and mountainous country. The animals' skins which compose the dresses of his three retainers also point to a similar conclusion. Besides the retainers, the wife of the chief is depicted, as well as two slaves who carry some objects on their shoulders. Unfortunately no light is cast upon the group by the inscription, which simply states that the cylinder belonged to "Gibil-dur (or Ne-Zicum), the brother of the king of Erech, the librarian, thy servant." All we can gather from it is that the famous library of Erech, which furnished Assur-bani-pal and his scribes with the original texts of the Izdubar Epic, was already in existence, and that the office of librarian was considered honourable enough to be borne by a brother of the reigning monarch.

If the legendary siege of Erech is not to be referred to the epoch of the Median conquest, it may have fallen at the time when the image of the goddess Nana was carried away from Erech by the Elamite king Kudur-nankhundi, 1635 years before the capture of Shushan, the capital of Elam, by the Assyrians (about B.C. 645), and consequently about B.C. 2280. A fragment which refers to this period in "Cuneiform Inscriptions," vol. iii. p. 38, relates the destruction wrought in the country by the Elamites, and makes

Kudur-nankhundi follow one of the other monarchs of an Elamite dynasty and exceed his predecessors in the injury he did to the country.

Putting together the detached notices of this period, the following may approximately represent the chronology, the dates being understood as round numbers.

? B.C. 2750, Elamites (Medes) overrun Babylonia.

B.C. 2280, Kudur-nankhundi, king of Elam, ravages Erech.

B.C. 1800, Khammuragas conquers Babylonia.

Although the dates transmitted through ancient authors are as a rule vague and doubtful, there are many independent notices which seem to point to somewhere about the twenty-third century before the Christian era for the foundation of the Babylonian and Assyrian power. Several of these dates are connected either directly or by implication with Nimrod, who first formed a united empire over these regions.

The following are some of these notices:—

Simplicius relates that Callisthenes, the friend of Alexander, sent to Aristotle from Babylon a series of stellar observations reaching back 1,903 years before the taking of Babylon by Alexander. This would make 1903 + 331 = B.C. 2234.

Berosus and Critodemus are said by Pliny to have made the inscribed stellar observations reach to 480 years before the era of Phoroneus; as the latter date was supposed to be about the middle of the eighteenth century B.C., 480 years before it comes also to about the period of Kudur-nankhundi.

Diodorus makes the Assyrian empire commence a thousand years or more before the Trojan war.

Ctesias and Cephalion make its foundation early in the twenty-second century B.C.

The two last statements, however, are probably derived from Ctesias, whose so-called history has been shown by cuneiform decipherment to have been a mere fiction put together out of misunderstood myths and fragments of theology. In any case, too, they apply only to the foundation of the Assyrian power, which was modern as compared with that of Babylonia, in spite of the assertion of Sargon, who boasts of having been preceded on the throne by 350 kings.

Of the latter part of the first tablet of the Izdubar Epic we have as yet no knowledge.

Chapter XII.
MEETING OF HEA-BANI AND IZDUBAR.

Dream of Izdubar.—Hea-bani.—His wisdom.—His
solitary life.—Izdubar's petition.—Zaidu.—Kharimtu and
Samkhat.—Tempt Hea-bani.—Might and fame of
Izdubar.—Speech of Hea-bani.—His journey to Erech.—
The midannu or tiger.—Festival at Erech.—Dream of
Izdubar.—Friendship with Hea-bani.

IN this chapter are included the fragments of what appear to be the second and third tablets or books. In this section of the story Izdubar comes prominently forward, and meets with Hea-bani. The notice of his mother Dannat appears in one of the tablets given in this chapter.

Izdubar, in the Babylonian and Assyrian sculptures, is always represented with a marked physiognomy, and his peculiarities can be seen by noticing the photograph from a Babylonian gem at the beginning of the book, the engraving from an Assyrian sculpture in the last chapter, and the engraving in page 249 showing Izdubar and Hea-bani struggling with wild animals. In all these cases, and in every other instance where Izdubar is represented, he is indicated as a man with masses of curls over his head and a large curly beard. The type is so marked and so distinct from either the Assyrian or the Babylonian one that it is hard to say to what race it should be attached.

The deity of Izdubar was Lugal-turda, the god who was changed into the bird of storm according to the old myth, from which it may be supposed that he was a native of the district of Amarda or Marad, where that god was worshipped. This district Mr. Smith thought was probably the Amordacia or Mardocæa of Ptolemy, but its situation is uncertain.

The fragments of the second and third tablets assume by their notices that Izdubar was already known as a mighty hunter, and it appears a little later that he claimed descent from the old Babylonian heroes, as he calls Xisuthrus, the Chaldean Noah, his "father."

TABLET II.

A single fragment which Mr. Smith believed to belong to this tablet has been found; it is K 3389, and contains part of the third and fourth columns of writing. It appears from this that Izdubar was then at Erech, and had a curious dream. He thought he saw the stars of heaven fall to the ground, and in their descent they struck upon his back. He then saw standing over him a terrible being, the aspect of whose face was fierce, and who was armed with claws, like the claws of lions. The greater part of the description of the dream is lost; it probably occupied Columns I. and II. of the second tablet. Thinking that the dream portended some fate to himself, Izdubar calls on all the wise men to explain it, and offers a reward to any one who can interpret the dream. Here the fragment K 3389 comes in:

COLUMN III.

- 1. .... *ru kili* I ....
- 2. .... he and the princes may he ...
- 3. .... in the vicinity send him,
- 4. .... may they ennoble his family,
- 5. .... at the head of his feast may he set thee
- 6. .... may he array thee in jewels and gold
- 7. .... may he enclose thee
- 8. .... in his .... seat thee
- 9. into the houses of the gods may he cause thee to enter
- 10. .... seven wives
- 11. .... cause illness in his stomach
- 12. .... went up alone
- 13. .... his heaviness to his friend
- 14. .... a dream I dreamed in my sleep
- 15. .... the stars of heaven fell to the earth
- 16. .... I stood still
- 17. .... his face
- 18. .... his face was terrible
-
- 19. .... like the claws of a lion, were his claws.
- 20. .... the strength in me
- 21. .... he slew
- 22. .... me
- 23. .... over me

- 24. ..... corpse ....

The first part of this fragment appears to recount the honours offered by Izdubar to any one who should interpret the dream. These included the ennobling of his family, his recognition in assemblies, his being invested with jewels of honour, and his wives being increased. A description of the dream of the hero, much mutilated, follows. The conduct of Nebuchadnezzar in the Book of Daniel, with reference to his dreams, bears some resemblance to that of Izdubar.

After this fragment we have again a blank in the story, and it would appear that in this interval application was made to a nondescript creature named Hea-bani that he would go to the city of Erech and interpret the dream of Izdubar.

Hea-bani appears, from the representations on seals and other objects on which he is figured, to have been a satyr or faun. He is always drawn with the feet and tail of an ox, and with horns on his head. He is said to have lived in a cave among the wild animals of the forest, and was supposed to possess wonderful knowledge both of nature and human affairs. In appearance he resembles the *se'irim* or hairy demons, half men, half goats, who inhabited the deserts and were a terror to passers-by. Reference is made to them in Lev. xvii. 7, 2 Chron. xi. 15, Is. xiii. 21, xxxiv. 14, from which we learn that worship was paid to them, and that they were supposed to be specially connected with the neighbourhood of Babylon. Hea-bani was angry at the request that he should abandon his solitary life for the friendship of Izdubar, and where our narrative reopens the god Samas is persuading him to accept the offer. It may be added that the name Hea-bani signifies "Hea created me," from which we may infer that the monster was believed to have originally ascended like Oannes out of the abysses of the sea.

COLUMN IV.

- 1. ... me

- 2. ... on my back

- 3. And Samas opened his mouth

- 4. and spake and from heaven said to him:

- 5. .... and the female Samkhat thou shalt choose

- 6. they shall array thee in trappings of divinity

- 7. they shall give thee the insignia of royalty

- 8. they shall make thee become great

- 9. and Izdubar thou shalt call and incline him towards thee

- 10. and Izdubar shall make friendship unto thee

- 11. he shall cause thee to recline on a grand couch

- 12. on a beautiful couch he shall seat thee

-

- 13. he will cause thee to sit on a comfortable seat a seat on the left

- 14. the kings of the earth shall kiss thy feet

- 15. he shall enrich thee and the men of Erech he shall make silent before thee

- 16. and he after thee shall take all ....

- 17. he shall clothe thy body in raiment and ....

- 18. Hea-bani heard the words of Samas the warrior

- 19. and the anger of his heart was appeased

- 20. .... was appeased

Here we are still dealing with the honours which Izdubar promises to the interpreter of his dream, and these seem to show that Izdubar had some power at Erech at this time; he does not, however, appear to have been an independent king, and it is probable that the next two columns of this tablet, now lost, contain negotiations for bringing Hea-bani to Erech, the subject being continued on the third tablet.

TABLET III.

This tablet is far better preserved than the two previous ones; it gives the account of the successful mission to bring Hea-bani to Erech, opening with a broken account of the wisdom of Hea-bani.

COLUMN I.

- 1. .... knows all things

- 2. .... and difficult

- 3. .... wisdom of all things

-

- 4. .... the knowledge that is seen and that which is hidden

- 5. .... bring word of peace to ....

- 6. from a far off road he will come and I rest and ....

- 7. .... on tablets and all that rests ....

- 8. .... and tower of Erech the lofty

- 9. .... beautiful

- 10. .... which like ....

- 11. .... I strove with him not to leave ....

- 12. .... god? who from ....

- 13. .... carry ....

- 14. .... leave ....

- (Many lines lost.)

COLUMN II.

- 1. Izdubar did not leave .....

- 2. Daughter of a warrior ....

- 3. their might ......

- 4. the gods of heaven, lord ......

- 5. thou makest to be sons and family? .....

- 6. there is not any other like thee ......

- 7. in the depth made ......

- 8. Izdubar did not leave, the son to his father day and night ......

- 9. he the ruler also of Erech ......

- 10. he their ruler and ......

- 11. made firm? and wise ......

- 12. Izdubar did not leave Dannat, the son to his mother ......

-

- 13. Daughter of a warrior, wife of .....

- 14. their might the god .... heard and ...

- 15. Aruru strong and great, thou Aruru hast made ......

- 16. again making his strength, one day his heart ......

- 17. he changed and the city of Erech ......

- 18. Aruru on hearing this, the strength of Anu made in the midst ......

- 19. Aruru put in her hands, she bowed her breast and lay on the ground

- 20. ... Hea-bani she made a warrior, begotten of the seed of the soldier Ninip

- 21. ...... covered his body, retiring in companionship like a woman,

- 22. the features of his aspect were concealed like the corn god

- 23. possessing knowledge of men and countries, in clothing clothed like the god Ner

- 24. with the gazelles he ate food in the night

- 25. with the beasts of the field he consorted in the day

- 26. with the creeping things of the waters his heart delighted

- 27. Zaidu catcher of men

- 28. in front of that field confronted him

- 29. the first day the second day and the third in the front of that field the same,

- 30. the courage of Zaidu dried up before him

- 31. and he and his beast entered into his house and

-

- 32. .... fear dried up and overcome

- 33. .... his courage grew before him

- 34. .... his face was terrible

COLUMN III.

- 1. Zaidu opened his mouth and spake and said to ......

- 2. My father the first leader who shall go ....

- 3. in the land of ......

- 4. like the soldier of Anu ......

- 5. shall march over the country ......
- 6. and firmly with the beast ......
- 7. and firmly his feet in the front of the field ...
- 8. I feared and I did not approach it
- 9. he filled the cave which he had dug
- 10. .....
- 11. I ascended on my hands to the ....
- 12. I did not reach to the .....

- 13. .... and said to Zaidu
- 14. .... Erech, Izdubar
- 15. .... ascend his field
- 16. .... his might
- 17. .... thy face
- 18. .... the might of a man
- 19. ......
- 20. .... like a chief
- 21. ...... field
- 22 to 24. three lines of directions.
-
- 25. According to the advice of his father ....
- 26. Zaidu went .....
- 27. he took the road and in the midst of Erech he halted
- 28. .... Izdubar ....
- 29. the first leader who shall go ....
- 30. in the land of ....
- 31. like the soldier of Anu ....
- 32. shall march over the country ....
- 33. and firmly with the beast ....

- 34. and firmly his feet ....

- 35. I feared and I did not approach it

- 36. he filled the cave which he had dug

- 37. ......

- 38. I ascended on my hands .....

- 39. I was not able to reach to the covert.

- 40. Izdubar to him also said to Zaidu:

- 41. go Zaidu and with thee Kharimtu, and Samkhat take,

- 42. and when the beast ... in front of the field

- 43 to 45. directions to the women how to entice Hea-bani.

- 46. Zaidu went and with him Kharimtu, and Samkhat he took, and

- 47. they took the road, and went along the path.

- 48. On the third day they reached the land where the flood happened.

- 49. Zaidu and Kharimtu in their places sat,

-

- 50. the first day and the second day in front of the field they sat,

- 51. the land where the beast drank of drink,

COLUMN IV.

- 1. the land where the creeping things of the water rejoiced his heart.

- 2. And he Hea-bani had made for himself a mountain

- 3. with the gazelles he ate food,

- 4. with the beasts he drank of drink,

- 5. with the creeping things of the waters his heart rejoiced.

- 6. Samkhat the enticer of men saw him

- 7 to 26. details of the actions of the female Samkhat and Hea-bani.

- 27. And Hea-bani approached Kharimtu then, who before had not enticed him.

- 28. And he listened .... and was attentive,

- 29. and he turned and sat at the feet of Kharimtu.

- 30. Kharimtu bent down her face,

- 31. and Kharimtu spake; and his ears heard

- 32. and to him also she said to Hea-bani:

- 33. Famous Hea-bani like a god art thou,

- 34. Why dost thou associate with the creeping things in the desert?

- 35. I desire thy company to the midst of Erech the lofty,

- 36. to the temple of Elli-tardusi the seat of Anu and Istar,

- 37. the dwelling of Izdubar the mighty giant,

- 38. who also like a bull towers over the chiefs.

- 39. She spake to him and before her speech,

- 40. the wisdom of his heart flew away and disappeared.

- 41. Hea-bani to her also said to Kharimtu:

- 42. I join to Samkhat my companionship,

- 43. to the temple of Elli-tardusi the seat of Anu and Istar,

- 44. the dwelling of Izdubar the mighty giant,

- 45. who also like a bull towers over the chiefs.

- 46. I will meet him and see his power,

COLUMN V.

- 1. I will bring to the midst of Erech a tiger,

- 2. and if he is able he will destroy it.

- 3. In the desert it is begotten, it has great strength,

- 4. ...... before thee

- 5. .... everything there is I know

- 6. Hea-bani went to the midst of Erech the lofty

- 7. .... the chiefs ... made submission

- 8. in that day they made a festival
- 9. ..... city
- 10. ..... daughter
- 11. ..... made rejoicing
- 12. ..... becoming great
- 13. ..... mingled and
- 14. ..... Izdubar rejoicing the people
- 15. went before him
- 16. A prince thou becomest glory thou hast
- 17. .... fills his body
- 18. .... who day and night
- 19. .... destroy thy terror
- 20. .... the god Samas loves him and
- 21. .... and Hea have given intelligence to his ears
- 22. he has come from the mountain
- 23. to the midst of Erech he will ponder thy dream
- 24. Izdubar his dream revealed and said to his mother
- 25. A dream I dreamed in my sleep
- 26. .... the stars of heaven
- 27. .... struck upon my back
- 28. .... of heaven over me
- 29. .... did not rise over it
- 30. .... stood over .....
- 31. .... him and
- 32. ..... over him
- 33. .... his ....
- 34. .... princess
- 35. .... me

- 36. ..... I know
- 37. ..... to Izdubar
-
- 38. ..... of heaven
- 39. ..... over thy back
- 40. ..... over thee
- 41. ..... did not rise over it
- 42. ..... my .....
- 43. ..... thee

There is one other mutilated fragment of this and the next column with part of a relation respecting beasts and a fragment of a conversation between Izdubar and his mother.

The whole of this tablet is curious, and it certainly gives the successful issue of the attempt to bring Hea-bani to Erech, and in very fragmentary condition the dream of the monarch.

It appears that the females Samkhat and Kharimtu prevailed upon Hea-bani to come to Erech and see the exploits of the giant Izdubar, and he declared that he would bring a *Midannu*, most probably a tiger, to Erech, in order to make trial of the strength of Izdubar, and to see if he could destroy it.

The Midannu is mentioned in the Assyrian texts as a fierce carnivorous animal allied to the lion and leopard; it is called *Midannu*, Mindinu, and Mandinu. In a list of animals it is associated with the *dumamu* or cat.

In the fifth column, after the description of the festivities which followed the arrival of Hea-bani, there appears a break between lines 15 and 16, some part of the original story being probably omitted here. The Assyrian copy probably is here defective, at least one line being lost. The portion here omitted seems to have stated that the following speech was made by the mother of Izdubar, who figures prominently in the earlier part of these legends.

Chapter XIII.
DESTRUCTION OF THE TYRANT KHUMBABA.

Mythical geography.—Forest region.—Khumbaba.—
Conversation.—Petition to Samas.—Journey to forest.—
Dwelling of Khumbaba.—Entrance to forest.—Meeting
with Khumbaba.—Death of Khumbaba.—Izdubar king.

THE wretchedly mutilated condition of the fragments that belong to the two next tablets or books of the Epic makes it impossible to ascertain their correct order and arrangement. The arrangement given here, accordingly, must be regarded as merely provisional. It may, however, be taken as certain that they all form part of the fourth and fifth tablets, and relate the contest between Izdubar and Khumbaba.

Khumbaba, the Kombabos of the Greeks, was the prototype of Geryon. He dwelt far away in the forest of pines and sherbin cedars, where the gods and spirits had their abode. It was, consequently, in the cold region of the Accadian Olympus, now Mount Elwend, that he was placed by the old mythology, and the similarity of his name to that of the Elamite god Khumba or Khumbume makes it possible that he was originally identical with the latter. In this case the antagonism between Khumbaba and Izdubar would have been merely a reflection of the antagonism that existed between the inhabitants of Babylonia and the subjects of the Elamite empire. Mr. Smith even thought that the overthrow of Khumbaba might have been an echo of the overthrow of some Elamite dynasty by a Chaldean one.

In the case of the fourth tablet Mr. Smith believed that he had found fragments of all six columns, but some of these fragments are useless until we have further fragments to complete them.

TABLET IV.

COLUMN I.

- 1. .... mu ....
- 2. .... thy ....
- 3. .... me, return
- 4. .... the birds shall rend him
- 5. .... in thy presence
- 6. .... of the forest of pine trees

- 7. .... all the battle

- 8. .... may the birds of prey surround him

- 9. .... that, his carcass may they destroy

- 10. .... to me and we will appoint thee king,

- 11. .... thou shalt direct after the manner of a king

- 12. [Izdubar] opened his mouth and spake,

- 13. and said to Hea-bani:

- 14. ... he goes to the great palace

- 15. .... the breast of the great queen

- 16. ..... knowledge, everything he knows

- 17. ...... establish to our feet

- 18. .... his hand

- 19. .... I to the great palace

- 20. .... the great queen

- (Probably over twenty lines lost here.)

COLUMN II.

- 1. .... enter

- 2. .... he raised

- 3. .... the ornaments of her ....

- 4. .... the ornaments of her breast

- 5. .... and her crown I divided

- 6. .... of the earth he opened

- 7. he .... he ascended to the city

- 8. he went up to the presence of Samas he made a sacrifice?

- 9. he built an altar. In the presence of Samas he lifted his hands:

- 10. Why hast thou established Izdubar, in thy heart thou hast given him protection,

- 11. when the son .... and he goes

- 12. on the remote path to Khumbaba.

- 13. A battle he knows not he will confront,

- 14. an expedition he knows not he will ride to,

-

- 15. for long he will go and will return,

- 16. to take the course to the forest of pine trees,

- 17. to Khumbaba of [whom his city may] he destroy,

- 18. and every one who is evil whom thou hatest ...

- 19. In the day of the year he will ....

- 20. May she not return at all, may she not ...

- 21. him to fix ....

(About ten lines lost here.)

Here we see that Izdubar, impressed with the magnitude of the task he had undertaken, makes a prayer and sacrifice to Samas to aid him in his task. The next fragment appears also to belong to this column, and may refer to preliminaries for sacrificing to Istar, with a view also to gain her aid in the enterprise.

This fragment of Column II. reads

- 1. .... neighbourhood of Erech ....

- 2. .... strong and ...

- 3. he burst open the road ....

- 4. and that city ....

- 5. and the collection ....

- 6. placed the people together ....

- 7. the people were ended ....

- 8. like of a king ....

- 9. which for a long time had been made ....

- 10. to the goddess Istar the bed ....

- 11. to Izdubar like the god Sakim ....

- 12. Hea-bani opened the great gate of the house of assembly ....

-
- 13. for Izdubar to enter ....
- 14. .... in the gate of the house ....

COLUMN III.

- 1. the corpse of ....
- 2. to ....
- 3. to the rising of ....
- 4. the angels ....
- 5. may she not return ....
- 6. him to fix ....
- 7. the expedition which he knows not ....
- 8. may he destroy also ....
- 9. of which he knows ....
- 10. the road ....

Five more mutilated lines, the rest of the column being lost.

This fragment shows Izdubar still invoking the gods for his coming expedition. Under the next column Mr. Smith placed a fragment, the position and meaning of which are quite unknown.

COLUMN IV.—UNCERTAIN FRAGMENT.

- 1. he was heavy ....
- 2. Hea-bani was ....
- 3. Hea-bani strong not rising ....
- 4. When ....
- 5. with thy song? ....
- 6. the sister of the gods faithful ....
- 7. wandering he fixed to ....
-
- 8. the sister of the gods lifted ....
- 9. and the daughters of the gods grew ....

- 10. I Hea-bani .... he lifted to ....

Somewhere here should be the story, now lost, of the starting of Izdubar on his expedition accompanied by his friend Hea-bani. The sequel shows they arrive at the palace or residence of Hea-bani, which is surrounded by a forest of pine and cedar, the whole being enclosed by some barrier or wall, with a gate for entrance. Hea-bani and Izdubar open this gate where the story reopens on the fifth column.

COLUMN V.

- 1. the sharp weapon

- 2. to make men fear him ....

- 3. Khumbaba poured a tempest out of his mouth ....

- 4. he heard the gate of the forest [open]

- 5. the sharp weapon to make men fear him [he took]

- 6. and in the path of his forest he stood and [waited]

- 7. Izdubar to him also [said to Hea-bani]

Here we see Khumbaba waiting for the intruders, but the rest of the column is lost; it appears to have principally consisted of speeches by Izdubar and Hea-bani on the magnificent trees they saw, and the work before them. A single fragment of Column VI., containing fragments of six lines, shows them still at the gate, and when the next tablet, No. V., opens, they had not yet entered.

TABLET V.

The fifth tablet is more certain than the last; it appears to refer to the conquest of Khumbaba. Only fragments of this tablet, which opens with a description of the retreat of Khumbaba, have as yet been discovered.

COLUMN I.

- 1. He stood and surveyed the forest

- 2. of pine trees, he perceived its height,

- 3. of the forest he perceived its approach,

- 4. in the place where Khumbaba went his step was placed,

- 5. on a straight road and a good path.

- 6. He saw the land of the pine trees, the seat of the gods, the sanctuary of the angels,

- 7. in front? of the seed the pine tree carried its fruit,

- 8. good was its shadow, full of pleasure,

- 9. an excellent tree, the choice of the forest,

- 10. .... the pine heaped ....

- 11. .... for one kaspu (7 miles) ...

- 12. .... cedar two-thirds of it ...

- 13. .... grown ....

- 14. .... like it ...

-

- (About 10 lines lost here.)

- 25. .... he looked ....

- 26. .... he made and he ....

- 27. .... drove to ....

- 28. .... he opened and ....

- 29. Izdubar opened his mouth and spake, [and said to Hea-bani]:

- 30. My friend ....

- 31. .... with their slaughter ....

- 32. .... he did not speak before her, he made with him ....

- 33. .... knowledge of war who made fighting,

- 34. in entering to the house thou shalt not fear ...

- 35. .... and like I take her also they ....

- 36. to an end may they seat ....

- 37. .... thy hand ....

- 38. .... took my friend first ....

- 39. .... his heart prepared for war, that year and day also

- 40. .... on his falling appoint the people

- 41. .... slay him, his corpse may the birds of prey surround
- 42. ...... of them he shall make
- 43. .... going he took the weight
- 44. they performed it, their will they established

- 45. .... they entered into the forest

COLUMN II.

(Five lines mutilated.)

- 6. they passed through the forest ....

- 7. Khumbaba ....
- 8. he did not come ....
- 9. he did not ....
- (Seven lines lost.)
- 17. heavy ....
- 18. Hea-bani opened his mouth ....
- 19. .... Khumbaba in ....
- 20. .... one by one and ....

(Many other broken lines.)

There are a few fragments of Columns III., IV., and V., and a small portion of Column VI., which reads:

- 1. .... cedar to ....
- 2. .... he placed and ....
- 3. .... 120 .... Hea-bani ....
- 4. .... the head of Khumbaba ....

- 5. .... his weapon he sharpened ....
- 6. .... tablet of the story of fate of ....

It appears from the various mutilated fragments of this tablet that Izdubar and Hea-bani conquer and slay Khumbaba and take his goods, but much is wanted to connect the fragments.

The conclusion of this stage of the story and triumph of Izdubar are given at the commencement of the sixth tablet. The conquest of Khumbaba gave Izdubar the crown and attributes of his fallen rival, who seems to have been a sun-god, and this caused Istar, who already appears as the bride of the sun in the myth of Tammuz, to woo the triumphant hero.

Chapter XIV.
THE ADVENTURES OF ISTAR.

Triumph of Izdubar.—Istar's love.—Her offer of marriage.—Her promises.—Izdubar's answer.— Tammuz.—Amours of Istar.—His refusal.—Istar's anger.—Ascends to Heaven.—The bull.—Slain by Izdubar.—Istar's curse.—Izdubar's triumph.—The feast.—Istar's despair.—Her descent to Hades.— Description.—The seven gates.—The curses.—Atsu-sunamir the Sphinx.—Release of Istar.—The dog of the dawn.—Lament for Tammuz.

IN this chapter are included the sixth and seventh tablets, which both primarily refer to the doings of Istar.

TABLET VI.

The sixth tablet is in better condition than any of the former ones, and allows of something like a connected translation.

COLUMN I.

- 1. .... his weapon, he made bright his weapon.

-

- 2. Like a bull his mountain he ascended after him.

- 3. He destroyed him and clothed himself with his spoils.

- 4. The ... he put on and the fastening of the crown he tore.

- 5. Izdubar his crown put on (and the fastening of the crown he tore).

- 6. For the favour of Izdubar the princess Istar lifted the eyes:

- 7. I will make thee also Izdubar my husband,[18]

- 8. thy oath to me shall be thy bond,

- 9. thou shalt be husband and I will be thy wife.

- 10. I will make (thy) chariot glisten with crystal and gold,

- 11. of which the body is gold and its horns are strong.

- 12. I will cause thy days to find gifts, O judge (?) of the great.

- 13. Into our house enter, mid the scent of the pines.

- 14. When thou enterest our house

- 15. may the river Euphrates kiss thy feet.

- 16. There shall be under thee kings, lords, and princes.

- 17. The tribute of the mountains and plains may they bring to thee as an offering.

- 18. May thy herds and flocks bring forth twins,

- 19. may the increase of the cows come unto (thee),

-

- 20. may thy (horse) be strong, without ceasing, in the chariot,

- 21. may (thy steed) in the yoke never have a rival.

- 22. (Izdubar) opened his mouth and speaks;

- 23. (he says) to the princess Istar:

- 24. .... to thee thy possession

- 25. .... body and rottenness (?)

- 26. .... baldness and famine

- 27. .... I keep back the instruments of divinity

- 28. .... instruments of royalty

- 29. .... storm (?)

- 30. .... he poured (?)

- 31. .... I lingered

- 32. .... I took thee

- 33. .... caused to enter

- 34. the door afterwards .... ended wind and showers

- 35. palace .... the hero

- 36. mouth .... check her

- 37. that sign .... carry her

- 38. body glorious (?) .... carry her

- 39. grand .... tower of stone
- 40. they have dwelt (in) the land of the enemy
- 41. may she .... her lord
- 42. never may he woo thee for ever
- 43. never may a god praise thee
- 44. I took also the torch? .... I loved thee

COLUMN II.

- 1. Rest thee and .....
- 2. as for Tammuz the lover of (thy) youth
- 3. year after year thou hast wearied him with thy love.
- 4. Allala the eagle also thou lovest and
- 5. thou didst strike him, and his wings thou didst break;
- 6. he stood in the forest, he begged for wings.
- 7. Thou lovest also a lion lusty in might,
- 8. thou didst tear out by sevens his claws.
- 9. Thou lovest also a horse glorious in war,
- 10. he yielded himself and thou didst weary his love overmuch.
- 11. For seven kaspu (fourteen hours) thou didst weary his love without ceasing,
- 12. troubled and thirsting thou didst weary him.
- 13. To his mother Silele thou didst send him wearied with thy love.
- 14. Thou lovest also the shepherd Tabulu,
- 15. of whom continually thou didst ask for thy stibium.
- 16. Every day he propitiated thee with offerings,
- 17. thou didst strike him and to a hyena thou didst change him;
- 18. his own village drove him away;
- 19. his dogs tore his wounds.
- 20. Thou lovest also Isullanu the husbandman of thy father,

- 21. who continually was subject to thy order;

- 22. each day had he made bright thy dish.

- 23. The eyes thou didst take from him and didst put him in chains,

- 24. (saying): O Isullanu, cut thy hand, eat (thy) eyes!

- 25. And thy hand thou didst bring out and thou didst strike? ....

- 26. Isullanu says to thee:

- 27. As for me what dost thou ask of me?

- 28. My mother, thou art not beautiful, and I eat not.

- 29. The food I have eaten is plentiful, even pain and waking;

- 30. trembling and faintness overcome me (?)

- 31. Thou didst hear also this ....

- 32. thou didst strike him; to a pillar[19] thou didst change him,

- 33. thou didst place him also in the midst of the land ....

- 34. that he rise not up, that he go not ....

- 35. And as for me dost thou love me, and like to him wilt thou [serve me]?

- 36. When Istar (heard) this,

- 37. Istar was angry and to heaven she ascended;

- 38. Istar went also to the presence of Anu her father,

- 39. to the presence of Anatu her mother she went and says:

- 40. My father, Izdubar hates me, and

COLUMN III.

- 1. Izdubar despises my beauty,

- 2. my beauty and my charms.

- 3. Anu opened his mouth and spake, and

- 4. says to the princess Istar:
- 5. My daughter thou shalt remove ....
- 6. and Izdubar will count thy beauty,
- 7. thy beauty and thy charms.

- 8. Istar opened her mouth and spake, and
- 9. says to Anu her father:
- 10. My father, create the bull of Anu[20] and
- 11. Izdubar ....
- 12. when he is filled ....
- 13. I will strike ....
- 14. I will join ....
- 15. ....
- 16. over ....

- 17. Anu opened his mouth and spake, and
- 18. says to the princess Istar:
- 19. .... thou shalt join ....
- 20. .... of noble names
- 21. .... *maskhi* ....
- 22. .... which is magnified ....

- 23. Istar opened her mouth and spake, and
-
- 24. says to Anu her father:
- 25. .... I will strike
- 26. .... I will break
- 27. .... of noble names
- 28. .... reducer

- 29. .... of foods
- 30. .... of him

(Some lines lost here.)

COLUMN IV.

(Some lines lost.)

- 1. .... warriors
- 2. .... to the midst
- 3. .... three hundred warriors
- 4. .... to the midst
- 5. .... slay Hea-bani
- 6. in two divisions he parted in the midst of it
- 7. two hundred warriors .... made, the bull of Anu ....
- 8. in the third division .... his horns
- 9. Hea-bani struck? .... his might
- 10. and Hea-bani pierced ....
- 11. the bull of Anu by his head he took hold of ....
- 12. by the thickness of his tail ....

- 13. Hea-bani opened his mouth and spake, and
- 14. says to Izdubar:
- 15. My friend, we have strengthened ....
-
- 16. when we overthrow ...
- 17. My friend, I see ....
- 18. and the might ....
- 19. may I destroy ....
- (Three lines lost.).
- 23. .... hands .... to Rimmon and Nebo
- 24. .... *tarka* .... *um* ....

- 25. .... Hea-bani took hold .... the bull of Anu
- 26. .... he .... also .... by his tail
- 27. .... Hea-bani

COLUMN V.

- 1. And Izdubar like a ....
- 2. the hero and (his friend)
- 3. in the vicinity of the middle of his horns ....
- 4. from the city they destroyed, the heart ....
- 5. to the presence of Samas ....
- 6. they had gone to the presence of Samas ....
- 7. he placed at the side the bulk (?) ....

- 8. And Istar ascended over the fortress of Erech the lofty,
- 9. she destroyed the bull, she uttered a curse:
- 10. Woe to Izdubar who has overthrown me, has slain the bull of Anu.
- 11. Hea-bani also heard this speech of Istar,
- 12. and he cut off the member of the bull of Anu and before her he laid it;
-
- 13. And what of it? since I conquered thee when him also (*i.e.* Izdubar)
- 14. I caused thee to listen to;
- 15. its skin also I have hung up at thy side.
- 16. Istar gathered her maidens
- 17. Samkhati and Kharimati,[21]
- 18. over the member of the bull of Anu a mourning she made.
- 19. Izdubar called on the people, the multitude
- 20. all of them:
- 21. with the thickness of his horns the young men were glorious,

- 22. 30 manehs of crystal (was) their substance,

- 23. the sharpness of the points was destroyed,

- 24. 6 gurs its mass altogether.

- 25. For the food of his god Lugal-turda he cut it up;

- 26. he seethed it and hangs it up in the rising of his fire;

- 27. in the river Euphrates they washed their hands.

- 28. They had been taken and gone

- 29. through the street of Erech riding,

- 30. the assembly of the warriors of Erech put trust in them.

- 31. Izdubar to the inhabitants of Erech

- 32. .... a proclamation made.

COLUMN VI.

- 1. "If anyone is of ability among the chiefs,

- 2. if any is noble among the men,

- 3. Izdubar is able among the chiefs,

- 4. Izdubar is noble among the men,

- 5. .... our strength

- 6. .... he has not

- 7. .... his ...."

- 8. Izdubar in his palace made a rejoicing,

- 9. the chiefs reclining lie on couches at night.

- 10. Hea-bani lies down, a dream he dreams.

- 11. Hea-bani came and the dream he explains,

- 12. and says to Izdubar.

TABLET VII.

The seventh tablet opens with the words, "My friend, what is this counsel the great gods are taking?" It is uncertain if any other portion of this tablet has been found, but part of a remarkable fragment, with a continuation of the story of Istar, has been placed here. It appears that the goddess, failing in her attempt in heaven to avenge herself on Izdubar for his slight, resolved to descend to hell, to search out, if possible, new modes of attacking him.

Columns I. and II. are lost, the fragments recommencing on Column III.

COLUMN III.

- 1. .... people? to destroy his hand approached
- 2. .... raise in thy presence
- 3. .... like before
-
- 4. .... Zaidu (shall accomplish) the wish of his heart
- 5. with the female Samkhat .... he brought
- 6. .... thee, the female Samkhat will expel thee
- 7. (homage) they did not perform ......
- 8. assemble thou a great assembly;
- 9. .... the strong one has caused thee to be struck, even thee.
- 10. ... goods of the house of thy fulness

After many lines destroyed, the story recommences in the fourth column.

COLUMN IV.

- 1. [To Hades the country whence none return] I turn myself,
- 2. I spread like a bird my hands.
- 3. I descend, I descend to the house of darkness, the dwelling of the god Irkalla:
- 4. to the house out of which there is no exit,
- 5. to the road from which there is no return:
- 6. to the house from whose entrance the light is taken,
- 7. the place where dust is their nourishment and their food mud.
- 8. Its chiefs also are like birds covered with feathers;
- 9. the light is never seen, in darkness they dwell.
- 10. In the house, O my friend, which I will enter,
- 11. for me is treasured up a crown;

-
- 12. with those wearing crowns who from days of old ruled the earth,

- 13. to whom the gods Anu and Bel have given names of rule.

- 14. Water (?) they have given to quench the thirst they drink limpid waters.

- 15. In the house, O my friend, which I will enter,

- 16. dwell the lord and the unconquered one,

- 17. dwell the priest and the great man,

- 18. dwell the worms of the deep of the great gods;

- 19. there dwells Etana, there dwells the god Ner,

- 20. (there dwells) the queen of the lower regions, Allat,

- 21. the mistress of the fields the mother of the queen of the lower regions before her submits,

- 22. and there is not any one that stands against her in her presence.

- 23. I will approach her and she will see me

- 24. ... and she will bring me to her

Here the story is again lost, Columns V. and VI. being absent. It would seem that Hea-bani is here telling his friend how he must die and descend into the house of Hades. Mr. Smith, however, thought that in the third column some one is speaking to Istar, trying to persuade her not to descend to Hades, while in the fourth column the goddess, who is suffering all the pangs of jealousy and hate, revels in the dark details of the description of the lower regions, and declares her determination to go there.

If this view is correct, this part of the legend would be connected with the beautiful story of the Descent of Istar into Hades which describes how the goddess descended into the lower world in search of her husband Tammuz, the Sun-god, who had been slain by the boar's tusk of winter. Tammuz became Adonis, the Phœnician *adonai* "lord," among the Greeks, to whom the story of Aphroditê and Adonis had been carried by the Phœnicians. The story is one which meets us in the mythologies of many races and nations throughout the world, and has grown in each case out of the winter-sleep of the sun and his resurrection in the spring. Its last echo in our own European folklore may be heard in the tale of the Sleeping Beauty. A calendar found among the banking records of the Egibi firm in Babylonia notes on the 15th day of the month Tammuz or June "an eclipse of the Moon," apparently in reference to the descent of the Moon-goddess Istar into Hades. The legend survives in a changed form in the Talmud (*Yoma 69b, Sanhedrim 60a*). Here it is said that after the Captivity the elders of the nation, headed by Ezra and Nehemiah, besought God that the demon of lust might be delivered into their hands. In spite of a prophetic voice which warned them of the consequences of their request, it was persisted in, and the demon was given up to them and imprisoned. But before three days were over, the whole course of the world was thrown into disorder. No eggs even were to be had, and the Jewish elders were obliged to confess their mistake and release the demon from his fetters.

The descent of Istar into Hades from K 162.

- 1. To Hades the land whence none return, the land (of darkness),
- 2. Istar daughter of Sin (the moon) her ear (inclined);
- 3. inclined also the daughter of Sin her ear,
- 4. to the house of darkness the dwelling of the god Irkalla,
- 5. to the house out of which there is no exit,
- 6. to the road from which there is no return,
- 7. to the house from whose entrance the light is taken,
- 8. the place where dust is their nourishment and their food mud.
- 9. Light is never seen, in darkness they dwell.
- 10. Its chiefs also are like birds covered with feathers,
- 11. over the door and bolts is scattered dust.
- 12. Istar on her arrival at the gate of Hades,
- 13. to the keeper of the gate a command she addresses:
- 14. Keeper of the waters, open thy gate,
- 15. open thy gate that I may enter.
- 16. If thou openest not the gate that I may enter,
- 17. I will strike the door, the bolts I will shatter,
- 18. I will strike the threshold and will pass through the doors;
- 19. I will raise up the dead to devour the living,

-
- 20. above the living the dead shall exceed in numbers.
- 21. The keeper opened his mouth and speaks,
- 22. he says to the princess Istar:
- 23. Stay, lady, thou dost not glorify her,
- 24. let me go and thy name repeat to the queen Allat.
- 25. The keeper descended and says to Allat:
- 26. This water (of life) thy sister Istar (comes to seek).
- 27. The queen of the great vaults (of heaven) ....
- 28. Allat on hearing this says:
- 29. Like the cutting off of the herb has (Istar) descended (into Hades),
- 30. like the lip of a deadly insect (?) she has ...
- 31. What will her heart bring me (*i.e.* matter to me), what will her anger (bring me)?
- 32: (Istar replies:) This water with (my husband)
- 33. like food would I eat, like beer would I drink.
- 34. Let me weep over the strong who have left their wives.
- 35. Let me weep over the handmaids who (have lost) the embraces of their husbands.
- 36. Over the only son let me mourn, who ere his days are come is taken away.
- 37. (Allat says:) Go keeper open thy gate to her,
- 38. bewitch her also according to the ancient rules.
- 39. The keeper went and opened his gate:
- 40. Enter, O lady, let the city of Cutha[22] receive thee;
-
- 41. let the palace of Hades rejoice at thy presence.
- 42. The first gate he caused her to enter and touched her, he threw down the great crown of her head.

- 43. Why, O keeper, hast thou thrown down the great crown of my head?

- 44. Enter, O lady, of Allat thus is the order.

- 45. The second gate he caused her to enter and touched her, he threw away the earrings of her ears.

- 46. Why, keeper, hast thou thrown away the earrings of my ears?

- 47. Enter, O lady, of Allat thus is the order.

- 48. The third gate he caused her to enter and touched her, he threw away the necklace[23] of her neck.

- 49. Why, keeper, hast thou thrown away the necklace of my neck?

- 50. Enter, O lady, of Allat thus is the order.

- 51. The fourth gate he caused her to enter and touched her, he threw away the ornaments of her breast.

- 52. Why, keeper, hast thou thrown away the ornaments of my breast?

- 53. Enter, O lady, of Allat thus is the order.

- 54. The fifth gate he caused her to enter and touched her, he threw away the gemmed girdle of her waist.

- 55. Why, keeper, hast thou thrown away the gemmed girdle of my waist?

-

- 56. Enter, O lady, of Allat thus is the order.

- 57. The sixth gate he caused her to enter and touched her, he threw away the bracelets of her hands and her feet.

- 58. Why, keeper, hast thou thrown away the bracelets of my hands and my feet?

- 59. Enter, O lady, of Allat thus is the order.

- 60. The seventh gate he caused her to enter and touched her, he threw away the covering robe of her body.

- 61. Why, keeper, hast thou thrown away the covering robe of my body?

- 62. Enter, O lady, of Allat thus is the order.

- 63. When for a long time Istar into Hades had descended,

- 64. Allat saw her and at her presence was arrogant;

- 65. Istar did not take counsel, at her she swore.

- 66. Allat her mouth opened and speaks,

- 67. to Namtar (the plague-demon) her messenger a command she addresses:

- 68. Go Namtar [take Istar from] me and

- 69. take her out to .... even Istar

- 70. diseased eyes (strike) her with,

- 71. diseased side (strike) her with,

- 72. diseased feet (strike) her with,

- 73. diseased heart (strike) her with,

- 74. diseased head (strike) her with,

- 75. strike her, the whole of her [strike with disease].

- 76. After Istar the lady [into Hades had descended],

-

- 77. with the cow the bull would not unite, and the ass the female ass would not approach;

- 78. the female slave in the streets would not let herself be touched.

- 79. The freeman ceased to give his command,

- 80. the female slave ceased to give her gift.

COLUMN II.

- 1. Papsukul, the messenger of the great gods bowed his face before (Samas);

- 2. ....

- 3. Samas (the sun-god) went and in the presence of his father the moon-god he stood,

- 4. into the presence of Hea the king he went in tears:

- 5. Istar into the lower regions has descended, she has not ascended back;

- 6. for a long time Istar into Hades has descended,

- 7. with the cow the bull will not unite, the ass the female ass will not approach;

- 8. the female slave in the street will not let herself be touched;

- 9. the freeman has ceased to give his command,

- 10. the female slave has ceased to give her gift.

- 11. Hea in the wisdom of his heart formed a resolution,

- 12. and made Atsu-sunamir[24] the sphinx:[25]

-

- 13. Go Atsu-sunamir towards the gates of Hades set thy face;

- 14. may the seven gates of Hades be opened at thy presence;

- 15. may Allat see thee and rejoice at thy presence;

- 16. when she shall be at rest in her heart, and her liver be appeased.

- 17. Conjure her by the name of the great gods.

- 18. Raise thy heads, to the roaring stream set thy ear;

- 19. may the lady (Istar) overmaster the roaring stream, the waters in the midst of it may she drink.

- 20. Allat on hearing this,

- 21. beat her breast, she bit her thumb,

- 22. she turned again, a request she asked not:

- 23. Go, Atsu-sunamir, may I imprison thee in the great prison,

- 24. may the garbage of the foundations of the city be thy food,

- 25. may the drains of the city be thy drink,

- 26. may the darkness of the dungeon be thy dwelling,

- 27. may a stake be thy seat,

- 28. may hunger and thirst strike thy offspring.

- 29. Allat her mouth opened and speaks,

- 30. to Namtar her messenger a command she addresses:

- 31. Go, Namtar, strike the firmly-fixed palace,

- 32. the *ashêrim*[26] adorn with stones of the dawn,

-

- 33. bid the spirits of earth come forth, on a throne of gold seat (them),

- 34. unto Istar give the waters of life and bring her before me.

- 35. Namtar went, he struck the firmly-fixed palace,

- 36. the *ashêrim* he adorned with stones of the dawn,

- 37. he brought forth the spirits of earth, on a throne of gold he seated (them).

- 38. To Istar he gave the waters of life and took her.

- 39. The first gate he passed her out of, and he restored to her the covering robe of her body.

- 40. The second gate he passed her out of, and he restored to her the bracelets of her hands and her feet.

- 41. The third gate he passed her out of, and he restored to her the gemmed girdle of her waist.

- 42. The fourth gate he passed her out of, and he restored to her the ornaments of her breast.

- 43. The fifth gate he passed her out of, and he restored to her the necklace of her neck.

- 44. The sixth gate he passed her out of, and he restored to her the earrings of her ears.

- 45. The seventh gate he passed her out of, and he restored to her the great crown of her head.

- 46. Since thou hast not paid, (he says) a ransom for thy deliverance to her (*i.e.* Allat), so to her again turn back

- 47. for Tammuz the husband of (thy) youth;

-

- 48. the glistening waters pour over (him), the drops (sprinkle upon him);

- 49. in splendid clothing dress him, with a ring of crystal adorn (him).

- 50. May Samkhat appease the grief (of Istar),

- 51. and, Kharimat,[27] give to her comfort.

- 52. The precious eye-stones also she destroyed not,

- 53. the wound of her brother (Tammuz) she heard, she smote (her breast), she, even Kharimat, gave her comfort;

- 54. the precious eye-stones, her amulets, she commanded not,

- 55. (saying): O my only brother, thou dost not lament for me.

- 56. In the day that Tammuz adorned me, with a ring of crystal, with a bracelet of emeralds, together with himself he adorned me,

- 57. with himself he adorned me; may men mourners and women mourners

- 58. on a bier place (him), and assemble the wake.

This remarkable text shows Istar fulfilling her threat and descending to Hades, but it does not appear that she had as yet accomplished her vengeance against Izdubar.

At the opening of the sixth tablet we have the final scene of the contest with Khumbaba. Izdubar, after slaying Khumbaba, takes the crown from the head of the monarch and places it on his own head, thus signifying that he assumed the empire. There were, as we are informed in several places, kings, lords, and princes, merely local rulers, but these generally submitted to the greatest power; and just as they had bowed to Khumbaba, so they were ready now to submit to Izdubar. The kingdom promised to Izdubar when he started to encounter Khumbaba now became his by right of superior force, and he entered the halls of the palace of Erech and feasted with his heroes.

We are thus brought to a curious part of the story, the romance of Izdubar and Istar. One of the strange and dark features of the Babylonian religion was the Istar or Venus worship, which was an adoration of the reproductive power of nature, accompanied by ceremonies which were a reproach to the country. The city of Erech, originally a seat of the worship of Anu, was now one of the foremost cities in this Istar worship. Tammuz, the young and beautiful Sun-god, the dead bridegroom of Istar, seems to be also spoken of as the brother of her handmaid Kharimat. This explains, as M. Lenormant has pointed out, the passage in Jeremiah xxii. 18, which preserves a portion of the wailing cry uttered by the worshippers of Tammuz or Adonis when celebrating his untimely death. This should be rendered: "Ah me, my brother, and ah me, my sister! Ah me, Adonis, and ah me, his lady!" Reference is made to the worship of Tammuz, which was carried on within the Temple itself at

Jerusalem, in Ezek. viii. 14, Amos viii. 10, (where we should translate "as at the mourning for the only son" Tammuz), and Zech. xii. 10, 11. Tammuz is the Semitic form of the Accadian Dumuzi which signified in that language "the only son."

BOWAREYEH MOUND AT WARKA (ERECH), SITE OF THE TEMPLE OF ISTAR.

The struggle with a bull on the part of Izdubar and Hea-bani, represented on the Babylonian cylinder figured on the next page, and numerous similar representations, refer to the struggle with the bull created by Anu to avenge the slight offered to Istar.

It would appear from the broken fragments of Column IV. that Hea-bani laid hold of the bull by the head and tail while Izdubar killed it, and Hea-bani in the engraving is represented holding the bull by its head and tail.

At the close of the sixth tablet the story is again lost, only portions of the third and fourth columns of the next tablet being preserved, but light is thrown on this portion of the narrative by the remarkable tablet describing the descent of Istar into Hades. It is possible that this tablet formed an episode in the sixth tablet of the Izdubar legends.

IZDUBAR AND HEA-BANI IN CONFLICT WITH THE LION AND BULL.

This tablet containing the descent of Istar into Hades was first noticed by Mr. Fox Talbot in the "Transactions of the Royal Society of Literature," but his attempt at a translation was a failure. Mr. Smith subsequently published a short notice of it in the "North British Review," and afterwards a translation of it in the "Daily Telegraph." Prof. Schrader brought out a monograph upon it in 1874, and both M. Lenormant and Dr. Oppert have worked at it. The most recent translation is one made into Italian by M. Lenormant in a publication entitled "Il mito di Adone-Tammuz," 1879, upon the basis of the one made by Dr. Oppert.

The story of the descent of Istar into Hades is one of the most beautiful myths in the Assyrian inscriptions; it has, however, received so much attention, and been so fully commented upon by various scholars, that little need be said on the subject here.

It is evident that we are dealing with the same goddess as the Istar, daughter of Anu, in the Izdubar legends, although she is here called daughter of Sin (the moon-god).

The description of the region of Hades is most graphic, and vividly portrays the sufferings of the prisoners there. Atsu-sunamir, created by Hea to deliver Istar, is described as a composite animal, half bitch and half man, with more than one head, and corresponds with the two dogs of the Hindu Rig-Veda, which have four eyes and broad snouts, and guard the road to the abode of Yama the king of the departed. They are also said to move among men, feasting on their lives, as the messengers of Yama; and as the offspring of Saramâ, the dawn, they are called Sârameyas, which Prof. Max Müller compares with the Greek Hermês. At any rate, the same conception of a dog of the dawn which guards the approach to the realm of Hades is found in the Greek Kerberos with his fifty heads (or three heads, according to later writers), as well as in the dog of Geryon named Orthros or "the dawn," who seems to be identical with the Vedic Vritra the demon of night. It would appear, therefore, that in the primitive mythology both of the Hindus and of the Accadians the "fleet" dawn was likened to a dog, sometimes regarded as carrying men away to the dark under-world, sometimes as bringing light to the under-world itself.

The latter part of the tablet is somewhat obscure, but refers to the custom of lamenting for Dumuzi or Tammuz.

Chapter XV.
ILLNESS AND WANDERINGS OF IZDUBAR.

Hea-bani and the trees.—Illness of Izdubar.—Death of
Hea-bani.—Journey of Izdubar.—His dream.—Scorpion
men.—The Desert of Mas.—Siduri and Sabitu.—Nes-Hea
the pilot.—Water of death.—Mua.—The conversation.—
Xisuthrus.

OF the three tablets in this section, the first one is very uncertain, and is put
together from two separate sources: the other two are more complete and
satisfactory.

TABLET VIII.

It is again uncertain if any of this tablet has been discovered; provisionally
some fragments of the first, second, third, and sixth columns of a tablet
which may belong to it are placed here, but the only fragment worth
translating at present is one given in Mr. Smith's "Assyrian Discoveries," p.
176. In some portions of these fragments there are references to the story of
Khumbaba, but as the fragment appears to refer to the illness of Izdubar it
probably belongs here.

K. 3588.

COLUMN I.

- 1. ....

- 2. Hea-bani (his mouth opened and spake and)
- 3. said to ....
- 4. I went (?) ....
- 5. in the ....
- 6. the door ....
- 7. of ....
- 8 and 9. ....
- 10. in ....
- 11. Hea-bani ....
- 12. with the door .... thy ...
- 13. the door on its sides does not ...

- 14. the creation of her ears they are not ...
- 15. for twenty kaspu (140 miles) I climbed up ...
- 16. as far as the pine tree a shrub (?) I had seen ...
- 17. thy tree (?) has not another ...
- 18. Six gars (120 feet) is thy height, two gars (40 feet) is thy breadth ....
- 19. thy street, thy blackness (?) thy rain ...
- 20. I made thee, I raised thee in the city of Nipur ....
- 21. yea I knew thy door like this ...
-
- 22. and this ...
- 23. I raised its face, I ...
- 24. I will fill thy bank (?) .....
- 25. .....
- 26. for he took ...
- 27. the pine tree, the cedar, ...
- 28. in its cover ...
- 29. thou also ....
- 30. may take ...
- 31. in the collection of everything ...
- 32. a great destruction ...
- 33. the whole of the trees ..
- 34. in thy land of the tree manubani ...
- 35. thy bush? is not strong ...
- 36. thy shadow is not great ...
- 37. and thy smell is not agreeable ...

- 38. The manubani tree was angry ...
- 39. made a likeness?

- 40. like the tree ...

- ......

The second, third, fourth and fifth columns appear to be entirely absent, the inscription reappearing on a fragment of the sixth column.

COLUMN II.

(Many lines lost.)

- 1. The dream which I saw ....

- 2. the tops of the mountain ....

-

- 3. ... he struck ....

- 4. he struck when thy royal raiment ....

- 5. he begat also in ....

- 6. He recounted to his friend Hea-bani the dream ...

- 7. My friend, the good omen of the dream ....

- 8. the dream was deceptive ....

- 9. My friend, the mountain which thou didst see ....

- 10. when I captured Khumbaba we ....

- 11. ... of his helpers Nitakh-garri ....

- 12. at the time of dawn ....

- 13. For twenty kaspu they journeyed a stage

- 14. at thirty kaspu they fixed

- 15. in the presence of Samas they dug out a pit (?) ....

- 16. Izdubar ascended also over ....

- 17. by the side of his house he crossed over ....

- 18. ... he brought the dream ....

- 19. he made it and the god ....

COLUMN III.

- 1. ... he brought the dream ....

- 2. he made it and the god ....

- 3. ... turban? ....

- 4. he cast him down and ....

- 5. the mountain like corn of the field ....

- 6. Izdubar at the destruction (?) set up ....

- 7. Anatu the troubler of men upon him struck,

-

- 8. and in the struggle his going he stayed.

- 9. He spake and said to his friend:

- 10. My friend thou dost not ask me why I am naked,

- 11. thou dost not inquire of me why I am spoiled,

- 12. because the god passed over, wherefore my limbs are hot.

- 13. My friend I saw a third dream;

- 14. that dream which I saw entirely disappeared.

- 15. They prayed; the god thunders on the ground.

- 16. He burnt up the exit of the darkness;

- 17. the lightning struck; a fire was kindled;

- 18. .... they took away; it rained death.

- 19. The glow also (disappeared), the fire sank,

- 20. .... they struck; it turned to a palm tree,

- 21. in the desert also thy lord took (his) path (?).

- 22. And Hea-bani his dream considered; he said to Izdubar:

- 23. .... Samas thy lord, the creator ....

The fourth and fifth columns of this tablet are lost. This part of the legend appears to refer to the illness of Izdubar.

COLUMN VI.

- 1. My friend ... the dream which is not ...

- 2. the day he dreamed the dream, the end ...

- 3. Hea-bani lay down also one day ...

- 4. which Hea-bani on (his) bed ...

- 5. the third day and the fourth day which ...

-

- 6. the fifth, and sixth, and seventh (days) ...

- 7. the eighth (and ninth, and tenth days) ....

- 8. when Hea-bani was sick ...

- 9. the eleventh and twelfth (days) ...

- 10. Hea-bani on (his) bed ...

- 11. Izdubar read also ...

- 12. Did my friend defend me ...

- 13. whenever in the midst of fight ...

- 14. I turn (?) to battle and ...

- 15. my friend who in battle ...

- 16. I in ......

It must here be noted that Mr. Smith's grounds for making this the eighth tablet were extremely doubtful, and it is possible that the fragments are of different tablets; but they fill up an evident blank in the story here, and they are consequently inserted pending further discoveries as to their true position.

In the first column Hea-bani appears to be addressing certain trees, and they are supposed to have the power of hearing and answering him. Hea-bani praises one tree and sneers at another, but from the mutilation of the text it does not appear why he acts so. We may conjecture he was seeking a charm to open a door he mentions, and that according to the story this charm was known to the trees. The fragment of the sixth column shows Hea-bani unable to interpret a dream, while Izdubar asks his friend to fight.

After this happened the violent death of Hea-bani, which added to the misfortunes of Izdubar; but no fragment of this part of the story is preserved.

TABLET IX.

This tablet is in a somewhat better state than the others, and all the narrative is clearer from this point, not a single column of the inscription being entirely lost. The ninth tablet commences with the sorrow of Izdubar at the death of Hea-bani.

COLUMN I.

- 1. Izdubar over Hea-bani his friend

- 2. bitterly weeps, and traverses the desert.

- 3. I have no judgment like Hea-bani here;

- 4. sickness entered into my stomach;

- 5. death I feared, and traverse the desert.

- 6. To the majesty of Xisuthrus, son of Ubara-tutu,

- 7. the road I am taking, and quickly I go;

- 8. to the lowlands of the mountains I take (my way) at night.

- 9. .... a (dream) I saw, and I feared.

- 10. I (bow) on my face, to Sin (the moon god) I pray;

- 11. and into the presence of the gods came my supplication;

- 12. Grant thou (health) to me, even unto me!

- 13. .... dream.

- 14. (Through) the dream (sent by) Sin (my) life had been gladdened.

- 15. Precious stones (?) ... to his hand.

- 16. He pulled out ..... his girdle

- 17. like a ... their ... he struck

- 18. he struck .... he smote, he broke

-

- 19. and .... they rejoiced, and

- 20. he threw (?) ....

- 21. he removed ....

- 22. the former name ....

- 23. the new name ....

(About eight lines lost here.)

The second column shows Izdubar in some fabulous region, whither he has wandered in search of Xisuthrus. Here he sees composite monsters with their feet resting in Hades and their heads reaching heaven. These beings are supposed to guide and direct the sun at its rising and setting. This passage is as follows:—

COLUMN II.

- 1. Of the mountains hearing him as many as ....
- 2. To the mountain of Masu in his course ....
- 3. who all day long guard the rising (sun).
- 4. Their crown was at the lattice of heaven,
- 5. below Hades was their footing.
- 6. Scorpion-men guard its gate,
- 7. burning with terribleness, and their appearance was death,
- 8. the greatness of their bulk overthrows the forests.
- 9. At the rising of the sun and the setting of the sun, they guard the sun, and
- 10. Izdubar saw them and fear and terror seized his face.
-
- 11. He took his counsel and approached before them.
- 12. The scorpion-man of his female asked:
- 13. Who has gone to us with his body the flesh of the gods?
- 14. To the scorpion-man his female answered:
- 15. His going (is) that of a god, but his feeble gait (is) that of a man.
- 16. The scorpion-man of the hero asked,
- 17. .... of the gods the word he recounts:
- 18. .... distant road
- 19. .... up to the presence
- 20. .... of which the passage is difficult.
- 21. ..... thy .... thou puttest on.

- 22. .... mountains situated.
- 23. .... thou puttest on.

The rest of this column is lost. In it Izdubar converses with the monsters, and where the third column begins he is telling them his purpose of seeking Xisuthrus.

COLUMN III.

- (1 and 2 lost.)
- 3. He Xisuthrus my father .....
- 4. who has been established also in the assembly (of the gods)
- 5. death and life [are known to him].
- 6. The scorpion-man opened his mouth (and spake);
- 7. they say to Izdubar:
-
- 8. Izdubar was not ....
- 9. of the mountain ....
- 10. for twelve kaspu (84 miles) [is the journey];
- 11. on the boundary of the field did he carry himself, and (there is) no light.
- 12. To the rising sun ....
- 13. to the setting sun ....
- 14. to the setting sun ....
- 15. they descended ....

In this mutilated passage, the monster describes the journey to be taken by Izdubar; there are now many lines wanting, until we come to the fourth column.

COLUMN IV.

- 1. In (his) sickness ....
- 2. in difficulty and ....
- 3. in lamentation and ....
- 4. again thou ....

- 5. the scorpion-man ....

- 6. (said) to Izdubar ....

- 7. Go Izdubar ....

- 8. the mountains of Mas ....

- 9. the mountains, the path (of the Sun) ....

- 10. may the women ....

- 11. the great gate of the land ....

- 12. Izdubar ....

- 13. for a memorial ....

- 14. the road of the sun ....

- 15. 1 kaspu (he went) ....

-

- 16. on the boundary of the field ....

- 17. he was not able (to look behind him).

- 18. 2 kaspu (he went) ....

This is the bottom of the fourth column; there are five lines lost at the top of the fifth column, and then the narrative reopens; the text is, however, mutilated and doubtful.

COLUMN V.

- 6. 4 (kaspu he went) ....

- 7. on the boundary (of the field)....

- 8. he was not able (to look behind him).

- 9. 5 kaspu (he went) ....

- 10. on the boundary of the field ....

- 11. he was not able (to look behind him).

- 12. 6 kaspu he went ....

- 13. on the boundary of the field did he carry himself (and there is no light).

- 14. He was not able (to look behind him).

- 15. 7 kaspu (he went) ....
- 16. on the boundary of the field was it situated and not ....
- 17. he was not able to look behind him.
- 18. 8 kaspu like a .... he mounts up;
- 19. on the boundary of the field (did he carry himself and) there is no light.
- 20. He was not able to look behind him.
- 21. 9 kaspu he went .... to the north
- 22. .... his face
-
- 23. (on the boundary of the field did he carry himself and) there is no light;
- 24. (he was not able) to look behind him.
- 25. (10 kaspu he went) .... him
- 26. .... a meeting
- 27. .... 4 kaspu
- 28. .... from the shadow of the sun
- 29. .... sight was established
- 30. to the forest of the trees of the gods in appearance it was equal.

IZDUBAR AMONG THE TREES OF THE GODS (?) FROM A BABYLONIAN CYLINDER FOUND IN CYPRUS BY GEN. DI CESNOLA.

- 31. Emeralds it carried as its fruit,

- 32. the branch refuses not to support a canopy.

- 33. Crystals they carry as shoots (?)

- 34. fruit they carry, and to the sight it is glistening.

Some of the words in this fragment are obscure, but the general meaning is clear. In the next column the wanderings of Izdubar are continued, and he comes to a country near the sea. Fragments of several lines of this column are preserved, but too mutilated to translate with certainty. The fragments are:—

COLUMN VI.

(About six lines lost.)

- 1. the pine tree ....

- 2. its nest of stone ....

- 3. not sweeping away the sea .... jet stones

- 4. like the tree of Elam and the tree of the prince .... emeralds

- 5. a locust ....

- 6. jet stone, ka stone .... the goddess Istar

- 7. like bronze and .... he carried

- 8. like .... obstacles

- 9. which .... the sea

- 10. it has, and .... may he raise

- 11. Izdubar [saw this] in his travelling,

- 12. on this sea he carried ....

- 13. Colophon. The women Siduri and Sabitu (who on the shore) of the sea dwelt.

- 14. .... tablet of the series: "When the hero Izdubar saw the fountain."

This tablet brings Izdubar to the region of the sea-coast, but his way is then barred by two women, one named Siduri and the other Sabitu. His further adventures are given on the tenth tablet, which opens:

TABLET X.

- 1. Siduri and Sabitu (who in the land beside the sea)

-

- 2. dwelt and ....

- 3. it was the moon, it was the moon ....

- 4. a covering of fire (?) ye accomplish.

- 5. Izdubar approached and ....

- 6. the ulcer covering (his) skin

- 7. he had the brand of the gods on (his) ....

- 8. there is shame of face on ....

- 9. to go on the distant path his face (was set).

- 10. Sabitu afar off pondered,

- 11. she counselled to her heart (this) plan.

- 12. Within herself also she (considered):

- 13. What is this message ....

- 14. May no one come straight in (his path).

- 15. When Sabitu saw him she entered (her gate);

- 16. her gate she entered and entered her ....

- 17. And he Izdubar had ears to (hear her);

- 18. he had struck his hands and made ....

- 19. Izdubar to her also even said (to Sabitu:)

- 20. Sabitu what didst thou see (that)

- 21. thy gate thou barrest ....

- 22. I force the door ....

The rest of this column is lost, but it must have described the meeting of Izdubar with a boatman named Ur-Hea or Lig-Hea, called Nes-Hea "the lion" or "dog of Hea" in Assyrian. In the second column they commence a journey by water together in a boat. But little of this column is preserved; two fragments only are given here.

- 1. .... he the word of his friend ....

- 2. .... the word of Hea-bani ....

- 3. .... I traverse (the desert).

- 4. .... (in) the dust he had ....

- 5. (the friend whom I have loved declared) lovingly; Hea-bani the friend whom I have loved made ....

- 6. (I am not as he) and would we had never gone up ....

- 7. (I did not make) the fortress of ....

- 8. (Izdubar to) her also speaks, even to Sabit:

- 9. (Again) O Sabit what is the way to Xisuthrus?

- 10. Explain the tokens of it to me; yea, explain the tokens of it to me.

- 11. If it be suitable the sea let me cross,

- 12. if it be not suitable the desert let me traverse.

- 13. Sabit to him also speaks, even to Izdubar:

- 14. There was no crossing (of the sea), O Izdubar, at any time,

- 15. and no one from remote times onwards has crossed the sea.

- 16. From crossing the sea Samas the hero I the mother prevented; (yet) Samas crossed, whoever

- 17. his mouth the passage .... its road,

- 18. and the well of the waters of death which extend before it

-

- 19. I approach, and, Izdubar, thou crossest the sea.

- 20. When thou hast come round to the waters of death, thou contrivest how

- 21. for Izdubar there is Ur-Hea the boatman of Xisuthrus.

- 22. Precious stones with him in the midst of the forest ....

- 23. .... may they see thy face.

- 24. .... and to cross with him if it is not suitable hasten behind him

- 25. .... upon hearing this,

- 26. .... an axe in the hand.

- 27. .... to their well he returns.

- 28, 29, 30. ....

- 31. .... Izdubar

- 32. .... and his lower part

- 33. .... the ship

- 34. .... (the waters) of death

- 35. .... wide

- 36. .... the field

- 37. .... to the river

- 38. .... ship

- 39. .... the well

- 40. .... the boatman

- 41. .... he descended

- 42. .... to thee

Here there are many lines lost, then recommencing the story proceeds on the third column.

COLUMN III.

- 1. my friend whom I have loved made ....

- 2. I am not as he and would we had never gone up ....

- 3. Izdubar to him also speaks, even to Ur-Hea;

- 4. Again, Ur-Hea, what (is the way to Xisuthrus?)

- 5. what are its signs explain to me; yea, explain (to me its signs).

- 6. If it be suitable the sea let me cross; if it be not suitable the desert let me traverse.

- 7. Ur-Hea to him also speaks, even to (Izdubar):

- 8. Thy hand, Izdubar, it prevents ....

- 9. thou hidest among the precious stones thou ...

- 10. the precious stones (are) a hiding-place [or canopy] and they are not ...

- 11. Take, Izdubar, an axe in (thy hands) ....

- 12. go down to the forest and a clearing of five *gar* (make).

- 13. Bury and make a tumulus; carry ....

- 14. Izdubar on his hearing this,

- 15. took the axe in his hand ....

- 16. he went down to the forest and a clearing of five *gar* (made):

- 17. he buried and made a tumulus; he carried ....

- 18. Izdubar and Ur-Hea rode (in the ship);

- 19. the ship the waves took and they ....

-

- 20. a journey of one month and fifteen days. On the third day in their course

- 21. Ur-Hea also reached the waters of death ....

COLUMN IV.

- 1. Ur-Hea to him also speaks, even to Izdubar:

- 2. The tablets O Izdubar ....

- 3. The waters of death smite; never mayest thou >enter the dome of the house (of the abyss).

- 4. The second time, the third time, and the fourth time go, O Izdubar ....

- 5. the fifth, sixth, and seventh time go, O Izdubar ....

- 6. the eighth, ninth, and tenth time go, O Izdubar ....

- 7. the eleventh and twelfth time go, O Izdubar ....

- 8. on the one hundred and twentieth time Izdubar finished ....

- 9. and he struck the middle of it ....

- 10. Izdubar seized the ....

- 11. on his wings an embankment he completed ...

- 12. Xisuthrus over him afar off pondered,

- 13. he counselled (this) plan within his heart.

- 14. With himself also he considered:

- 15. Why is the hiding-place of the ship ....

- 16. and the pilot ....

- 17. the man who went also is not; and ....

- 18. I ponder, and I do not ....

- 19. I ponder, and I do not....

- 20. I ponder, and I do not....

IZDUBAR, COMPOSITE FIGURES, AND UR-HEA IN THE BOAT; FROM AN EARLY BABYLONIAN CYLINDER.

Here there is a blank, the extent of which is uncertain, and where the narrative recommences it is on a small fragment of the third and fourth columns of another copy. It appears that the lost lines record the meeting between Izdubar and a female being named Mu-seri-ina-namari, or the "Waters of dawn at daylight." In the account of the Deluge, Mu-seri-ina-namari is mentioned as bringing the black clouds from the horizon of heaven. It was here, beyond the circular boundary of the earth, and on the shores of the ocean which surrounded it, that Izdubar is now supposed to be.

It is curious that, whenever Izdubar speaks to this being, the name Mua is used, while, whenever Izdubar is spoken to, the full name Mu-seri-ina-namari occurs. Where the story reopens Izdubar is informing Mua of his first connection with Hea-bani and his offers to him when he desired him to come to Erech.

COLUMN III. (fragment).

- 1. for my friend....

- 2. free thee....

- 3. weapon....

- 4. bright star....

COLUMN IV. (fragment).

- 1. On a beautiful couch I will seat thee,

- 2. I will cause thee to sit on a comfortable seat on the left,

- 3. the kings of the earth shall kiss thy feet.

- 4. I will enrich thee and the men of Erech I will make silent before thee,

- 5. and I after thee will take all....

- 6. I will clothe thy body in raiment and....

- 7. Mu-seri-ina-namari on hearing this

- 8. his fetters loosed ....

The speech of Mua to Izdubar and the rest of the column are lost, the narrative recommencing on Column V. with another speech of Izdubar.

COLUMN V. (fragment).

- 1. .... to me

- 2. .... my ... I wept

- 3. .... bitterly I spoke

- 4. .... my hand

- 5. .... ascended to me

- 6. .... to me

- 7. .... hyæna of the desert

COLUMN V.

- 1. Izdubar opened his mouth and said to Mu

- 2. .... my presence?

- 3. .... not strong

- 4. .... my face

- 5. .... lay down in the field,

- 6. .... of the mountain, the hyæna of the field,

- 7. Hea-bani my friend .... the same.

- 8. No one else was with us, we ascended the mountain.

- 9. We took it and the city we destroyed.

- 10. We conquered also Khumbaba who in the forest of pine trees dwelt.

- 11. Again why did his fingers lay hold to slay the lions?

- 12. Thou wouldst have feared and thou wouldst not have .. all the difficulty.

- 13. And he did not succeed in slaying the same;

- 14. his heart failed, and he did not strike .... over him I wept,

- 15. he covered also my friend like a corpse in a grave,

- 16. like a lion? he tore? him

- 17. like a lioness? placed .... field

- 18. he was cast down to the face of the earth

- 19. he broke? and destroyed his defence? ....

- 20. he was cut off and given to pour out? ....

- 21. Mu-seri-ina-namari on hearing this

Here the record is again mutilated, but Izdubar further informs Mua what he did in conjunction with Hea-bani. Where the story reopens on Column VI. Izdubar relates part of their adventure with Khumbaba.

COLUMN VI.

- 1. .... taking
- 2. .... to thee
- 3. .... thou art great
- 4. .... all the account

- 5. .... forest of pine trees
- 6. .... went night and day
- 7. .... the extent of Erech the lofty
- 8. .... he approached after us
- 9. .... he opened the land of forests
- 10. .... we ascended
- 11. .... in the midst like thy mother
- 12. .... cedar and pine trees
- 13. .... with our strength
- 14. .... silent
- 15. .... he of the field
- 16. .... by her side
- 17. .... the Euphrates

Here again our narrative is lost, and where we again meet the story Izdubar is conversing with Xisuthrus. The conversation is contained in the broken fifth column of K 3382, first noticed and copied by Mr. Pinches.

COLUMN V.

- 1. .... Mua
- 2. ..... my ...

- 3. .... they are not like.

- 4. .... before me.

- 5. .... traversed the desert.

- 6. .... the glare of the desert.

- 7. .... the same.

- 8. .... the mountain.

- 9. .... we destroy.

- 10. .... (among) the royal tree (and) the pine they dwell.

- 11. .... lions.

- 12. .... times to come.

- 13. .... were slain, the same.

- 14. .... over him I wept.

- 15. .... burial.

- 16. .... him.

- 17. .... the desert.

- 18. .... over me; thou hast gone round ....

- 19. .... I turned back; the ship (?) I ....

- 20. (my friend) whom I have loved declared lovingly; Hea-bani my friend (made) ....

- 21. (I) am not as he, and would we had never gone up; I did not make a fortress ....

-

- 22. Izdubar to him also speaks, even to Xisuthrus:

- 23. Thus may I go and Xisuthrus afar off, who has conversed with him, may I see.

-

- 24. I went round, I went through all countries;

- 25. I passed through difficult lands;

- 26. I crossed all seas.

- 27. A good .... they did not dwell before me.

- 28. I exhausted myself through weakness; with my .... the crown I filled.

- 29. .... the house I did not reach, and my clothing was decayed.

- 30. .... of a leopard, a tiger, a raging winged bull ....

- 31. their (lairs) I approached; their skins I stripped off ....

- 32. .... may they bar its gate; with much bitumen ....

- 33. .... the contents ....

- 34. .... the sides ....

- 35. (Xisuthrus) to him speaks, even to Izdubar:

- 36. .... O Izdubar, sickness ....

- 37. .... gods and men ....

- 38. .... thy (father) and thy mother made ....

We now come to a fragment which forms the reverse of the tablet already translated, and recounts the visit of Izdubar to the two women Siduri and Sabitu. This reads as follows:—

- 1. I was angry (?) ....

- 2. If at any time we built a house, if ever we establish ....

- 3. If ever brothers fixed ....

-

- 4. If ever hatred is in ....

- 5. If ever the river makes a (great) flood.

- 6. (If ever) reviling within the mouth ....

- 7. the face that will bow before Samas ....

- 8. from of old is not ....

- 9. Spoiling and death together ....

- 10. of death the image they guarded not ....

- 11. The man or servant on approaching (death),

- 12. the spirits of the earth the great gods are they.

- 13. The goddess Mammetu maker of fate, to them their fate brings,

- 14. she has fixed death and life;

- 15. of death its days are not known.

COMPOSITE FIGURES (SCORPION MEN); FROM AN ASSYRIAN CYLINDER.

This statement closes the tenth tablet and leads to the next question of Izdubar and its answer, which includes the story of the Flood.

The present division of the legends has its own peculiar difficulties; in the first place it does not appear how Hea-bani was killed. Possibly he fell in an attempt to slay a lion.

The land of Mas or desert of Mas over which Izdubar travels in this tablet is the desert on the west of the Euphrates, and the name reminds us of the Biblical Mash who is called a son of Aram in Genesis x. 23; on the sixth column the fragments appear to refer to some bird with magnificent feathers like precious stones, seen by Izdubar on his journey.

Chapter XVI.
THE STORY OF THE FLOOD AND CONCLUSION.

Eleventh tablet.—The gods.—Sin of the world.—Command to build the ark.—Its contents.—The building.—The Flood.—Destruction of people.—Fear of the gods.—End of Deluge.—Nizir.—Resting of ark.—The birds.—The descent from the ark.—The sacrifice, covenant, and rainbow.—Speeches of gods.—Translation of Adra-Khasis.—Cure of Izdubar.—His return.—Lament over Hea-bani.—Resurrection of Hea-bani.—Burial of warrior.—Age and composition of the Deluge tablet.—Comparison with Genesis.—Syrian nation.—Connection of legends.—Points of contact.—Duration of Deluge.—Mount of descent.—Ten generations.—Early cities.

THE eleventh tablet of the Izdubar series is the one which first attracted attention, and is certainly the most important on account of its containing the story of the Flood. This tablet is the most perfect in the series, scarcely any line being entirely lost. A new fragment of it, belonging to another edition of the story, has been recently brought to the museum by Mr. Hormuzd Rassam.

TABLET XI.

COLUMN I.

- 1. (Izdubar) to him also speaks even to Xisuthrus afar off:

- 2. O Xisuthrus,

- 3. (why) dost thou not again (to me) as I (to thee)?

- 4. (why) dost thou not again (to me) as I (to thee)?

- 5. .... my heart to make war

- 6. .... I come up after thee,

- 7. when thou didst take, and in the assembly of the gods didst obtain life.

- 8. Xisuthrus to him also speaks, even to Izdubar:

- 9. Let me reveal to thee (Izdubar) the story of my preservation,

- 10. and the judgment of the gods let me relate to thee.

- 11. The city Surippak the city which thou knowest on the Euphrates is placed,

- 12. that city is ancient and the gods are within it.

- 13. To make a deluge [*or* whirlwind] the great gods have brought their heart;

- 14. even he their father, Anu,

- 15. their king, the warrior Bel,

- 16. their throne-bearer, Ninip,

- 17. their minister, the lord of Hades, Nin-si-kha (wife of) Hea with them sat, and

- 18. their will he (*i.e.* Hea) repeated: to his minister the minister of the city of Kis, he declared what he had (in mind);[28]

- 19. his minister heard and proclaimed attentively:

- 20. Man of Surippak, son of Ubara-tutu,

- 21. build a house, make a ship to preserve the sleep of plants (and) living beings;

- 22. store the seed and vivify life,

- 23. cause also the seed of life of every kind to go up into the midst of the ship.

- 24. The ship which thou shalt make,

- 25. 600 cubits (shall be) its measure in length,

- 26. 60 cubits the amount of its breadth and its height.

- 27. ... and on the deep cover it, even it, with a roof.

- 28. I understood and say to Hea my lord:

- 29. The building of the ship which thou commandest thus,

- 30. .... I shall have made,

- 31. .... the sons of the host and the old men.

- 32. (Hea opened his mouth and) speaks and says to me his servant:

- 33. ...... thou shalt say unto them,
- 34. ...... he has rejected me and
- 35. ...... it is upon me
- 36. .... like caves ....
- 37. ... may I judge above and below ....
- 38. ... close the ship ...
-
- 39. ... at the season which I will make known to you,
- 40. into it enter and the door of the ship turn.
- 41. Into the midst of it thy grain, thy furniture, thy goods,
- 42. thy wealth, thy woman slaves, thy handmaids, and the sons of the host,
- 43. (the beasts) of the field, the wild animals of the field, as many as I would protect,
- 44. I will send to thee, and thy door shall guard (them).

- 45. Adrakhasis[29] his mouth opened and speaks, and
- 46. says to Hea his lord:
- 47. No one a ship has made ...
- 48. in the lower part of the ship has shut up ....
- 49. .... and may I see the ship ....
- 50. .... in the lower part of the ship ....
- 51. the building of the ship which thou commandest me (thus),
- 52. which in ....

COLUMN II.

- 1. strong ....
- 2. on the fifth day .... it rose.
- 3. In its circuit 14 in all (were) its girders.
- 4. 14 in all it contained ... above it

- 5. I placed its roof; it .... I enclosed it.

-

- 6. I rode in it the sixth time; I divided its passages the seventh time;

- 7. its interior I divided the eighth time.

- 8. Leaks for the waters within it I cut off.

- 9. I saw the rents and the wanting parts I added.

- 10. 3^{30} *sari* of bitumen I poured over the outside.

- 11. 3^{30} *sari* of bitumen I poured over the inside.

- 12. 3 *sari* of men carrying baskets, who carried on their heads food.

- 13. I added a *saros* of food which the people should eat;

- 14. two *sari* of food the boatmen shared.

- 15. To .... I sacrificed oxen

- 16. I (established) .... each day

- 17. I (established) .... beer, food, and wine;

- 18. (I collected them) like the waters of a river, and

- 19. (I collected) like the dust of the earth, and

- 20. (in the ship) the food with my hand I placed.

- 21. (Through the help of) Samas the seaworthiness of the ship was accomplished.

- 22. ... they were strong and

- 23. the tackling of the ship I caused to bring above and below.

- 24. .... they went in two-thirds of it.

- 25. All I possessed I collected it, all I possessed I collected it in silver,

- 26. all I possessed I collected it in gold,

-

- 27. all I possessed I collected it in the seed of life of all kinds.

- 28. I caused everything to go up into the ship, my slaves and my handmaids,

- 29. the beast of the field, the wild animal of the field, the sons of the people all of them, I caused to go up.

- 30. The season Samas fixed and

- 31. he spake saying: In the night I will cause it to rain from heaven heavily,

- 32. enter into the midst of the ship and shut thy door.

- 33. That season came round (of which)

- 34. he spake saying: In the night I will cause it to rain from heaven heavily.

- 35. Of the day I reached its evening,

- 36. the day of watching fear I had.

- 37. I entered into the midst of the ship and shut my door.

- 38. On closing the ship to Buzur-sadi-rabi the boatman

- 39. the habitation I gave with its goods.

- 40. Mu-seri-ina-namari

- 41. arose, from the horizon of heaven a black cloud.

- 42. Rimmon in the midst of it thundered, and

- 43. Nebo and the Wind-god went in front,

- 44. the throne-bearers went over the mountain and plain,

- 45. Nergal the mighty removes the wicked,

- 46. Ninip goes in front, he casts down,

- 47. the spirits of earth carried destruction,

- 48. in their terror they shake the earth;

- 49. of Rimmon his flood reached to heaven.

- 50. The darkened (earth to a waste) was turned,

COLUMN III.

- 1. the surface of the earth like .... they covered,

- 2. (it destroyed all) living beings from the face of the earth;

- 3. the raging (deluge) over the people, reached to heaven.

- 4. Brother saw not his brother, men did not know one another. In heaven

- 5. the gods feared the whirlwind and

- 6. sought a refuge; they ascended to the heaven of Anu.

- 7. The gods like dogs were fixed, in a heap did they lie down.

- 8. Spake Istar like a child,

- 9. the great goddess uttered her speech:

- 10. All to clay are turned and

- 11. that which I in the presence of the gods prophesied (even evil has happened).

- 12. As I prophesied in the presence of the gods evil,

- 13. to evil (were devoted) all my people, the trouble I prophesied thus:

-

- 14. I the mother have begotten my people, and

- 15. like the young of the fishes they fill the sea. And

- 16. the gods because of the spirits of earth are weeping with me.

- 17. The gods on seats are seated in lamentation,

- 18. covered were their lips for the coming evil.

- 19. Six days and nights

- 20. passed, the wind, the whirlwind, (and) the storm, overwhelmed.

- 21. On the seventh day at its approach the rain was stayed, the raging whirlwind

- 22. which had smitten like an earthquake,

- 23. was quieted. The sea began to dry, and the wind and deluge ended.

- 24. I watched the sea making a noise,

- 25. and the whole of mankind was turned to clay,

- 26. like reeds the corpses floated.

- 27. I opened the window, and the light smote upon the fortress of my nostrils.

- 28. I was grieved and sat down; I weep,

- 29. over the fortress of my nostrils went my tears.

- 30. I watched the regions at the boundary of the sea,

- 31. towards all the twelve points of the compass (there was) no land.

- 32. In the country of Nizir rested the ship;

- 33. the mountain of Nizir stopped the ship, and to pass over it it was not able.

- 34. The first day, the second day, the mountain of Nizir stopped the ship.

-

- 35. The third day, the fourth day, the mountain of Nizir stopped the ship.

- 36. The fifth day, the sixth day, the mountain of Nizir stopped the ship.

- 37. On the seventh day at its approach

-

- 38. I sent forth a dove and it left. The dove went, it returned, and

- 39. a resting-place it did not find, and it came back.

- 40. I sent forth a swallow and it left. The swallow went, it returned, and

- 41. a resting-place it did not find, and it came back.

- 42. I sent forth a raven and it left.

- 43. The raven went, and the carrion on the water it saw, and

- 44. it did eat, it swam, and turned away, it did not come back.

- 45. I sent (the animals) forth to the four winds, I sacrificed a sacrifice,

- 46. I built an altar on the peak[31] of the mountain,

- 47. by sevens vessels I placed,

- 48. at the bottom of them I spread reeds, pines, and juniper.

- 49. The gods smelt the savour, the gods smelt the good savour;

-

- 50. the gods like flies over the sacrificer gathered.

- 51. From afar also the great goddess at her approach

- 52. lifted up the mighty arches (*i.e.* the rainbow) which Anu had created as his glory.

- 53. The crystal of those gods before me (*i.e.* the rainbow) never may I forget;

COLUMN IV.

- 1. those days I devised with longing that I might never forget.

- 2. 'May the gods come to my altar,

- 3. may Bel never come to my altar,

- 4. for he did not consider and had made a whirlwind,

- 5. and my people he consigned to the abyss.'

- 6. From afar also Bel at his approach

- 7. saw, the ship he stopped; Bel was filled with anger against the gods and the spirits of heaven:

- 8. 'Let no one come out alive, never may a man live in the abyss.'

- 9. Ninip his mouth opened, and spake; he says to the warrior Bel:

- 10. 'Who is it except Hea that forms a resolution?

- 11. and Hea knows and all things he ...'

- 12. Hea his mouth opened and spake, he says to the warrior Bel:

- 13. 'Thou messenger of the gods, warrior,

- 14. as thou didst not consider a deluge thou madest.

- 15. The doer of sin bore his sin, the blasphemer bore his blasphemy.

- 16. Never may the just prince be cut off, never may the faithful (be destroyed).

- 17. Instead of thy making a deluge, may lions come and men be diminished;

- 18. instead of thy making a deluge, may hyænas come and men be diminished;

- 19. instead of thy making a deluge, may a famine happen and the country be (destroyed);

- 20. instead of thy making a deluge, may pestilence come and men be destroyed.

- 21. I did not reveal the judgment of the gods.

- 22. To Adrakhasis (Xisuthrus) a dream I sent, and the judgment of the gods he heard.'

- 23. Again also Bel considers, (*literally*, again consideration was considered); he approaches the midst of the ship.

- 24. He took my hand and caused me to ascend up,

- 25. he caused (me) to ascend; he united my wife to my side;

- 26. he turned unto us and fixes himself in covenant with us; he approaches us:

- 27. 'Formerly Adrakhasis (was) mortal, but

- 28. again also Adrakhasis and his wife to live as gods are taken away, and

- 29. Adrakhasis also dwells in a remote place at the mouth of the rivers.'

- 30. They took me, and in a remote place at the mouth of the rivers they caused me to dwell.

- 31. Again also as for thee whomsoever the gods have chosen also,

- 32. for the health which thou seekest and askest,

- 33. the bulwarks shall be mounted six days and seven nights,

- 34. like one who sits in the vicinity of his nest,

- 35. a way like a storm shall be laid upon him.

- 36. Adrakhasis to her also says, even to his wife:

- 37. I announce that the chief who has sought health

- 38. the way like a storm shall be laid upon him.

- 39. His wife to him also says even to Adrakhasis afar off:

- 40. Turn him, and let the man be sent away;

- 41. by the road that he came may he return in peace,

- 42. thro' the great gate going forth let him return to his country.

- 43. Adrakhasis to her also says, even to his wife:

- 44. The pain of the man pains thee,

- 45. mount the bulwarks; his baldness place on his head.

- 46. And the day when he had mounted the side of the ship,

- 47. she mounted, his baldness she placed on his head.

-

- 48. And the day when he had mounted the side of the ship,

- 49. first the *sabusat* of his baldness,

- 50. second the *mussukat*, third the *radbat*, fourth she opened his *zikaman*,

- 51. fifth the *sibu* she placed, sixth the *bassat*,

COLUMN V.

- 1. seventh in the outlet she turned him and let the man go free.

- 2. Izdubar to him also says even to Xisuthrus afar off:

- 3. In this way thou wast compassionate (?) over me,

- 4. quickly thou hast begotten me, and thou hast set eyes (on me).

- 5. Xisuthrus to him also says even to Izdubar.

- 6. .... thy baldness,

- 7. .... I separated thee,

- 8. .... thy baldness,

- 9. second the *mussukat*, third the *radbat*,

- 10. fourth I opened thy *zikaman*,

- 11. fifth the *sibu* I placed, sixth the *bassat*,

- 12. seventh in the opening I turned thee.

- 13. Izdubar to him also says even to Xisuthrus afar off:
- 14. ...... Xisuthrus whither may I go?
-
- 15. ...... they shipped
- 16. ...... dwelling in death,
- 17. ...... his tail dies also.

- 18. Xisuthrus to him also says even to Nis-Hea the boatman:
- 19. Nis-Hea, may thy (oar) accomplish a passage for thee.
- 20. He who ..... on the shore of (the gods) ....
- 21. the man whom thou goest before, disease has covered his body;
- 22. illness has overmastered the strength of his limbs.
- 23. Take him, Nis-Hea, to cleanse carry him,
- 24. may he cleanse his disease in the water like purity,
- 25. may he cast off his illness, and may the sea carry it away, may health cover his skin,
- 26. may it restore the hair of his head,
- 27. the hair clothing, the covering of his loins.
- 28. That he may go to his country, that he may take his road,
- 29. never may the hair become old and alone may he be alone (*i.e.* unrivalled).
- 30. Nis-Hea took him, to cleanse he carried him,
- 31. his disease in the water like purity (beauty) he cleansed,
-
- 32. he cast off his illness, and the sea carried it away, health covered his skin,
- 33. the hair of his head was restored, the hair clothing the covering of his loins.
- 34. That he might go to his country, that he might take his road,
- 35. the hair he did not cast off, but alone he was alone.

- 36. Izdubar and Nis-Hea rode in the ship,
- 37. where he had placed them they rode.

- 38. His wife to him also says even to Xisuthrus afar off:
- 39. Izdubar goes away, he is at rest, he performs
- 40. what thou hast given (him to do), and returns to his country.
- 41. And he even Izdubar lifted up the oar (?);
- 42. the ship touched the shore.
- 43. Xisuthrus to him also says even to Izdubar:
- 44. Izdubar, thou goest away, thou art at rest, thou performest
- 45. what I gave thee (to do), and thou returnest to thy country.
- 46. Let the story of my preservation be revealed, O Izdubar,
- 47. and let the judgment of the gods be related to thee.
- 48. This account (?) like ....
- 49. its renown (?) like the Amurdin tree ....
-
- 50. if he takes the whole of it in the hand ....
- 51. To Izdubar he revealed this in his hearing, and ....
- 52. he bound together heavy stones ....

COLUMN VI.

- 1. they dragged it and to the deep ....
- 2. he even Izdubar took the animal ....
- 3. he cut the heavy stones ....
- 4. one homer he poured out in libation to it for his ship.

- 5. Izdubar to him also says even to Nis-Hea, the boatman:
- 6. O Nis-Hea, the whole of this, even the whole of the story,
- 7. of which a man in his heart shall take its story,

- 8. may he bring it to the midst of Erech the lofty, may he complete (it) like ....

- 9. .... splendour (which) is diminished ....

- 10. May I record and return to perform my vengeance (?).

- 11. For 10 kaspu (70 miles) they journeyed the stage, for 20 kaspu (140 miles) they made hostility;

- 12. Izdubar saw a well which the waters were excavating.

- 13. He turned to the bright waters and smells (?) the waters; .... grant me thy image (?)

- 14. .... the men he approached and (their) goods he took away (?)

-

- 15. at his return they tore the hair.

- 16. Izdubar approached (?) ....

- 17. over the fortress of his nostrils coursed his tears, and he says to Nis-Hea the boatman:

- 18. What is it to me, Nis-Hea, that my hands rest?

- 19. What is it to me that my heart lives?

- 20. I have not done good to my own self;

- 21. and yet the lion of the earth does good (to himself).

- 22. Again for 20 kaspu (140 miles) alone I take the way, and

- 23. when I had opened the .... I heaped up the tackling,

- 24. the sea against its long wall I urged.

- 25. And he left the ship by the shore, 20 kaspu (140 miles) they journeyed the stage.

- 26. For 30 kaspu (210 miles) they performed the labour, they came into the midst of Erech the lofty.

- 27. Izdubar to him also says, even to Nis-Hea the boatman:

- 28. Ascend, Nis-Hea, over the fortress of Erech go;

- 29. the foundation-stone is scattered, the bricks of its interior are not made,

- 30. and its foundation is not laid to thy height (?);

- 31. 1 *saros* (is) thy city, 1 *saros* the plantations, 1 *saros* the boundary of the temple of Nantur the house of Istar,

- 32. 3 *sari* together the city of Erech ...

The opening line of the next tablet is preserved, it reads: "The gad-fly in the house of the serving-man was left." After this the story is again lost for several lines, and where it reappears Izdubar is mourning for Hea-bani.

The fragments of this tablet are:—

COLUMN I.

- 1. The gad-fly in the house of the serving-man was left.

(Several lines lost.)

- 1. Izdubar (lamented thus over Hea-bani his friend:)

- 2. If to ....

- 3. to happiness thou (art not admitted);

- 4. a shining cloak (thou dost not wear),

- 5. like a misfortune (?) thou ....

- 6. Fat (and) goodly food thou dost not share;

- 7. to (come to) its savour they do not choose thee.

- 8. The bow against the ground thou dost not aim,

- 9. what the bow has struck escapes thee:

- 10. the staff to thy hands thou dost not lift,

- 11. the captive will not curse thee:

- 12. sandals to thy feet thou dost not bind,

- 13. a thrust against the ground thou dost not make.

- 14. Thy wife whom thou lovest thou dost not kiss,

- 15. thy wife whom thou hatest thou dost not strike;

- 16. thy child whom thou lovest thou dost not kiss,

- 17. thy child whom thou hatest thou dost not strike.

-

- 18. The destruction of the earth has seized thee.

- 19. Ninazu, of darkness the mother, of darkness, of darkness,

- 20. her illustrious stature as his mantle covers him, and

- 21. her feet like a deep well beget [*or* darken] him.

This is the bottom of the first column. The next column has lost all the upper part: it appears to have contained the remainder of this lament, an appeal to one of the gods on behalf of Hea-bani, and a repetition of the lamentation, the third person being used instead of the second. The fragments commence in the middle of this:

- 1. his wife whom he hates he strikes,

- 2. his child whom he loves he kisses;

- 3. his child whom he has hated he strikes,

- 4. the destruction of the earth takes him.

- 5. Ninazu, of darkness the mother of darkness, of darkness!

- 6. Her illustrious stature as a mantle covers him,

- 7. her feet like a deep well beget him.

- 8. Lo! Hea-bani from the earth to .....

- 9. The plague-demon did not take him, fever did not take him, the earth took him.

- 10. The resting-place of Nergal the unconquered did not take him, the earth took him.

- 11. The place of the battle of heroes did not strike him, the earth took him.

-

- 12. Lo! .... ni son of the goddess Ninsun[32] for his servant Hea-bani wept;

- 13. to the house of Bel alone he went.

- 14. "Father Bel, a gad-fly to the earth struck me,

- 15. a deadly wound to the earth struck me,"

COLUMN III.

- 1. Hea-bani who to rest (was not admitted),

- 2. the plague-demon did not take him, (the earth took him);

- 3. the resting-place of Nergal the unconquered did not take him, (the earth took him).

- 4. In the place of the battle of heroes they did not (strike him, the earth took him).

- 5. Father Bel, a judgment did not take him.

- 6. Father Sin, the gad-fly (struck him);

- 7. a deadly wound (to the earth struck him).

- 8. Hea-bani who to rest (was not admitted),

- 9. the plague-demon did not take him, (the earth took him);

- 10. the resting-place of Nergal (the unconquered did not take him).

- (About 12 lines lost, containing a repetition of this passage.)

- 23. The plague-demon ....

-

- 24. the resting-place of Nergal the unconquered (did not take him);

- 25. the place of the battle of heroes did not (take him).

- 26. Father Hea ....

- 27. To the warrior Merodach ....

- 28. Heroic warrior (Merodach) ....

- 29. he created him the word ....

- 30. the spirit ....

- 31. To his father ....

- 32. the heroic warrior Merodach (son of Hea)

- 33. created him the word, the earth opened, and

- 34. the spirit (or ghost) of Hea-bani like dust from the earth (arose):

- 35. ..... and thou explainest,

- 36. he pondered and repeated this:

COLUMN IV.

- 1. Tell, my friend, tell, my friend,
- 2. the secrets of the earth which thou hast seen, tell (me).
- 3. I cannot tell thee, my friend, I cannot tell thee,
- 4. (how) can I tell thee the secrets of the earth which I have seen?
- 5. ..... I sit weeping
- 6. ..... may I sit and may I weep
- 7. ..... of growth and thy heart rejoiced
- 8. ..... thou growest old, the worm entered
- 9. ..... of youth and thy heart rejoiced
-
- 10. ..... dust filling
- 11. ..... he passed over
- 12. ..... he passed over
- 13. ..... I saw

Here there is a serious blank in the inscription, about twenty lines being lost, and Mr. Smith has conjecturally inserted a fragment which appears to belong to this part of the narrative. It is very curious from the geographical names it contains.

- 1. .... I poured out ....
- 2. .... which thou trusted ....
- 3. .... city of Babylon *ri* ....
- 4. .... which he was blessed ....
- 5. .... may he mourn for my fault ....
- 6. .... may he mourn for him and for ....
- 7. .... Kisu and Kharsak-kalama, may he mourn .....
- 8. .... his .... Cutha ....
- 9. .... Eridu? and Nipur ....

The rest of Column IV. is lost, and of the next column there are only remains of the first two lines.

COLUMN V.

- 1. like a good prince who ....

- 2. like ....

Here there are about thirty lines missing, the story recommencing with Column VI., which is perfect.

COLUMN VI.

- 1. On a couch he reclines and

-

- 2. pure water drinks.

- 3. He who in battle is slain, thou seest and I see.

- 4. His father (and) his mother (support) his head,

- 5. (and) his wife addresses the corpse.

- 6. His friends in the field (are standing),

- 7. thou seest and I see.

- 8. His spoil on the ground is uncovered,

- 9. of his spoil he has no oversight.

- 10. Thou seest and I see.

- 11. His tender orphans long for bread; the food

- 12. which in the tents is placed is eaten.

- 13. The twelfth tablet of the legends of Izdubar.

- 14. Like the ancient copy written and made clear.

XISUTHRUS OR NOAH AND IZDUBAR; FROM AN EARLY BABYLONIAN CYLINDER.

This passage closes the great Epic of the ancient Chaldeans, which even in its present mutilated form is of the greatest importance in relation to the civilization, manners, and customs of that early people. The main feature in this part of the Izdubar legends is the description of the Flood in the eleventh tablet, which evidently refers to the same event as the Flood of Noah in Genesis.

The episode of the Flood has been introduced into the Izdubar Epic in accordance with the principle upon which it has been formed. The eleventh tablet or book answers to the sign of Aquarius and the month called "the rainy" by the Accadians, and it was therefore rightly occupied by the story of the Flood. The compiler of the Epic seems to have used for this purpose two independent poems relating to the event; at least it is otherwise difficult to account for the repetitions observable in certain lines which sometimes differ slightly from one another, as well as for certain inconsistencies which the skill of the compiler has not been able entirely to remove. Thus according to I. 13, the Deluge was caused by all "the great gods;" according to II. 30, by Samas only; according to IV. 4, 5, by Bel. There is little doubt that many independent versions of the history of the Deluge were current in a poetical form; indeed, a fragment of one of these, containing the original Accadian text along with the Assyrian translation has been preserved, and the version found in Berosus differs in several notable points from the version embodied in the great Chaldean Epic.

The fragment of the variant version of which the Accadian text has been preserved is as follows:—

- 1. .... then like a bowl of sacrificial wine the mountain ....

- 2. .... country to country ran together.

- 3. The female-slave to her mother (?) it had caused to ascend.

-

- 4. The freeman from the house of his fecundity it had caused to go forth.

- 5. The son from the house of his father it had caused to go forth

- 6. The doves from their cotes had fled away.

- 7. The raven on its wing it had caused to ascend.

- 8. The swallow from his nest it had caused to depart.

- 9. The oxen it had scattered, the lambs it had scattered.

- 10. (It was) the great days when the evil spirits hunt.

- 11. The universe they subjected unto themselves.

- 12. Among the bricks of the foundations (they dealt destruction).

- 13. The earth like a potsherd (they shattered).

- 14. Bel and Beltis the supreme ones the mighty tablets (of destiny consulted).

- 15. The foot to the earth they did not (put).

- 16. The highways of the earth they did not (tread).

If we compare the Babylonian account of the Deluge contained in the Epic with the account in Genesis we shall find some differences between them; but if we consider the differences that existed between the two countries of Palestine and Babylonia these variations do not appear greater than we should expect. Chaldea was essentially a mercantile and maritime country, well watered and flat, while Palestine was a hilly region with no great rivers, and the Jews were shut out from the coast, the maritime regions being mostly in the hands of the Philistines and Phœnicians. There was a total difference between the religious ideas of the two peoples, the Jews believing in one God, the creator and lord of the Universe, while the Babylonians worshipped gods and lords many, every city having its local deity, and these being joined by complicated relations in a poetical mythology, which was in marked contrast to the severe simplicity of the Jewish system. With such differences it was only natural that, in relating the same stories, each nation should colour them in accordance with its own ideas, and stress would naturally in each case be laid upon points with which they were familiar. Thus we should expect beforehand that there would be differences in the narrative such as we actually find, and we may also notice that the cuneiform account does not always coincide even with the account of the same events given by Berosus from Chaldean sources, from which, as already observed, we may infer that there was more than one version of the story of the Deluge current in Babylonia itself.

The great value of the inscriptions describing the Flood consists in the fact that they form an independent testimony to the Biblical narrative at a much earlier date than any other evidence. The principal points in the two narratives compared in their order will serve to show the correspondences and differences between the two. It must, however, be remembered that the Biblical narrative is composed of two different accounts of the Flood, generally known as the Elohistic and Jehovistic, and, as M. Lenormant has observed, it is with the union of the two in our present Hebrew text rather than with either one of them alone that the Babylonian version corresponds. The repetitions observable in the Hebrew text are not to be found in the cuneiform text.

		Genesis:		Babylonian
		Elohist.	Jehovist.	Account.
1.	Announcement of the Deluge	vi. 11-13.	vi. 5-8.	i. 12-23.
2.	Command to build the ark	vi. 14-16.		i. 20-27.
3.	What was to enter the ark	vi. 19-21.	vii. 2, 3.	i. 41-43.
4.	Size of the ark	vi. 15, 16.		i. 25, 26.
5.	Speech of Xisuthrus			i. 45-52.
6.	The building of the ark	vi. 22.	vii. 5.	ii. 2-24.
7.	The coating within and without with bitumen.	vi. 14.		ii. 10, 11.
8.	Food taken in the ark.	vi. 21.		ii. 12-20.

9.	The coming of the Flood	vii. 10-12.	vii. 10.	ii. 14, &c.
10.	Destruction of the people	vii. 21, 22.	vii. 23.	iii. 2-15.
11.	Duration of the Deluge	vii. 12, 24.	vii. 17.	iii. 19-21.
12.	Assuaging of the waters	viii. 1.	viii. 2.	iii. 21-23.
13.	Opening of window		viii. 6.	iii. 27.
14.	Ark rests on a mountain	viii. 4.		iii. 33-36.
15.	Sending forth of the birds		viii. 6-12.	iii. 38-44.
16.	Order to leave the ark	viii. 15-17.		
17.	Leaving the ark	viii. 18, 19.		iii. 45.
18.	Building the altar and sacrifice		viii. 20.	iii. 46-48.
19.	The savour of the offering		viii. 21.	iii. 49.
20.	A deluge not to happen again	ix. 11.	viii. 21, 22.	iv. 15-20.
21.	The Covenant	ix. 9-11.		iv. 26.
22.	The rainbow a pledge of the covenant	ix. 13-17.		iii. 51, 52.
23.	The Deluge caused by the sin of men	vi. 11-13.	vi. 5-7.	iv. 14, 15.
24.	Noah saved by his righteousness		vi. 8., vii. 1.	iv. 16.

25.	The translation of the patriarch (in Genesis of Enoch)	v. 24.	iv. 28-30.

One of the first points that strike us on comparing the Biblical and cuneiform accounts together is that they both agree in representing the Flood as a punishment for the sins of mankind. This agreement is rendered remarkable by the absence of such a moral cause in the legends of a deluge current among other nations; it is wanting even in the version of the Babylonian account given by Berosus. Equally remarkable is the agreement of the two accounts in the narrative of the sending forth of the birds, two of which, the raven and the dove, are the same in both. Some of the actual phrases and words found in Genesis are also found in the cuneiform tablet; though sometimes they are modified, as when Genesis says of the entrance of Noah into the ark: "The Lord shut him in;" whereas in the Babylonian narrative the closing of the door is ascribed to Xisuthrus himself.

Positive discrepancies, however, occur between the two records. Thus they differ as regards the size of the ark. According to the cuneiform account, its length and breadth were in the proportion of ten to one and the height and breadth were the same; but the Bible makes the proportion as six to one, and describes the height as being thirty cubits and the breadth fifty. The version of the story given by Berosus, on the other hand, agrees in this matter neither with Genesis nor with the tablet from Erech. It measures the ark by stadia and not by cubits, makes the proportion of its length and breadth as five to two, and says nothing of the height.

Another difference may be found in the description of the patriarch who escapes the Flood. Xisuthrus is a king who enters the ark with his servants, people, and pilot, while in the Bible only Noah and his family are saved. So, too, no reference is made in the Babylonian account to the distinction between the clean and unclean animals mentioned by the Jehovist, though seven was a sacred number among the Babylonians. The most remarkable difference, however, between the two accounts is with respect to the duration of the Deluge. On this point the inscription gives seven days for the Flood, and seven days for the resting of the ark on the mountain, while the Elohist puts the commencement of the Flood on the 17th day of the second month (Marchesvan) and its termination on the 27th day of the second month in the following year, making a total duration of one lunar year and eleven days. This exactly accords with the climatic conditions of Babylonia, where the rains begin at the end of November. The Euphrates and Tigris then begin to rise, the country is inundated in March, the seventh month of the Hebrew narrative, and from the end of May onwards the waters go down. According to the Jehovist, however, the Deluge is announced to Noah only seven days before it takes place; the waters are at their height for forty days and then decrease during another forty days, after which the patriarch sends out the birds at intervals of seven days, so that it was not till twenty-one days after he has first opened the window that he finally leaves the ark. This is in practical agreement with the cuneiform account, since seven was a sacred number among the Babylonians just as forty is in the Old Testament. As M. Lenormant points out, the date of the 15th of Dæsius (or May) given by Berosus must be due to a scribe's error, since this would place the Flood at a time when the waters were going down. There is again a difference as to the mountain on which the ark rested; Nizir, the place mentioned in the cuneiform text, being east of Assyria, and its mountain, also called "the mountain of the world" where the gods were supposed to dwell, being the present peak of Elwend, while the mountains of Ararat mentioned in the Bible were north of Assyria, near Lake Van. It is evident that different traditions have placed the mountain of the ark in totally different positions, and there is not positive proof as to which is the earlier traditionary spot. The word Ararat is connected with a word *Urdhu*, meaning "highland," and might be a general term for any part of the hilly country to the north-east of Assyria.

It is interesting to find references in the Jehovistic account to the sacred Babylonian number seven and the seven-day week. Just as Xisuthrus set vessels by sevens on the altar of sacrifice, so Noah offered clean beasts and fowls which had been taken by sevens into the ark. And the narrative of the sending-out of the birds contains a clear reference to the seven-day week, which was known from very early times to the Accadians, who had named each day after one of the seven planets. The Sabbath also, which occurred on the 7th, 14th, 19th, 21st and 28th days of the lunar month, was rigorously observed by them. They called it "a day of completion of labours," or "a day unlawful to work upon," and a sort of saints' calendar for the month of the intercalatory Elul says that upon it "the shepherd of many peoples may not eat the flesh of *birds* (?) or cooked fruit. The garments of his body he must not change. White robes he may not put on. Sacrifice he may not offer. The king in his chariot may not ride. He may not legislate in royal fashion. A place of garrison the general by word of mouth may not appoint. Medicine for the sickness of the body one may not apply." The very word *Sabattu* or Sabbath was used by the Assyrians, and a bilingual tablet explains it as "a day of rest for the heart."

One striking difference between the descriptions of the Deluge given in the Old Testament and in the Epic of Izdubar is due to the fact that the Hebrews were an inland people, whereas the Accadians were a maritime, or rather fluviatile one. Hence it is that while the ark is called in the Babylonian version "a ship," it is called *têbâh*, that is, "a coffer" in Genesis. In Genesis, too, nothing is said about launching the ark, testing its seaworthiness, or entrusting it to a pilot. However, the narrative in Genesis preserves a recollection of the bitumen for which the Babylonian plain was famous, and like the cuneiform narrative states that the ark was pitched.

Some of the other differences observable in the two accounts are evidently due to the opposite religious systems of the two countries, but there is again a curious point in connection with the close of the Chaldean legend: this is the translation of the hero of the Flood.

In the Book of Genesis it is not Noah but the seventh patriarch Enoch who is translated, three generations before the Flood.

There appears to have been some connection or confusion between Enoch and Noah in ancient tradition; both are holy men, and Enoch is said, like Noah, to have predicted the Flood.

It is a curious fact that the dynasty of gods, with which Egyptian mythical history commences, resembles in some respects the list of antediluvian kings of Babylonia given by Berosus as well as the list of antediluvian patriarchs in Genesis.

This dynasty has sometimes seven, sometimes ten reigns, and in the Turin Papyrus of kings, which gives ten reigns, there is the same name for the seventh and tenth kings, both being called Horus, and the seventh king is stated to have reigned 300 years, which is the length of life of the seventh patriarch Enoch after the birth of his son.

Here are the three lists of Egyptian gods, Hebrew patriarchs, and Chaldean kings.

Egypt.	Patriarchs.	Chaldean Kings.
Ptah.	Adam.	Alorus.
Ra.	Seth.	Alaparus.
Su.	Enos.	Almelon.
Seb.	Cainan.	Ammenon.
Hosiri.	Mahalaleel.	Amegalarus.
Set.	Jared.	Daonus. (Dun in the inscriptions.)
Hor.	Enoch.	Ædorachus.

Tut.	Methuselah.	Amempsin.
Ma.	Lamech.	Otiartes (Opartes).
Hor.	Noah.	Xisuthrus.

It is well known that Enos, like Adam, signifies "man;" hence some writers have supposed that the list of Noah's ancestors was originally counted from Enos, so that Lamech, Noah's father, would have been the seventh in descent. There is, moreover, a curious resemblance between the names of the descendants of Seth and those of the descendants of Cain, Methuselah, indeed, being apparently more correctly written Methusael (Gen. iv. 18), which is the Assyrian *Mutu-sa-ili*, "Man of God." Now Lamech, the descendant of Cain, is the seventh from Adam. It may be noticed that Irad or Jared is the same word as the Assyrian *Arad*, "servant," and *Arad* or *Ardutu* is the Assyrian rendering of the Accadian Ubara, the first part of the name of the father of Xisuthrus, who is actually called Ardates by Abydenus.

Mr. George Smith believed that the real connection between the traditions of Babylonia and Palestine would never be cleared up until the literature of the Syrian population which intervened is recovered. It is very possible that light may be thrown upon the question by the excavations now being made at Jerablus, the site of Carchemish, the capital of the ancient Hittites. Terah may be the same word as Tarkhu, who seems to have been worshipped as a god by the Hittites; and Lucian has preserved a legend of the Flood and the patriarch Sisythes, who is evidently the Xisuthrus of the Babylonians, which was current at Hierapolis or Mabug, a little to the south of Jerablus. In this legend the ark has become a coffer, Sisythes and his family are alone preserved, and the Flood was sent to punish the wickedness of mankind.

There is one point which still deserves notice: these traditions are not fixed to any localities in or near Palestine, but even on the showing of the Jews themselves, belong to the neighbourhood of the Euphrates valley, and Babylonia in particular; this of course is clearly stated in the Babylonian inscriptions and traditions.

Eden, according even to the Jews, was by the Euphrates and Tigris; the cities of Babylon, Larancha, and Sippara were supposed by the Babylonians to have been founded before the Flood. Surippak was the city of the ark, the mountains east of the Tigris were the resting-place of the ark, Babylon was the site of the tower, and Ur of the Chaldees the birthplace of Abraham. These facts and the further statement that Abraham, the father and first leader of the Hebrew race, migrated from Ur to Harran in Syria, and from thence to Palestine, are all so much evidence in favour of the hypothesis that

Chaldea was the original home of these stories, and that the Jews received them originally from the Babylonians; but on the other hand there are such striking differences in some parts of the legends, particularly in the names of the patriarchs before the Flood, that it is evident further information is required before we can determine how or when they were received by the Jews.

To pass, now, to the twelfth tablet of the Izdubar Epic, a curious fragment has been provisionally placed by Mr. Smith in the fourth column, in which Izdubar appears to call on his cities to mourn with him for his friend. This tablet is remarkable for the number of cities mentioned as already existing in the time of Izdubar. Combining this notice with other early inscriptions, the statements of Berosus and the notice of the cities of Nimrod in Genesis, we get the following list of the oldest known cities in the Euphrates valley:—

- 1. Babylon and its suburb
- 2. Borsippa.
- 3. Cutha.
- 4. Larsa.
- 5. Surippak, called Larancha by Berosus.
- 6. Eridu.
- 7. Nipur.
- 8. Erech.
- 9. Calneh.
- 10. Sippara. (Sepharvaim.)
- 11. Kisu (or Kis).
- 12. Ganganna.
- 13. Amarda or Marad.
- 14. Ur
- 15. Nisin or Karrak.
- 16. Agané.
- 17. Duban or Duran.
- 18. Abnunna or Mullias.

- 19. Zirghul.

To these we may also add the great cities of Assyria:—

- 20. Assur, the primitive capital.

- 21. Ninua or Nineveh.

- 22. Calah.

- 23. Resen (Assyrian Res-eni, "the head of the spring.")

So far as the various statements go, all these cities and probably many others were in existence in the time of Nimrod, and some of them even before the Flood; the fact that the Babylonians four thousand years ago believed their cities to be of such antiquity, shows that they were not recent foundations, and the attainments of the people at that time in the arts and sciences prove that their civilization had already known ages of progress. The legendary epoch of Izdubar must be considered at present as the commencement of the united monarchy in Babylonia, and as marking the first of the series of great conquests in Western Asia; but how far back we have to go from our earliest known monuments to reach this era we cannot now tell.

Every nation has its hero, and it was only natural that when the Accadian kings of Ur at last succeeded in establishing an united empire throughout Babylonia, the legends of the national hero should be coloured by the new conception of imperial unity.

Chapter XVII.
CONCLUSION.

Notices of Genesis.—Correspondence of names.—
Abram.—Ur of Chaldees.—Ishmael.—Sargon of
Agané.—His birth.—Concealed in ark.—Creation.—
Garden of Eden.—Oannes.—Berosus.—Izdubar
legends.—Babylonian seals.—Egyptian names.—Assyrian
sculptures.

SCATTERED through various cuneiform inscriptions are other notices, names, or passages, connected with the Book of Genesis. Although the names of the Genesis patriarchs are not in the inscriptions which give the history of the mythical period, nevertheless some of the patriarchal names of Genesis are found here and there in the inscriptions.

The name Adam is in the Creation legends, but only in a general sense as man, as in Gen. i. 26, 27, 28.; v. 1, not as a proper name. Several of the other names of antediluvian patriarchs correspond with Babylonian words and roots, such as Methusael (Gen. iv. 18), which is the Assyrian *mutu-sa-ili*, "man of God," and has been changed into Methuselah (Gen. v. 21) in order to assimilate it to the genius of the Hebrew language, or Noah, the Assyrian nukhu, "rest;" but, besides these, certain names appear as proper names also in Babylonia, among them Cainan, Lamech, and Laban.

Cainan is found as the name of a Babylonian town Kan-nan; the inhabitants of which were sometimes called Kanunai, which must not be confounded with the name of the Canaanites or "lowlanders," originally the inhabitants of the coastland of Phœnicia and then, by extension, of all Palestine.

Lamech has already been pointed out by Palmer ("Egyptian Chronicles," vol. i. p. 56), in the name of the deified Phœnician patriarch Diamich; this name is found in the cuneiform texts as Dumugu and Lamga, two forms of the Accadian name of the moon.

The two wives of Lamech, Adah and Zillah, seem to be the Assyrian *edhutu* or *edhatu* "darkness," and *tsillatu* "the shades of night;" and the names of his two sons Jabal and Jubal are but varying forms of the Assyrian *abil* "son." Dr. Oppert long ago pointed out that this Assyrian word was the origin of the name Abel which has been assimilated in spelling to a Hebrew word signifying "mere breath."

Some of the names of the patriarchs after the Flood are found as names of towns in Syria, but not in Babylonia; among these are Reu or Ragu, Serug, and Harran.

Laban, on the other hand, as was first noticed by Dr. Delitzsch, is mentioned in a list of gods given in a cuneiform tablet (published in the "Cuneiform Inscriptions of Western Asia," iii. 66, 6.)

MUGHEIR, THE SITE OF UR OF THE CHALDEES.

The name of Abramu or Abram is found in the Assyrian inscriptions in the time of Esarhaddon. After the captivity of the ten tribes, some of the Israelites prospered in Assyria, and rose to positions of trust in the empire. Abram was one of these, he was sukulu rabu or "great attendant" of Esarhaddon, and was eponym in Assyria, B.C. 677. Various other Hebrew names are found in Assyria about this time, including Pekah, Hoshea, and several compounded with the two Divine names Elohim and Jehovah, showing that both these names were in use among the Israelites. The presence of proper names founded on the Genesis stories, like Abram, and the use at this time of these forms of the Divine name, should be taken into consideration in discussing the evidence of the antiquity of Genesis.

Ur, now represented by the mounds of Mugheir, on the western bank of the Euphrates to the south of Babylon, was the capital of the earliest Accadian dynasty with which we are acquainted. It was specially devoted to the worship of the moon-god, the ruins of whose temple have been discovered there. Ur was the birthplace of Abraham, in whom we must see one of those Semitic intruders who settled among the Accadians, and after adopting their culture and civilization finally succeeded in overcoming and supplanting them. It is probable that it is called *Ur Casdim*, "Ur of the Casdim," in Genesis only proleptically, since Casdim appears to be the representative of an Assyrian word meaning "conquerors"—a suitable epithet for the Semitic tribes after

- 230 -

their conquest of Babylonia. The Greek names Chaldean and Chaldea are of much later date, being derived from the Kaldai, a small tribe settled on the Persian Gulf and first mentioned in the ninth century B.C., who under Merodach-Baladan (B.C. 721-709) possessed themselves of Babylonia and became so integral a portion of its inhabitants as to give their name to the whole of them in classical times.

Some of the Genesis names are found at a comparatively early date, the first which appears on a contemporary monument being Ishmael. In the reign of Khammuragas among the witnesses to some documents at Larsa in Babylonia, appears a man named "Abuha son of Ishmael."

After the time of Abraham the book of Genesis is concerned with the affairs of Palestine, and of the countries in its immediate vicinity, and it has no connection with Babylonian history and traditions; however, the cuneiform records contain one story which has a striking likeness to that of Moses in the ark, and which, although not within the period covered by Genesis, is of great interest in connection with the early history of the Jews.

Sargina or Sargon I. was a Babylonian monarch who reigned in the city of Agané about B.C. 1800. The name of Sargon signifies the right, true, or legitimate king, and may have been assumed on his ascending the throne. Sargon was probably of obscure origin, and hence the myth that attached itself to him in later popular belief. This curious story is found on fragments of tablets from Kouyunjik, and reads as follows:

- 1. Sargina the powerful king the king of Agané am I.

- 2. My mother was a princess, my father I did not know, a brother of my father chose the mountains.

- 3. In the city of Azupiranu which by the side of the river Euphrates is situated

- 4. (my) mother the princess conceived me; in an inaccessible place she brought me forth.

- 5. She placed me in a basket of rushes, with bitumen my exit she sealed up.

-

- 6. She launched me on the river which did not drown me.

- 7. The river carried me, to Akki the irrigator it brought me.

- 8. Akki the irrigator in tenderness of bowels lifted me up;

- 9. Akki the irrigator as his child brought me up,

- 10. Akki the irrigator as his woodman set me,

- 11. and in my woodmanship Istar loved me.

- 12. 45? years the kingdom I ruled,

- 13. the people of the black heads I governed, I ..

- 14. over rugged countries in many chariots of bronze I rode,

- 15. I governed the upper countries,

- 16. I ruled? over the chiefs of the lower countries.

- 17. To the sea coast three times I advanced, Dilvun (in the Persian Gulf) submitted,

- 18. Durankigal bowed, &c. &c.

After this follows an address to any king who should at a later time notice the inscription.

This myth is but a repetition of the oft-told story, how the hero of noble birth is born in secret, is exposed to death, but is rescued and brought up in a humble sphere of life until the time comes when his true origin and character are revealed, and he becomes a mighty prince and conqueror. The legend was told of Perseus in Greece, of Romulus in Italy, of Cyrus in Persia. But just as Cyrus was a real personage upon whom the legend was fastened, so too Sargon was a real personage, who founded the great library of Aganè, and extended his conquests as far as the island of Cyprus, which he conquered in the third year of his reign.

The most hazardous of the theories put forward in the preceding chapters is the one which identifies Izdubar with Nimrod, and makes him reign in the legendary period of Babylonian history. This theory is founded on several plausible, but probably merely superficial grounds; and if any one accepts Mr. Smith's view on the point, it will be only for similar reasons to those which caused him to propose it; namely, because, failing this, we have no clue whatever to the age and position of the most famous hero in Oriental tradition.

We must never lose sight of the fact that, apart from the more perfect and main parts of these texts, both in the decipherment of the broken fragments and in the various theories projected respecting them, the Assyrian scholar must change his opinions many times, and no doubt any accession of new material would change again our views respecting the parts affected by it. These theories and conclusions, however, although not always correct, have, on their way, assisted the inquiry, and have led to the more accurate knowledge of the texts; for certainly in cuneiform matters we have often had to advance through error to truth.

In adopting Mr. Smith's theory for the position of Nimrod, one thing is certainly clear: he is placed as low in the chronology as it is possible to make him.

The stories and myths given in the foregoing pages have, probably, very different values; some are genuine traditions—some compiled to account for natural phenomena, and some pure romances. At the head of their history and traditions the Babylonians placed an account of the creation of the world; and, although different forms of this story were current, in certain features they all agreed. Beside the account of the present animals, they related the creation of legions of monster forms which disappeared before the human epoch, and they accounted for the great problem of humanity— the presence of evil in the world—by making out that it proceeded from the original chaos, the spirit of confusion and darkness, which was the origin of all things, and which was even older than the gods.

The principal story of the Creation, given in Chapter V., substantially agrees, as far as it is preserved, with the Biblical account. According to it, there was a chaos of watery matter before the Creation, and from this all things were generated.

We have then a considerable blank, the contents of which we can only conjecture, and after this we come to the creation of the heavenly orbs.

The fifth tablet in the series relates how God created the constellations of the stars, the signs of the zodiac, the planets and other stars, the moon and the sun. After another blank we have a fragment which relates to the creation of wild and domestic animals; it is curious here that the original taming of domestic animals was even then so far back in the history of the race that all knowledge of it was lost, and the "animals of the city," or domestic animals, were considered different creations from the "animals of the desert," or "field," or wild animals.

We next come to the war between the dragon and powers of evil, or chaos, on one side and the gods on the other. The gods have weapons forged for them, and Merodach undertakes to lead the heavenly host against the dragon. The war, which is described with spirit, ends of course in the triumph of the principle of good, and the overthrow of primeval anarchy.

In Chapter V. another account of the Creation is given which differs materially from the first. The principal feature in the second account is the description of the eagle-headed men with their family of leaders—this legend clearly showing the origin of the eagle-headed figures represented on the Assyrian sculptures.

It is probable that some of these Babylonian legends contained detailed descriptions of the Garden of Eden, which seems to have been the district of Eridu in the south of Babylonia, as Sir Henry Rawlinson believes.

There are coincidences in respect to the geography of the region and its name which render the identification very probable; of the four rivers in each case, two, the Euphrates and Tigris, are identical; then, again, the known fertility of the region, its name sometimes Gan-duni, so similar to Gan-eden (the Garden of Eden), and other considerations, all tend towards the view that it is the Paradise of Genesis.

There are evidences of the belief in the tree of life, which is one of the most common emblems on the seals and larger sculptures, and is even used as an ornament on dresses; a sacred tree is also several times mentioned in the legends and hymns, but at present there is no direct connection known between the tree and the Fall, although the gem engravings render it very probable that there was a legend of this kind like the one in Genesis.

In the history of Berosus mention is made of a composite being, half man, half fish, named Oannes, who was supposed to have appeared out of the sea and to have taught the Babylonians all their learning. The Babylonian and Assyrian sculptures have made us familiar with the figure of Oannes, and have so far given evidence that Berosus has truly described this mythological figure; but it is a curious fact that the legend of Oannes, which must have been one of the Babylonian stories of the Creation, has not yet been recovered. In fact, as previously noticed (p. 12), there is only one fragment which can be at all referred to it, and this has been accidentally preserved among a series of extracts from various Accadian works in a bilingual reading-book compiled for the use of Assyrian students of Accadian. The fragment is as follows:—

OANNES. FROM NIMROUD SCULPTURE.

- 1. To the waters their god
- 2. has returned:
- 3. to the house of bright things
- 4. he descended (as) an icicle:
- 5. on a seat of snow
- 6. he grew not old in wisdom.

The legend of Oannes, whose name may possibly be the Accadian Hea-khan, "Hea the fish," concerned the Babylonians only, and so did not interest the Assyrians, who did not care to have it in their libraries.

Besides the legend of Oannes, however, there are evidently many stories of early times still unknown, or only known by mere fragments or allusions.

The fables given in Chapter IX. form a series quite different in character from the legends, and the only excuse for inserting them here is the need of exhibiting as clearly and fully as possible the literature of the great epoch which produced the Genesis tablets.

Most of the other stories apparently relate to the great period before the Flood, when celestial visitors came to and from the earth, and the inhabitants of the world were very distinctly divided into the good and bad, but the stories are only fables with a moral attached, and have little connection with Babylonian history.

Two of these stories are very curious, and may hereafter turn out to be of great importance; one is the story of the sin committed by the god Zu, and the other the story of Atarpi.

Berosus in his history has given an account of ten Chaldean kings who reigned before the Flood, and the close of this period is well known from the descriptions of the Deluge in the Bible, the Deluge tablet, and the work of the Greek writer. According to Berosus several of the Babylonian cities were built before the Flood, and various arts were known, including writing. The enormous reigns given by Berosus to his ten kings, making a total of 432,000 years, force us to discard the idea that the details are historical, although there may be some foundation for his statement of a civilization before the Deluge. The details given in the inscriptions describing the Flood leave no doubt that both the Bible and the Babylonian story describe the same event, and the Flood becomes the starting-point for the modern world in both histories. According to Berosus 86 kings reigned for 34,080 years after the Flood down to the Median conquest. If these kings are historical, it is doubtful if they formed a continuous line, and they could scarcely cover a longer period than 2,000 years. The Median or Elamite conquest took place about B.C. 2700, and, if we allow the round number 2,000 years for the previous period, it will make the Flood fall about B.C. 4700. In a fragmentary inscription with a list of Babylonian kings, some names are given which appear to belong to the 86 kings of Berosus, but our information about this period is so scanty that nothing can be said about this dynasty, and a suggestion as to the date of the Deluge must be received with more than the usual grain of salt.

We can see, however, that there was a civilized race in Babylonia before the Median Conquest, the progress of which must have received a rude shock when the country was overrun by the uncivilized Eastern borderers.

Among the fragmentary notices of this semi-mythical period is the portion of the inscription describing the building of the Tower of Babel and the dispersion.

It is probable from the fragments of Berosus that the incursions and dominion of the Median Elamites lasted about two hundred years, during which the country suffered greatly from them.

The legends of Izdubar or Nimrod commence with a description of the evils brought upon Babylonia by foreign invasion, the conquest and sacking of the city of Erech being one of the incidents in the story. Izdubar, a famous hunter, who claimed descent from a long line of kings, reaching up to the time of the Flood, now comes forward; he has a dream, and after much trouble a half-human creature named Hea-bani is persuaded by Zaidu, the hunter, and two females, to come to Erech and interpret the dream of Izdubar. Hea-bani, having heard the fame of Izdubar, brings to Erech a midannu or tiger to test his strength, and Izdubar slays it. After these things, Izdubar and Hea-bani become friends, and, having invoked the gods, they start to attack the tyrant Khumbaba. Khumbaba dwelt in a thick forest, surrounded by a wall, and here he was visited by the two friends, who slew him and carried off his spoils.

Izdubar was now proclaimed king, and extended his authority over the Babylonian world, his court and palace being at Erech. The goddess Istar, daughter of Anu according to one myth, of Bel according to another, of Sin, the moon god, according to a third, who had loved the shepherd Tammuz, the Sun-god, fell in love with Izdubar. He refused her offers, and the goddess, angry at his answer, ascended to heaven and petitioned her father Anu to create a bull for her, to be an instrument of her vengeance. Anu complied, and created the bull, on which Izdubar and Hea-bani collected a band of warriors and went against it. Hea-bani took hold of the animal by its head and tail, while Izdubar slew it.

Istar on this cursed Izdubar, and descended to Hades to attempt once more to summon unearthly powers against the hero. She descends to the infernal regions, which are vividly described, and, passing through their seven gates, is ushered into the presence of the queen of the dead. The world of love goes wrong in the absence of Istar, and on the petition of the gods she is once more brought to the earth, ultimately Anatu, her mother, satisfying her vengeance by striking Izdubar with a loathsome disease.

Hea-bani, the friend of Izdubar, is now killed, and Izdubar, mourning his double affliction, abandons his kingdom and wanders into the desert to seek the advice of Xisuthrus his ancestor, who had been translated for his piety and now dwelt with the gods.

Izdubar now had a dream, and after this wandered to the region where gigantic composite monsters held and controlled the rising and setting sun: from these he learned the road to the region of the blessed, and, passing across a great waste of sand, arrived at a region where splendid trees were laden with jewels instead of fruit.

Izdubar then met two females, named Siduri and Sabitu, after an adventure with whom he found a boatman named Nes-Hea, who undertook to navigate him to the region where Xisuthrus dwelt.

Coming near the dwelling of the blessed, he found it surrounded by the waters of death, which he had to cross in order to reach the land of which he was in search.

On arriving at the other side, Izdubar was met by Mu-seri-ina-namari, "the waters of dawn at daybreak," who engaged him in conversation about Hea-bani, and then Xisuthrus, taking up the conversation, described to him the Deluge. Izdubar was afterwards cured of his illness and returned with Nes-Hea to Erech, where he mourned anew for his friend Hea-bani, and on intercession with the gods the ghost of Hea-bani arose from the ground where the body had lain.

The details of this story, and especially the accounts of the regions inhabited by the dead, are very striking, and illustrate, in a wonderful manner, the religious views of the people.

It is worth while here to pause, and consider the evidence of the existence of the legends recounted in the preceding pages from the close of the mythical period down to the seventh century B.C.

We have first the seals: of these there are some hundreds in European museums, and among the earliest are many specimens carved with scenes from the Genesis legends; some of these are a good deal older than B.C. 2000, others may be ranged at various dates down to B.C. 1500.

With three exceptions, which are of Assyrian origin, all the seals engraved in the present volume are Babylonian. One very fine and early example is photographed as the frontispiece of the book. The character and style of the cuneiform legend which accompanies this shows it to be one of the most ancient specimens; it is engraved on a hard jasper cylinder in bold style, and is a remarkable example of early Babylonian art. Many other similar cylinders of the same period are known; the relief on them is bolder than on the later seals, on which from about B.C. 1600 or 1700, a change in the inscriptions becomes general.

The numerous illustrations to the present work, which have been collected from these early Babylonian seals, will serve to show that the legends were well known, and formed part of the literature of the country before the second millennium B.C.

After B.C. 1500, the literature of Babylonia is unknown, and we lose sight of all evidence of its legends for some centuries. In the meantime Egypt supplies a few notices bearing on the subject, which serve to show that knowledge of them was still kept up. Nearly thirteen hundred years before the Christian era one of the Egyptian poems likens a hero to the Assyrian chief, Kazartu, a great hunter. Kazartu probably means a "strong" or "powerful" one, and it has already been suggested that the reference is to the hero Nimrod. A little later, in the period extending from B.C. 1000 to 800, we have in Egypt several persons named Namurot, which seems to be an echo of the name of the mighty hunter.

On the revival of the Assyrian empire, about B.C. 990, we come again to numerous references to the Genesis legends, and these continue through almost every reign down to the close of the empire. The Assyrians carved the sacred tree and cherubim on their walls, they depicted in the temples the struggle between Merodach and the dragon, they decorated their portals with the figure of Izdubar strangling a lion, and carved the struggles of Izdubar and Hea-bani with the lion and the bull even on their stone vases.

Just as the sculptures of the Greek temples, the paintings on the vases and the carving on their gems were taken from their myths and legends, so the series of myths and legends belonging to the valley of the Euphrates furnished materials for the sculptor, the engraver, and the painter, among the ancient Babylonians and Assyrians.

In this way we have continued evidence of the existence of these legends down to the time of Assur-bani-pal, B.C. 673 to 626, who caused the present known copies to be made for his library at Nineveh.

Search in Babylonia would, no doubt, yield much earlier copies of all these works, but that search has not yet been instituted, and for the present we have to be contented with our Assyrian copies. Looking, however, at the world-wide interest of the subjects, and at the important evidence which perfect copies of these works would undoubtedly give, there can be no doubt that further progress will be made in research and discovery, and that all that is here written will one day be superseded by newer texts and fuller and more perfect light.

FOOTNOTES

1 The native account of the Deluge shows that this name must be corrected to Opartes, the native name being Ubara-Tutu.

2 A common title of the early Accadian kings is "shepherd," pointing to the fact that the Accadians had led a pastoral life before their settlement and organization in the Babylonian plain.

3 Assyrian, Tiamtu, "the deep."

4 Assyrian, Apsu, "the ocean."

5 Assyrian, Mummu, "chaos."

6 Assyrian, Lakhmu or Lakhvu; and Lakhama or Lakhva.

7 Though Lakhmu properly represented Anu or Anatu, he sometimes takes the place of the Solar hero Ninip as husband of Gula, "the great" goddess.

8 The seven "sheep (or oxen) of the hero" Tammuz (Orion), of which the first was "the plough-handle," perhaps Benelnash. One of the others was "the shepherd of the heavenly flock" or Arcturus.

9 This is Dr. Oppert's rendering of a line which is so mutilated as to make any attempt at translation extremely doubtful.

10 The word used here is Accadian (*ba-an-an-me*).

11 Since, however, a bilingual tablet states that the pronunciation of the Accadian word for "the desert" which lay on the west side of the Euphrates (where Ur was built) was *edinna*, it is possible that "the Garden of Eden" of Genesis may be the cultivated portion of *edinna*, "the desert," in the neighbourhood of Eridu.

12 The seven *mustakridhât* of Syria, the seven days between February the 25th and March 3rd, when evil spirits are supposed to have special power.

13 This is the Assyrian translation. The Accadian original has simply "men of death." The lightnings are still regarded as serpents by the Canadian Indians who call the thunder their hissing (Baring-Gould, "Curious Myths," ii. p. 146).

14 A constellation which rose heliacally in Marchesvan or October. The word means "Dog of death."

15 Compare Jer. li. 34.

16 This is the reading of the original Accadian text. The Assyrian translation has, "was his establisher."

17 Itak had his worshippers as well as Dibbara. Thus an Accadian seal in the possession of Dr. Huggins bears a legend stating that it belonged to "Ruru-lukh, the servant of Itak, the street-traverser." The god is represented on this seal as a man in a flounced dress, to whom a kid is being offered, and is symbolized by two animals one of which looks like a locust, the other like a monkey.

18 Another copy of the legend reads "lover."

19 Literally, "a thing hung up."

20 Or "bull of heaven." It was a constellation, perhaps Taurus.

21 "Joy" and "Seduction."

22 A great necropolis seems to have existed in Cutha.

23 Literally "precious stones."

24 That is, "Go forth, cause it to be light!"

25 Literally "the man who is a female dog," or "lion."

26 Literally "stone stakes" or "cones," the symbols of the goddess Ashêrah. Cf. 1 Kings vii. 15-22.

27 Tillili, the Accadian name of Kharimat, is here used. Tillili was the wife of the Sun-god Alala symbolized by the eagle, which we are told was "the symbol of the southern" or "meridian sun." What Sir H. Rawlinson calls the monotheistic party among the Babylonians resolved Tillili into Anatu and Alala into Anu.

28 This last sentence is found only in the fragment discovered by Mr. Rassam.

29 Or: He then intelligently.

30 The fragment brought to England by Mr. Rassam reads 6.

31 The word used here is *ziggurrat*, which is employed to denote the towers attached to Babylonian temples. These towers were commonly used as observatories.

32 Bricks have been found at Warka or Erech bearing the name of a certain king Sin-kudur, who calls himself the son of this same goddess, and describes himself as the builder of the temple of Anu at Erech.

www.ingramcontent.com/pod-product-compliance
Ingram Content Group UK Ltd.
Pitfield, Milton Keynes, MK11 3LW, UK
UKHW031825270325
456796UK00002B/310

9 789366 381657